A*List VOCA

중학 고난도

A*List

How to Use 이 책의 구성과 특징

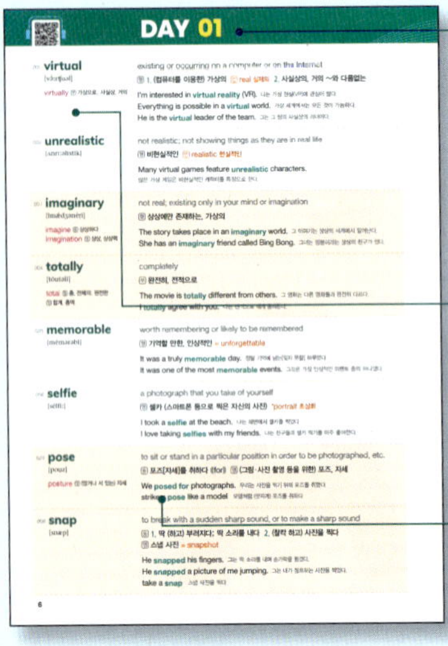
DAY 01

virtual
virtually
existing or occurring on a computer or on the Internet
1. (컴퓨터를 이용한) 가상의 real 실제의 2. 사실상의, 거의 ~와 다름없는
I'm interested in virtual reality (VR).
Everything is possible in a virtual world.
He is the virtual leader of the team.

unrealistic
not realistic; not showing things as they are in real life
비현실적인 realistic 현실적인
Many virtual games feature unrealistic characters.

imaginary
imagine
imagination
not real; existing only in your mind or imagination
상상에만 존재하는, 가상의
The story takes place in an imaginary world.
She has an imaginary friend called Bing Bong.

totally
total
completely
완전히, 전적으로
The movie is totally different from others.
I totally agree with you.

memorable
worth remembering or likely to be remembered
기억할 만한, 인상적인 = unforgettable
It was a truly memorable day.
It was one of the most memorable events.

selfie
a photograph that you take of yourself
셀카 (스마트폰 등으로 찍은 자신의 사진) *portrait 초상화
I took a selfie at the beach.
I love taking selfies with my friends.

pose
posture
to sit or stand in a particular position in order to be photographed, etc.
포즈[자세]를 취하다 (for) (그림·사진 촬영 등을 위한) 포즈, 자세
We posed for photographs.
strike a pose like a model

snap
to break with a sudden sharp sound, or to make a sharp sound
1. 딱 (하고) 부러지다; 딱 소리를 내다 2. (찰칵 하고) 사진을 찍다
스냅 사진 = snapshot
He snapped his fingers.
He snapped a picture of me jumping.
take a snap

6

1 **새 교육과정 중학 교과서 필수 어휘와 고등 교과서 빈출 어휘를 완벽 반영한 640개의 표제어**

DAY별로 18개의 단어와 2개의 숙어를 쉽고 빠르게 익힐 수 있는 8주 완성 학습 플랜을 제시합니다.

2 **연관성 높은 단어들을 2개씩 짝지어 외우는 주제별 구성**

주제별로 연관된 어휘끼리 짝지어 학습하면 더 쉽고 빠르게 단어를 암기할 수 있습니다.

3 **암기 효과를 극대화하는 교과서 빈출 숙어 및 구문 표현 컬러 표기**

단어의 의미와 용법을 즉각적으로 파악할 수 있어 영어 문장 이해의 든든한 밑바탕이 됩니다.

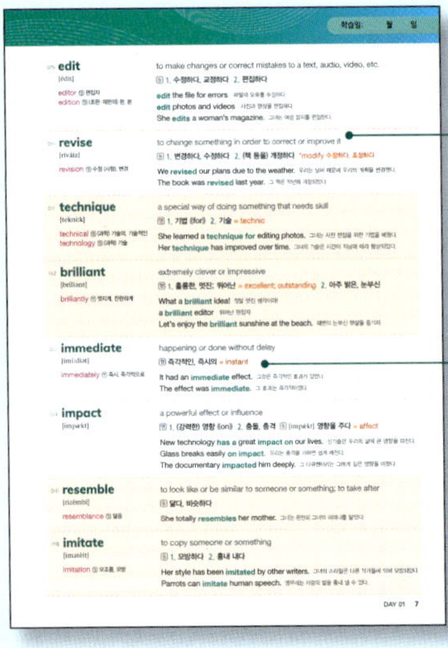
학습일: 월 일

edit
editor
edition
to make changes or correct mistakes to a text, audio, video, etc.
1. 수정하다, 교정하다 2. 편집하다
edit the file for errors
edit photos and videos
She edits a woman's magazine.

revise
revision
to change something in order to correct or improve it
1. 변경하다, 수정하다 2. (책 등을) 개정하다 *modify 수정하다, 조정하다
We revised our plans due to the weather.
The book was revised last year.

technique
technical
technology
a special way of doing something that needs skill
1. 기법 (for) 2. 기술 = technic
She learned a technique for editing photos.
Her technique has improved over time.

brilliant
brilliantly
extremely clever or impressive
1. 훌륭한, 멋진; 뛰어난 = excellent; outstanding 2. 아주 밝은, 눈부신
What a brilliant idea!
a brilliant editor
Let's enjoy the brilliant sunshine at the beach.

immediate
immediately
happening or done without delay
즉각적인, 즉시의 = instant
It had an immediate effect.
The effect was immediate.

impact
a powerful effect or influence
1. (강력한) 영향 (on) 2. 충돌, 충격 영향을 주다 = affect
New technology has a great impact on our lives.
Glass breaks easily on impact.
The documentary impacted him deeply.

resemble
resemblance
to look like or be similar to someone or something; to take after
닮다, 비슷하다
She totally resembles her mother.

imitate
imitation
to copy someone or something
1. 모방하다 2. 흉내 내다
Her style has been imitated by other writers.
Parrots can imitate human speech.

DAY 01 7

4 **실력 Up 영영풀이**

영어로만 단어의 뜻을 설명해 보는 영영풀이로 자연스럽게 영어식 표현에 익숙해집니다.

5 **누적 반복되는 연관 단어/숙어와 풍부한 추가 어휘**

자연스러운 반복 학습과 함께 유의어, 반의어, 파생어, 참고 어휘 등 관련된 어휘를 함께 익힐 수 있어 단어에 대한 이해와 활용 능력을 더욱 넓힐 수 있습니다.

QR코드로 바로 듣는 MP3

각 DAY별 어휘의 발음과 예문을 바로 듣고 따라 읽으며 소리로도 익힐 수 있는 QR코드 삽입

QR코드로 바로 연결되는 어휘 학습앱

표지의 QR코드를 통해 어휘 학습이 가능한 앱으로 바로 연결

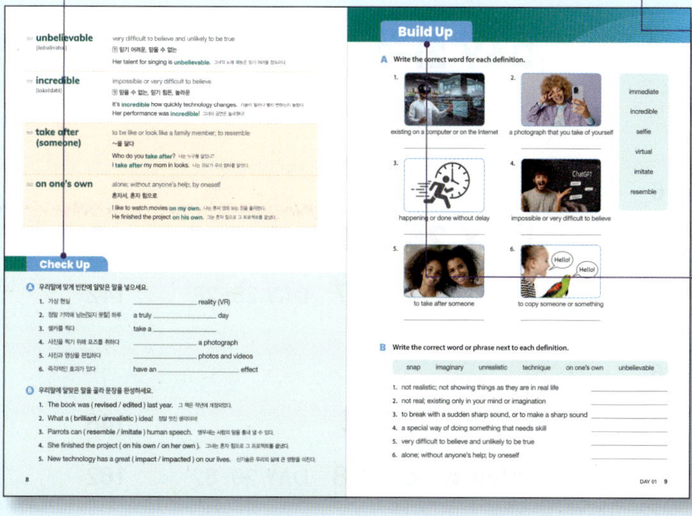

6 각 DAY별로 학습한 어휘를 점검할 수 있는 Check Up

오늘 배운 단어를 문제를 통해 확인하며 얼마나 외웠는지 스스로 점검할 수 있습니다.

7 영영풀이 테스트로 심화 학습이 가능한 Build Up

시각효과를 통한 연상작용의 극대화와 심화 테스트를 통해 단어를 더 오래 기억할 수 있습니다.

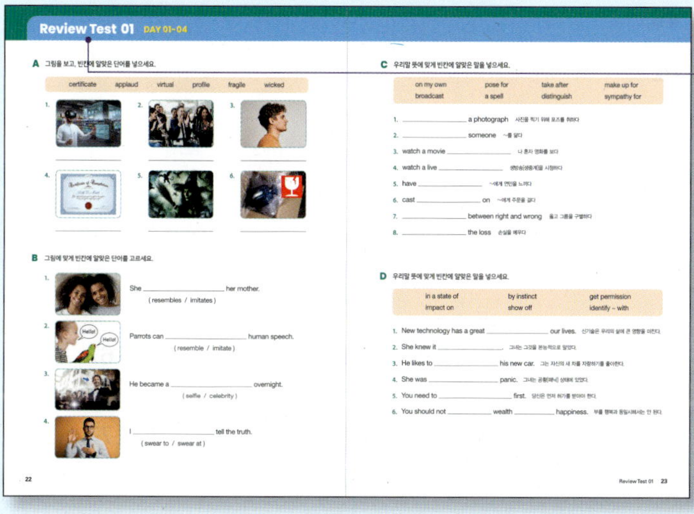

8 누적된 어휘를 반복 확인할 수 있는 Review Test

4일차를 학습한 후 유의어, 반의어, 숙어 등 다양한 문제를 풀어 보며 누적된 어휘를 반복 확인할 수 있습니다.

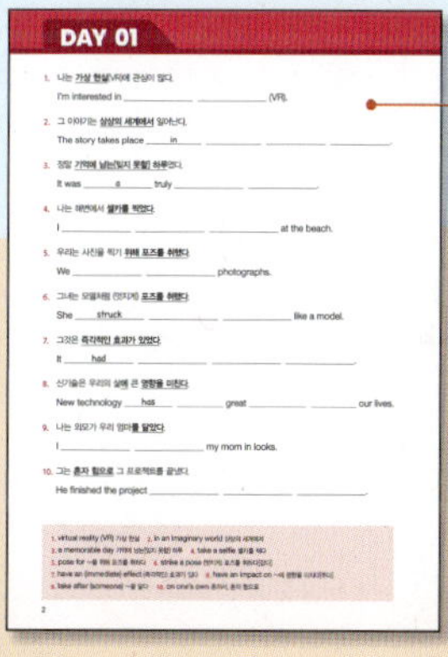

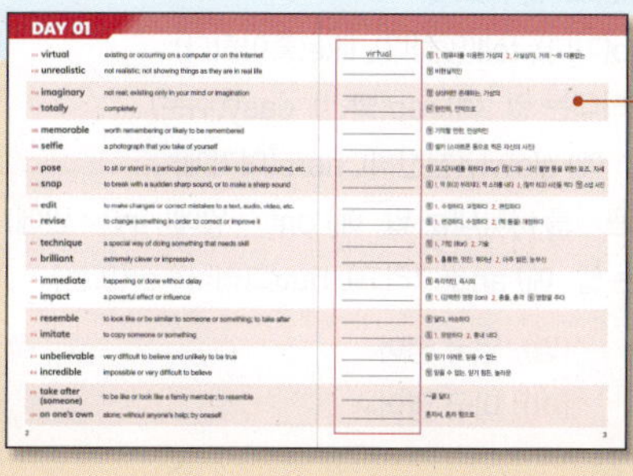

9 실력 Up 숙어·구문 표현 연습장

10 휴대하며 외우는 어휘 암기장

〈숙어·구문 표현 연습장〉과 간편히 휴대하며 암기할 수 있는 〈어휘 암기장〉으로 단어를 더 오래 기억할 수 있습니다.

Contents 차례

이 책에 나오는 품사와 약어

1	**명사**	명 사람, 사물, 동물 등의 이름을 나타내는 말 예) friend(친구), cat(고양이)
2	**대명사**	대 명사를 대신하는 말 예) you(너), she(그녀), it(그것)
3	**동사**	동 동작이나 상태를 나타내는 말 예) go(가다), tell(말하다), like(좋아하다)
4	**형용사**	형 상태, 성질, 모양, 크기, 수량 등을 나타내는 말 예) red(빨간), easy(쉬운)
5	**부사**	부 동사, 형용사, 부사 등을 꾸며주는 말 예) slowly(천천히), here(여기에)
6	**전치사**	전 명사, 대명사 앞에서 다른 단어와의 관계를 나타내는 말 예) on(~ 위에), in(~ 안에)
7	**접속사**	접 단어와 단어, 문장과 문장을 이어주는 말 예) and(그리고), but(그러나), or(또는)

*유의어 유 비슷한 의미를 갖는 말 *(영) 영국 영어
*반의어 반 반대의 의미를 갖는 말 *(미) 미국 영어

Study Planner 학습 계획표

하루에 1 DAY씩 8주 완성

각 DAY별로 학습한 날짜를 써 나가며 단어 실력을 키워 봅시다.

Week 1	DAY 01	DAY 02	DAY 03	DAY 04	Review Test 01
1차 학습일					
2차 학습일					

Week 2	DAY 05	DAY 06	DAY 07	DAY 08	Review Test 02
1차 학습일					
2차 학습일					

Week 3	DAY 09	DAY 10	DAY 11	DAY 12	Review Test 03
1차 학습일					
2차 학습일					

Week 4	DAY 13	DAY 14	DAY 15	DAY 16	Review Test 04
1차 학습일					
2차 학습일					

Week 5	DAY 17	DAY 18	DAY 19	DAY 20	Review Test 05
1차 학습일					
2차 학습일					

Week 6	DAY 21	DAY 22	DAY 23	DAY 24	Review Test 06
1차 학습일					
2차 학습일					

Week 7	DAY 25	DAY 26	DAY 27	DAY 28	Review Test 07
1차 학습일					
2차 학습일					

Week 8	DAY 29	DAY 30	DAY 31	DAY 32	Review Test 08
1차 학습일					
2차 학습일					

DAY 01

001 **virtual** [və́ːrʧuəl]

virtually 부 가상으로; 사실상, 거의

existing or occurring on a computer or on the Internet

형 1. (컴퓨터를 이용한) 가상의 반 real 실제의 2. 사실상의, 거의 ~와 다름없는

I'm interested in **virtual reality** (VR). 나는 가상 현실(VR)에 관심이 많다.
Everything is possible in a **virtual** world. 가상 세계에서는 모든 것이 가능하다.
He is the **virtual** leader of the team. 그는 그 팀의 사실상의 리더이다.

002 **unrealistic** [ʌnriːəlístik]

not realistic; not showing things as they are in real life

형 비현실적인 반 realistic 현실적인

Many virtual games feature **unrealistic** characters.
많은 가상 게임은 비현실적인 캐릭터를 특징으로 한다.

003 **imaginary** [imǽdʒənèri]

imagine 동 상상하다
imagination 명 상상, 상상력

not real; existing only in your mind or imagination

형 상상에만 존재하는, 가상의

The story takes place in an **imaginary** world. 그 이야기는 상상의 세계에서 일어난다.
She has an **imaginary** friend called Bing Bong. 그녀는 빙봉이라는 상상의 친구가 있다.

004 **totally** [tóutəli]

total 형 총, 전체의; 완전한
명 합계, 총액

completely

부 완전히, 전적으로

The movie is **totally** different from others. 그 영화는 다른 영화들과 완전히 다르다.
I **totally** agree with you. 나는 전적으로 네게 동의한다.

005 **memorable** [mémərəbl]

worth remembering or likely to be remembered

형 기억할 만한, 인상적인 = unforgettable

It was a truly **memorable** day. 정말 기억에 남는[잊지 못할] 하루였다.
It was one of the most **memorable** events. 그것은 가장 인상적인 이벤트 중의 하나였다.

006 **selfie** [sélfiː]

a photograph that you take of yourself

명 셀카 (스마트폰 등으로 찍은 자신의 사진) *portrait 초상화

I took a **selfie** at the beach. 나는 해변에서 셀카를 찍었다.
I love taking **selfies** with my friends. 나는 친구들과 셀카 찍기를 아주 좋아한다.

007 **pose** [pouz]

posture 명 (앉거나 서 있는) 자세

to sit or stand in a particular position in order to be photographed, etc.

동 포즈[자세]를 취하다 ((for)) 명 (그림·사진 촬영 등을 위한) 포즈, 자세

We **posed for** photographs. 우리는 사진을 찍기 위해 포즈를 취했다.
strike a **pose** like a model 모델처럼 (멋지게) 포즈를 취하다

008 **snap** [snæp]

to break with a sudden sharp sound, or to make a sharp sound

동 1. 딱 (하고) 부러지다; 딱 소리를 내다 2. (찰칵 하고) 사진을 찍다
명 스냅 사진 = snapshot

He **snapped** his fingers. 그는 딱 소리를 내며 손가락을 튕겼다.
He **snapped** a picture of me jumping. 그는 내가 점프하는 사진을 찍었다.
take a **snap** 스냅 사진을 찍다

009 **edit**
[édit]

editor 명 편집자
edition 명 (초판·재판의) 판, 본

to make changes or correct mistakes to a text, audio, video, etc.
동 1. 수정하다, 교정하다 2. 편집하다

edit the file for errors 파일의 오류를 수정하다
edit photos and videos 사진과 영상을 편집하다
She **edits** a woman's magazine. 그녀는 여성 잡지를 편집한다.

010 **revise**
[riváiz]

revision 명 수정 (사항), 변경

to change something in order to correct or improve it
동 1. 변경하다, 수정하다 2. (책 등을) 개정하다 *modify 수정하다, 조정하다

We **revised** our plans due to the weather. 우리는 날씨 때문에 우리의 계획을 변경했다.
The book was **revised** last year. 그 책은 작년에 개정되었다.

011 **technique**
[tekní:k]

technical 형 (과학) 기술의, 기술적인
technology 명 (과학) 기술

a special way of doing something that needs skill
명 1. 기법 ((for)) 2. 기술 = technic

She learned a **technique for** editing photos. 그녀는 사진 편집을 위한 기법을 배웠다.
Her **technique** has improved over time. 그녀의 기술은 시간이 지남에 따라 향상되었다.

012 **brilliant**
[bríliənt]

brilliantly 부 멋지게, 찬란하게

extremely clever or impressive
형 1. 훌륭한, 멋진; 뛰어난 = excellent; outstanding 2. 아주 밝은, 눈부신

What a **brilliant** idea! 정말 멋진 생각이야!
a **brilliant** editor 뛰어난 편집자
Let's enjoy the **brilliant** sunshine at the beach. 해변의 눈부신 햇살을 즐기자.

013 **immediate**
[imí:diət]

immediately 부 즉시, 즉각적으로

happening or done without delay
형 즉각적인, 즉시의 = instant

It had an **immediate** effect. 그것은 즉각적인 효과가 있었다.
The effect was **immediate**. 그 효과는 즉각적이었다.

014 **impact**
[ímpækt]

a powerful effect or influence
명 1. (강력한) 영향 ((on)) 2. 충돌, 충격 동 [impǽkt] 영향을 주다 = affect

New technology **has a** great **impact on** our lives. 신기술은 우리의 삶에 큰 영향을 미친다.
Glass breaks easily **on impact**. 유리는 충격을 가하면 쉽게 깨진다.
The documentary **impacted** him deeply. 그 다큐멘터리는 그에게 깊은 영향을 미쳤다.

015 **resemble**
[rizémbl]

resemblance 명 닮음

to look like or be similar to someone or something; to take after
동 닮다, 비슷하다

She totally **resembles** her mother. 그녀는 완전히 그녀의 어머니를 닮았다.

016 **imitate**
[ímətèit]

imitation 명 모조품, 모방

to copy someone or something
동 1. 모방하다 2. 흉내 내다

Her style has been **imitated** by other writers. 그녀의 스타일은 다른 작가들에 의해 모방되었다.
Parrots can **imitate** human speech. 앵무새는 사람의 말을 흉내 낼 수 있다.

017 **unbelievable**
[ənbəlívəbəl]

very difficult to believe and unlikely to be true

형 믿기 어려운, 믿을 수 없는

Her talent for singing is **unbelievable**. 그녀의 노래 재능은 믿기 어려울 정도이다.

018 **incredible**
[inkrédəbl]

impossible or very difficult to believe

형 믿을 수 없는, 믿기 힘든, 놀라운

It's **incredible** how quickly technology changes. 기술이 얼마나 빨리 변하는지 놀랍다.
Her performance was **incredible**! 그녀의 공연은 놀라웠다!

019 **take after (someone)**

to be like or look like a family member; to resemble

~을 닮다

Who do you **take after**? 너는 누구를 닮았니?
I **take after** my mom in looks. 나는 외모가 우리 엄마를 닮았다.

020 **on one's own**

alone; without anyone's help; by oneself

혼자서, 혼자 힘으로

I like to watch movies **on my own**. 나는 혼자 영화 보는 것을 좋아한다.
He finished the project **on his own**. 그는 혼자 힘으로 그 프로젝트를 끝냈다.

Check Up

A 우리말에 맞게 빈칸에 알맞은 말을 넣으세요.

1. 가상 현실 ________________ reality (VR)
2. 정말 기억에 남는[잊지 못할] 하루 a truly ________________ day
3. 셀카를 찍다 take a ________________
4. 사진을 찍기 위해 포즈를 취하다 ________________ a photograph
5. 사진과 영상을 편집하다 ________________ photos and videos
6. 즉각적인 효과가 있다 have an ________________ effect

B 우리말에 알맞은 말을 골라 문장을 완성하세요.

1. The book was (**revised** / **edited**) last year. 그 책은 작년에 개정되었다.
2. What a (**brilliant** / **unrealistic**) idea! 정말 멋진 생각이야!
3. Parrots can (**resemble** / **imitate**) human speech. 앵무새는 사람의 말을 흉내 낼 수 있다.
4. She finished the project (**on his own** / **on her own**). 그녀는 혼자 힘으로 그 프로젝트를 끝냈다.
5. New technology has a great (**impact** / **impacted**) on our lives. 신기술은 우리의 삶에 큰 영향을 미친다.

Build Up

A Write the correct word for each definition.

immediate	incredible	selfie	virtual	imitate	resemble

1. 

existing on a computer or on the Internet

____

2. 

a photograph that you take of yourself

____

3. 

happening or done without delay

____

4. 

impossible or very difficult to believe

____

5. 

to take after someone

____

6. 

to copy someone or something

____

B Write the correct word or phrase next to each definition.

snap	imaginary	unrealistic	technique	on one's own	unbelievable

1. not realistic; not showing things as they are in real life ______________________
2. not real; existing only in your mind or imagination ______________________
3. to break with a sudden sharp sound, or to make a sharp sound ______________________
4. a special way of doing something that needs skill ______________________
5. very difficult to believe and unlikely to be true ______________________
6. alone; without anyone's help; by oneself ______________________

DAY 02

021 **broadcast**
[brɔ́ːdkæst]

to send out a program on television or radio **(broadcast-broadcast)**
동 방송하다 명 방송, 방영

The game will be **broadcast** live tomorrow. 그 경기는 내일 생중계될 것이다.
watch a live **broadcast** 생방송[생중계]을 시청하다

022 **channel**
[ʧǽnl]

a television or radio station
명 1. (TV 등의) 채널 2. 수로, 해협

What's on **Channel** 5 tonight? 오늘 밤 5번 채널에서는 뭘 하지?
I changed the **channel** to watch the show. 나는 그 쇼를 보기 위해 채널을 돌렸다.
the English **Channel** 영국 해협

023 **fame**
[feim]
famous 형 유명한

the state of being known or recognized by many people
명 명성, 명망

Thanks to the talent show, he won instant **fame**.
그 경연 프로그램 덕분에 그는 즉각적인 명성을 얻었다.
bring **fame** and fortune 명성과 부를 가져오다

024 **celebrity**
[səlébrəti]

a famous person
명 유명 인사, (유명) 연예인 = (비격식) celeb

He became a **celebrity** overnight. 그는 하룻밤 사이에 유명인이 되었다.
TV **celebrities** 텔레비전 유명 연예인들

025 **interview**
[íntərvjùː]

a meeting where a famous person is asked questions for a magazine, etc.
명 1. 인터뷰, 회견 ((with)) 2. 면접(시험) 동 인터뷰를 하다

They had an **interview with** the pop star. 그들은 그 팝스타와 인터뷰를 했다.
I have a job **interview** tomorrow. 나는 내일 취업 면접이 있다.

026 **profile**
[próufail]

a side view of someone's head
명 1. 옆얼굴, 측면 2. 인물 소개, 프로필 *outline 개요, 윤곽(선)

He has a handsome **profile**. 그는 옆얼굴이 잘생겼다.
introduce a brief **profile** of the actor 그 배우의 간략한 프로필을 소개하다

027 **passion**
[pǽʃən]
passionate 형 열정적인, 열렬한

a very strong feeling about a subject
명 열정, 격정, 열망 ((for))

He has a **passion for** his work. 그는 자신의 일에 대한 열정이 있다.

028 **applaud**
[əplɔ́ːd]
applause 명 박수(갈채)

to express approval or praise by clapping
동 박수를 치다, 갈채를 보내다

The audience **applauded** loudly. 관객들이 크게 박수를 쳤다.

029 **cast**
[kæst]

to choose actors to play particular parts in a play or movie **(cast-cast)**
동 1. 배역을 정하다, 캐스팅하다 2. 던지다 명 (영화 등의) 출연자들, 배역

The director **cast** her in the lead role. 그 감독은 그녀를 주연으로 캐스팅했다.
The die is **cast.** 주사위는 (이미) 던져졌다.
introduce **the cast of** the movie 그 영화의 출연진을 소개하다

---

030 **supervise**
[súːpərvàiz]
supervisor 명 감독관, 관리자

to be in charge of; to watch and direct
동 감독하다, 관리하다 *direct 지휘하다, 총괄하다

The director will **supervise** the entire shoot. 감독은 모든 촬영을 감독할 것이다.

---

031 **rival**
[ráivəl]
rivalry 명 경쟁(의식)

a person, company, or organization that competes with another
명 경쟁자, 경쟁 상대 유 competitor 경쟁자, (시합) 참가자

They have been **rivals** for a long time. 그들은 오랫동안 경쟁자였다.

---

032 **instinct**
[ínstiŋkt]
instinctive 형 본능적인
instinctively 부 본능적으로, 직감적으로

a natural tendency to behave in a particular way
명 1. 본능 2. 직감 = intuition

She knew it **by instinct.** 그녀는 그것을 본능적으로 알았다.
Her **instincts** have always been right. 그녀의 직감은 늘 옳았다.

---

033 **insult**
[insʌ́lt]

to say or do something that is rude or offensive to someone
동 모욕하다 명 [ínsʌlt] 모욕, 모욕적인 말[행동]

He **insulted** her in front of her friends. 그는 그녀의 친구들 앞에서 그녀를 모욕했다.
She took his comments as an **insult.** 그녀는 그의 말을 모욕으로 받아들였다.

---

034 **offend**
[əfénd]
offensive 형 모욕적인, 불쾌한

to make someone upset or angry
동 1. 기분 상하게[화나게] 하다 2. 불쾌감을 주다

She was deeply **offended** by his comments. 그녀는 그의 발언에 몹시 기분이 상했다.
She **felt offended** by his joke. 그녀는 그의 농담에 불쾌감을 느꼈다.

---

035 **pity**
[píti]
pitiful 형 가엾은

a feeling of sadness or sympathy for someone or something
명 1. 동정, 연민, 불쌍히 여김 ((for)) 2. 유감 동 동정하다

I **felt pity for** him. 나는 그에게 동정심을 느꼈다[그를 불쌍히 여겼다/그가 딱했다].
It's a pity that you can't come with us. 네가 우리와 함께 갈 수 없다니 안타깝다.
She **pitied** the little child. 그녀는 그 어린아이를 불쌍히 여겼다.

---

036 **sympathy**
[símpəθi]
sympathetic 형 동정적인; 동조하는

the feeling of being sorry for someone (who is in a bad situation)
명 1. 연민, 동정심 ((for)) 2. 동의[동조], 지지 ((with))

I **have sympathy for** the less fortunate. 나는 불우한 사람들에게 연민을 느낀다.
She was **in sympathy with** my view. 그녀는 내 의견에 동조했다.

037 **dramatic**
[drəmǽtik]
dramatically 부 극적으로

sudden and extreme; exciting or impressive
형 1. 급격한, 극적인 2. 감격적인, 인상적인

bring a **dramatic** change 극적인 변화를 가져오다
Our team achieved a **dramatic** victory. 우리 팀이 감격적인 승리를 거두었다.

038 **twist**
[twist]
twisted 형 꼬인, 뒤틀린

an unexpected change or development in a story or situation
명 (예상 밖의) 전환, 반전 동 1. 구부리다 2. 돌리다, 비틀다

The movie features a dramatic **twist**. 그 영화는 극적인 반전을 특징으로 한다.
twist a wire 철사를 구부리다
The story **twists and turns** until the end. 그 이야기는 끝까지 반전을 거듭한다.

039 **show off**

to try to impress others by talking about your abilities or possessions
(~을) 자랑하다, 으스대다, 과시하다 *show-off 과시적인 사람, 잘난 척하는 사람

He likes to **show off** his new car. 그는 자신의 새 차를 자랑하기를 좋아한다.
Stop **showing off**. 살난 척 솜 그만해. / 그만 자랑해라.

040 **be scheduled to**

to be planned to do something
~할 예정이다

The movie **is scheduled to** be released in July. 그 영화는 7월에 개봉될 예정이다.
The meeting **is scheduled to** start at 10:00 AM. 회의는 오전 10시에 시작될 예정이다.

Check Up

A 우리말에 맞게 빈칸에 알맞은 말을 넣으세요.

1. 생방송[생중계]을 시청하다 — watch a live ____________
2. 명성과 부를 가져오다 — bring ____________ and fortune
3. 하룻밤 사이에 유명인이 되다 — become a ____________ overnight
4. 간략한 프로필을 소개하다 — introduce a brief ____________
5. ~에게 동정심을 느끼다[~을 불쌍히 여기다] — feel ____________ for
6. 극적인 반전 — a dramatic ____________

B 우리말에 알맞은 말을 골라 문장을 완성하세요.

1. They (**have rivals** / **have been rivals**) for a long time. 그들은 오랫동안 경쟁자였다.
2. She knew it (**instinct** / **by instinct**). 그녀는 그것을 본능적으로 알았다.
3. She was (**insulted** / **offended**) by his comments. 그녀는 그의 발언에 기분이 상했다.
4. I have (**sympathy for** / **sympathy with**) the less fortunate. 나는 불우한 사람들에게 연민을 느낀다.
5. Stop (**show off** / **showing off**). 잘난 척 좀 그만해. / 그만 자랑해라.

Build Up

A Write the correct word for each definition.

applaud	celebrity	profile	insult	channel	supervise

1. 

a television or radio station

____

2. 

a famous person

____

3. 

to express approval or praise by clapping

____

4. 

a side view of someone's head

____

5. 

to watch and direct

____

6. 

to say or do something that is rude

____

B Write the correct word or phrase next to each definition.

interview	passion	broadcast	be scheduled to	cast	sympathy

1. to send out a program on television or radio __________
2. a very strong feeling about a subject __________
3. to choose actors to play particular parts in a play or movie __________
4. the feeling of being sorry for someone (who is in a bad situation) __________
5. to be planned to do something __________
6. a meeting where a famous person is asked questions for a magazine, etc. __________

041 **weird**
[wiərd]

very strange or unusual and difficult to explain
형 기이한, 기묘한, 기괴한 유 strange, odd 이상한

have a **weird** dream 기이한 꿈을 꾸다
There was a **weird** sound coming from the basement. 지하실에서 이상한 소리가 났다.

042 **wicked**
[wíkid]

morally wrong and bad
형 1. 사악한 2. 짓궂은, 장난기 있는

The musical features the Good Witch and the **Wicked** Witch.
그 뮤지컬에는 착한 마녀와 사악한 마녀가 나온다.
a story about the **Wicked** Witch of the West in *The Wizard of Oz*
〈오즈의 마법사〉에 나오는 사악한 서쪽 마녀에 관한 이야기
give a **wicked** smile 짓궂은[음흉한] 미소를 짓다

043 **spell**
[spel]

words that are thought to have magic power
명 주문, 마법 ((on)) 동 철자를 말하다

a magic **spell** 마법의 주문
She **cast a spell on** the monkeys. 그녀는 그 원숭이들에게 주문을 걸었다.
Her name is **spelled** E-l-p-h-a-b-a. 그녀의 이름은 E-l-p-h-a-b-a라고 쓴다.

044 **enable**
[inéibl]

able 형 할 수 있는

to make it possible for someone to do something
동 ~을 할 수 있게 하다, ~을 가능하게 하다 ((to)) = allow

The magic spell **enabled** them **to** fly. 그 마법의 주문은 그들을 날 수 있게 했다.
Your dream **enables** you **to** reach for the stars. 너의 꿈은 네가 별에 닿을 수 있게 해 준다.

045 **distinct**
[distíŋkt]

distinctly 부 뚜렷하게, 명백하게
distinctive 형 특이한, 눈에 띄는

clearly different or separate
형 1. 뚜렷이 다른[구별되는], 별개의 ((from)) 2. 뚜렷한, 분명한

The two groups are completely **distinct from** each other. 그 두 그룹은 서로 완전히 다르다.
She has a **distinct** American accent. 그녀는 뚜렷한 미국 억양을 가지고 있다.

046 **distinguish**
[distíŋgwiʃ]

to recognize the difference between two people or things
동 1. 구별하다 ((between A and B)) 2. 특징 짓다, 차이를 나타내다 ((A from B))

It's important to **distinguish between** right **and** wrong. 옳고 그름을 구별하는 것은 중요하다.
Language **distinguishes** human beings **from** animals. 언어는 인간을 동물과 구별 짓는다.

047 **insight**
[ínsàit]

the ability to see and understand the truth about people or situations
명 통찰력 ((into)) *perception 자각, 통찰력

a writer of great **insight** 대단한 통찰력이 있는 작가
He has deep **insight into** life. 그는 인생에 대한 깊은 통찰력을 가지고 있다.

048 **perspective**
[pərspéktiv]

a way of thinking about something
명 관점, 시각 = viewpoint

The novel is written from a child's **perspective**. 그 소설은 아이의 시각[관점]에서 쓰여졌다.
Let's see the issue from a different **perspective**. 이 문제를 다른 관점에서 살펴보자.

049 **fragile**
[frǽdʒəl]

easily broken or damaged

형 1. 깨지기[부서지기] 쉬운 2. 취약한, 허술한 반 durable 내구성이 있는, 오래가는

fragile glass 깨지기 쉬운 유리
Their friendship is **fragile**. 그들의 우정은 쉽게 깨질 수 있다[허약하다].

050 **delicate**
[délikət]
delicacy 명 여림; 섬세함

needing to be dealt with very carefully; easily damaged or broken

형 1. 연약한, 다치기[부서지기] 쉬운 = fragile 2. 섬세한 3. 미묘한, 다루기 힘든

Handle it with care. It's very **delicate**. 그것을 조심해서 다루세요. 깨지기[다치기] 쉬워요.
It requires a **delicate** touch. 그것은 섬세한 손길을 필요로 한다.
a **delicate** situation 미묘한 상황

051 **cautious**
[kɔ́ːʃəs]
cautiously 부 조심스럽게

being careful about what you say or do, especially to avoid danger or mistakes

형 조심스러운, 신중한 ((about)) 유 careful 조심하는

Be **cautious** not to drop it. 그것을 떨어뜨리지 않도록 조심해.
She is **cautious about** making big decisions. 그녀는 큰 결정을 내리는 데 신중하다.

052 **caution**
[kɔ́ːʃən]

great care and attention; a warning or a piece of advice

명 1. 조심, 신중 2. 주의, 경고 동 주의[경고]를 주다 ((against/about))

This should be treated **with caution**. 이것은 조심해서 다뤄져야 한다.
I **cautioned** him **against** ignoring the instructions.
나는 그에게 지침을 무시하지 말라고 주의를 주었다.

053 **sensitive**
[sénsətiv]
sense 명 감각 동 감지하다, 느끼다

easily hurt or damaged

형 예민한, 민감한, 세심한 ((about/to)) 반 insensitive 둔감한

She is very **sensitive about** her weight. 그녀는 자신의 몸무게에 아주 예민하다.
a soap for **sensitive** skin 민감한 피부를 위한 비누
a **sensitive** topic 민감한 주제

054 **sensible**
[sénsəbl]

reasonable, practical, and showing good judgment

형 분별 있는, 현명한

It's not **sensible** to go out alone at night. 밤에 혼자 나가는 것은 분별 있는 행동이 아니다.
That was a **sensible** decision. 그것은 현명한 결정이었다.

055 **humble**
[hʌ́mbl]

not proud; not thinking of yourself as better than other people

형 1. 겸손한 2. (신분 등이) 미천한, 낮은

a very **humble** person 아주 겸손한 사람
He comes from a **humble** background. 그는 미천한 집안 출신이다.

056 **modest**
[mádist]
modestly 부 겸손하게; 적당히

not too proud or confident about yourself or your abilities

형 1. 겸손한 ((about)) = humble 2. 적당한, 보통의, 수수한

He was very **modest about** his achievements. 그는 자신의 성취에 대해 아주 겸손했다.
a **modest** little house 수수한 작은[아담한] 집

057 **essential**

[isénʃəl]

essence 명 본질, 정수

extremely important and necessary

형 1. 필수적인 ((for/to)) = vital 2. 본질적인, 근본적인

Hard work is **essential for** your success. 노력은 성공에 필수적이다.
It's essential to book in advance. 미리 예약하는 것이 필수이다.
the **essential** difference between him and me 그와 나의 본질적인 차이

058 **dedicate**

[dédikèit]

dedicated 형 전념하는, 헌신적인
dedication 명 전념, 헌신

to give a lot of your time and effort to something

동 1. (시간·노력을) 바치다, 헌신하다 = devote 2. (책 등을) 헌정하다 ((to))

He **dedicated** his life **to** helping the poor. 그는 일생을 가난한 이들을 돕는 데 바쳤다.
This book is **dedicated to** my parents. 이 책을 나의 부모님께 바칩니다.

059 **make up with (someone)**

to end an argument with someone and to become friends again

~와 화해하다

Did you **make up with** Glinda? 너 글린다랑 화해했니?
I hope they can **make up with** each other soon. 나는 그들이 곧 서로 화해할 수 있기를 바란다.

060 **make up for**

to make a bad situation better, or replace something that has been lost

(손실 등을) 메우다, 보충하다, 만회하다 = compensate

He worked hard to **make up for** the loss. 그는 손실을 메우기 위해 열심히 일했다.
I bought flowers to **make up for** my mistake. 나는 내 실수를 만회하기 위해 꽃을 샀다.

Check Up

A 우리말에 맞게 빈칸에 알맞은 말을 넣으세요.

1. 기이한 꿈을 꾸다 — have a ______________ dream
2. ~에게 주문을 걸다 — cast a ______________ on
3. 대단한 통찰력이 있는 작가 — a writer of great ______________
4. 깨지기 쉬운 유리 — ______________ glass
5. 섬세한 손길을 필요로 하다 — require a ______________ touch
6. 조심해서 다루다 — treat with ______________

B 우리말에 알맞은 말을 골라 문장을 완성하세요.

1. The magic spell (**enabled** / **dedicated**) them to fly. 그 마법의 주문은 그들을 날 수 있게 했다.
2. It's important to (**distinct** / **distinguish**) between right and wrong. 옳고 그름을 구별하는 것은 중요하다.
3. The novel is written from a child's (**insight** / **perspective**). 그 소설은 아이의 시각[관점]에서 쓰여졌다.
4. That was a (**sensible** / **sensitive**) decision. 그것은 현명한 결정이었다.
5. He worked hard to (**make up with** / **make up for**) the loss. 그는 손실을 메우기 위해 열심히 일했다.

Build Up

A Write the correct word for each definition.

cautious
humble
sensitive
wicked
fragile
distinct

1. 

morally wrong and bad

2. 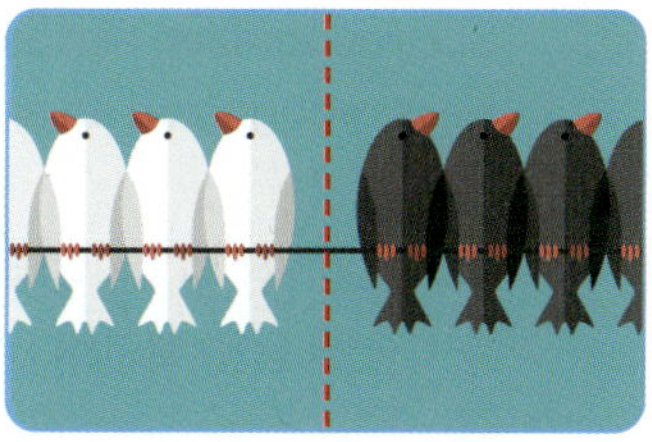

clearly different or separate

3. 

easily broken or damaged

4. 

being careful about what you say or do

5. 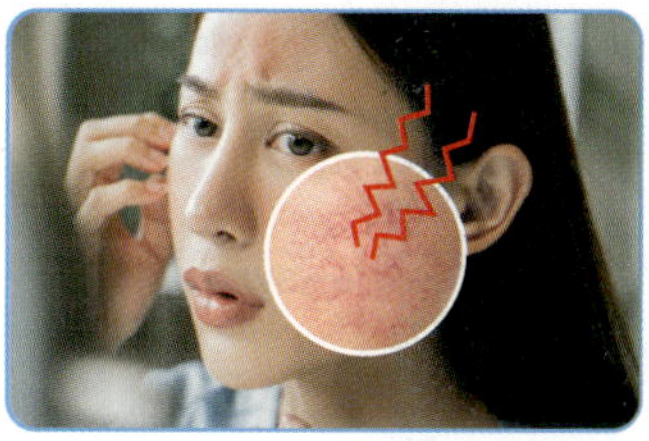

easily hurt or damaged

6. 

not proud

B Write the correct word or phrase next to each definition.

enable	insight	distinguish	dedicate	make up with	modest

1. to make it possible for someone to do something
2. to recognize the difference between two people or things
3. not too proud or confident about yourself or your abilities
4. to give a lot of your time and effort to something
5. to end an argument with someone and to become friends again
6. the ability to see and understand the truth about people or situations

DAY 04

061 **recognize**
[rékəgnàiz]
recognition 명 알아봄, 인식; 인정

to know someone or something (because you have seen or heard them before)
동 1. (누구·무엇인지) 알아보다 2. 인정하다; (~으로) 인정받다 ((as))

She **recognized** him as soon as she saw him. 그녀는 그를 보자마자 알아봤다.
He is **recognized as** an expert in this field. 그는 이 분야의 전문가로 인정받고 있다.

---

062 **identify**
[aidéntəfài]
identity 명 신원; 정체성
identification (ID) 명 신분 증명(서)

to recognize and correctly name someone or something
동 1. (신원 등을) 확인하다, 알아보다 ((as)) 2. 찾다, 발견하다

The police **identified** the man. 경찰이 그 남자의 신원을 확인했다.
She **identified** him **as** the thief. 그녀는 그를 도둑으로 확인했다(지목했다).
Scientists have **identified** the cause of the disease. 과학자들은 그 병의 원인을 밝혀냈다.

---

063 **fake**
[feik]

not real, but made to look or seem real
형 가짜의, 모조의 유 false 인조의, 가짜의 명 모조품 = imitation 반 original 원본

carry a **fake** ID card 가짜[위조] 신분증을 소지하다
The painting was identified as a **fake**. 그 그림은 모조품으로 밝혀졌다.

---

064 **genuine**
[dʒénjuin]
genuinely 부 진심으로

real or true; not fake or false
형 1. 진짜의, 진품의 2. 진심 어린, 진실된 = sincere

It's not a **genuine** Picasso. 그것은 피카소 진품이 아니다.
a **genuine** concern for the poor 가난한 사람들에 대한 진심 어린 걱정[관심]
She is a very **genuine** person. 그녀는 아주 진실된 사람이다.

---

065 **swear**
[swɛər]

to make a serious promise to do something **(swore-sworn)**
동 1. 맹세하다 ((to)) = vow 2. 욕을 하다 ((at))

I **swear to** tell the truth. 나는 진실을 말할 것을 맹세한다.
He **swore at** them loudly. 그는 그들에게 큰 소리로 욕을 했다.

---

066 **ensure**
[inʃúər]
sure 형 확신하는, 확실한

to make sure that something happens
동 반드시 ~하게 하다, 보장하다 유 guarantee 보증하다

We must **ensure** the safety of kids. 우리는 아이들의 안전을 보장해야 한다.
Please **ensure** that the door is locked. 문이 잠겨 있는지 확인해 주세요.

---

067 **shameful**
[ʃéimfəl]
shame 명 부끄러움, 수치심
shamefully 부 창피스럽게

bad enough to make you feel ashamed
형 수치스러운, 창피한, 부끄러운 = disgraceful

It was **shameful** behavior. 그것은 부끄러운 행동이었다.

---

068 **ashamed**
[əʃéimd]

feeling shame or embarrassment about someone or something
형 부끄러운, 창피한 ((of)) 반 proud 자랑스러운

You should be **ashamed of** yourself. 너는 네 자신을 부끄러워해야 한다.
He **felt ashamed of** his behavior. 그는 자신의 행동에 부끄러움을 느꼈다.

069 **state**
[steit]
statement 명 진술

the condition that something or someone is in
명 1. 상태, 형편 2. (미국 등의) 주 동 (정식으로) 진술하다

He was **in a state of** panic. 그는 공황[패닉] 상태에 있었다.
Alaska is the largest **state** in the U.S. 알래스카는 미국에서 가장 큰 주이다.
Please **state** your full name for the record. 기록을 위해 당신의 성명을 말씀해 주세요.

070 **status**
[stéitəs]

the official or social position of a person or group
명 1. (법적) 신분 2. (사회적) 지위 3. (진행) 상황 *situation 상황, 처지 *condition (건강) 상태

his **status** as a British citizen 그의 영국 시민으로서의 신분
He has a high social **status**. 그는 높은 사회적 지위를 가지고 있다.
a **status** report on the project 그 프로젝트에 대한 현황 보고서

071 **certificate**
[sərtífikət]

an official document that states that certain facts are true
명 1. 증서, 증명서 2. 수료증, 자격증

a birth **certificate** 출생 증명서
He received a **certificate** after finishing the course. 그는 그 과정을 마친 후 수료증을 받았다.

072 **valid**
[vǽlid]
validity 명 유효함; 타당성

legally or officially acceptable
형 1. (법적으로) 유효한 2. (논리적으로) 타당한, 정당한 반 invalid 무효한; 근거 없는

a **valid** passport 유효한 여권
There is no **valid** reason to reject their requests. 그들의 요청을 거부할 타당한 이유가 없다.

073 **permit**
[pərmít]

to allow something to happen, especially by rules or laws
동 허락하다, 허가하다 ((to)) = allow, let 명 [pə́:rmit] 허가(증)

They **permitted** him **to** leave. 그들은 그가 떠나는 것을 허락했다.
Smoking is not **permitted** here. 여기서는 흡연이 허락되지 않는다(금지되어 있다).
a work **permit** 취업 허가증

074 **permission**
[pərmíʃən]

the act of allowing someone to do something
명 허락, 허가, 승인 유 approval 승인

You need to **get permission** first. 당신은 먼저 허가를 받아야 한다.
You can't park here **without permission**. 당신은 허가 없이 여기에 주차할 수 없다.

075 **approve**
[əprú:v]
approval 명 승인

to officially accept a plan, proposal, etc.
동 1. (공식적으로) 승인하다 2. 찬성하다 ((of)) 반 disapprove 승인[찬성]하지 않다

The committee **approved** the budget. 위원회는 그 예산을 승인했다.
He doesn't **approve of** smoking. 그는 흡연에 찬성하지 않는다.

076 **consent**
[kənsént]

to agree to something; to give your permission for something
동 동의하다, 허락하다 ((to)) 반 refuse 거절하다 명 동의, 승낙 = agreement, permission

They finally **consented to** the plan. 그들은 마침내 그 계획(안)에 동의했다.
You need your parents' **consent** to participate. 참가하려면 부모님의 동의가 필요하다.

077 **qualify**
[kwάləfài]
qualification 명 자격, 자격증

to give someone the right to do something
동 1. 자격을 주다; 자격이 있다 ((for)) 2. 자격(증)을 얻다 ((as))

This course will **qualify** you to teach yoga.
이 과정은 당신에게 요가를 가르칠 수 있는 자격을 줄 것이다.
She **qualifies for** the scholarship. 그녀는 장학금을 받을 자격이 있다(요건에 부합한다).
She **qualified as** a doctor last year. 그녀는 작년에 의사 자격을 얻었다(자격증을 땄다).

078 **grant**
[grænt]

to give or allow someone something, usually in an official way
동 1. (공식적으로) 주다, 수여하다 유 give 주다 2. (법적으로) 승인하다 *allow 허락하다

grant permission 허가해 주다
They were **granted** citizenship. 그들은 시민권을 부여받았다.

079 **identify A with B**

to consider A to be the same as B
A를 B와 동일시하다

Many people **identify** quality **with** price. 많은 사람들이 품질을 가격과 동일시한다.
You should not **identify** wealth **with** happiness. 부를 행복과 동일시해서는 안 된다.

080 **can tell**

to be able to recognize someone or something
(~을) 구별하다, (~라는 것을) 알 수 있다

Can you **tell** if it's a genuine diamond or not?
너는 그것이 진짜 다이아몬드인지 아닌지 구별할 수 있니?
I **could tell** it was him by his voice. 나는 그의 목소리로 그라는 것을 알 수 있었다.

Check Up

A 우리말에 맞게 빈칸에 알맞은 말을 넣으세요.

1. 가짜[위조] 신분증을 소지하다 — carry a ________________ ID card
2. 피카소 진품 — a ________________ Picasso
3. ~에 부끄러움을 느끼다 — feel ________________ of
4. 공황[패닉] 상태에 있다 — be in ________________ panic
5. 출생 증명서 — a birth ________________
6. 유효한 여권 — a ________________ passport

B 우리말에 알맞은 말을 골라 문장을 완성하세요.

1. She (**qualified** / **identified**) him as the thief. 그녀는 그를 도둑으로 확인했다(지목했다).
2. I (**swear to** / **swear at**) tell the truth. 나는 진실을 말할 것을 맹세한다.
3. We must (**enable** / **ensure**) the safety of kids. 우리는 아이들의 안전을 보장해야 한다.
4. You need to (**get permission** / **grant permission**) first. 당신은 먼저 허가를 받아야 한다.
5. He doesn't (**approve for** / **approve of**) smoking. 그는 흡연에 찬성하지 않는다.

Build Up

A **Write the correct word for each definition.**

recognize	shameful	consent	certificate	genuine	swear

1. 

to know someone or something

____

2. 

The Museum of Modern Art, New York

real or true; not fake or false

____

3. 

to make a serious promise

____

4. 

bad enough to make you feel ashamed

____

5. 

an official document that states that certain facts are true

____

6. 

to agree to something

____

B **Write the correct word or phrase next to each definition.**

qualify	approve	identify A with B	ensure	permit	status

1. to make sure that something happens ______________
2. the official or social position of a person or group ______________
3. to allow something to happen, especially by rules or laws ______________
4. to officially accept a plan, proposal, etc. ______________
5. to give someone the right to do something ______________
6. to consider A to be the same as B ______________

Review Test 01 DAY 01-04

A 그림을 보고, 빈칸에 알맞은 단어를 넣으세요.

certificate　applaud　virtual　profile　fragile　wicked

1. 
____

2. 
____

3. 
____

4. 

____

5. 
____

6. 
____

B 그림에 맞게 빈칸에 알맞은 단어를 고르세요.

1. 

She __________ her mother.
(resembles / imitates)

2. 

Parrots can __________ human speech.
(resemble / imitate)

3. 

He became a __________ overnight.
(selfie / celebrity)

4. 

I __________ tell the truth.
(swear to / swear at)

C 우리말 뜻에 맞게 빈칸에 알맞은 말을 넣으세요.

on my own	pose for	take after	make up for
broadcast	a spell	distinguish	sympathy for

1. ____________ a photograph 사진을 찍기 위해 포즈를 취하다
2. ____________ someone ~를 닮다
3. watch a movie ____________ 나 혼자 영화를 보다
4. watch a live ____________ 생방송[생중계]을 시청하다
5. have ____________ ~에게 연민을 느끼다
6. cast ____________ on ~에게 주문을 걸다
7. ____________ between right and wrong 옳고 그름을 구별하다
8. ____________ the loss 손실을 메우다

D 우리말 뜻에 맞게 빈칸에 알맞은 말을 넣으세요.

in a state of	by instinct	get permission
impact on	show off	identify ~ with

1. New technology has a great ____________ our lives. 신기술은 우리의 삶에 큰 영향을 미친다.
2. She knew it ____________. 그녀는 그것을 본능적으로 알았다.
3. He likes to ____________ his new car. 그는 자신의 새 차를 자랑하기를 좋아한다.
4. She was ____________ panic. 그녀는 공황[패닉] 상태에 있었다.
5. You need to ____________ first. 당신은 먼저 허가를 받아야 한다.
6. You should not ____________ wealth ____________ happiness. 부를 행복과 동일시해서는 안 된다.

E 밑줄 친 단어와 비슷한 뜻을 가진 단어를 고르세요.

1. What a brilliant idea!

a. different　　b. distinct　　c. excellent

2. It had an immediate effect.

a. total　　b. instant　　c. complete

3. Be cautious not to drop it.

a. delicate　　b. fragile　　c. careful

4. He was very modest about his achievements.

a. shameful　　b. humble　　c. responsible

F 밑줄 친 단어와 반대의 뜻을 가진 단어를 고르세요.

1. Everything is possible in a virtual world.

a. imaginary　　b. real　　c. magic

2. It's not a genuine Picasso.

a. fake　　b. weird　　c. real

3. You should be ashamed of yourself.

a. shameful　　b. proud　　c. dedicated

4. They finally consented to the plan.

a. permitted　　b. granted　　c. refused

G 주어진 영영풀이에 알맞은 단어를 고르세요.

1. not real; existing only in your mind or imagination

   a. virtual   b. imaginary   c. modest

2. worth remembering or likely to be remembered

   a. forgettable   b. unbelievable   c. memorable

3. impossible or very difficult to believe

   a. incredible   b. brilliant   c. unrealistic

4. to say or do something that is rude or offensive to someone

   a. insult   b. offend   c. supervise

5. to make it possible for someone to do something

   a. impossible   b. unable   c. enable

6. needing to be dealt with very carefully; easily damaged or broken

   a. dedicate   b. delicate   c. sensitive

H 빈칸에 알맞은 동사 형태를 넣어 문장을 완성하세요.

1. Her style has been ______________ by other writers. (imitate)
2. The game will be ______________ live tomorrow. (broadcast)
3. This book is ______________ my parents. (dedicate to)
4. He is ______________ an expert in this field. (recognize as)

DAY 05

081 **opportunity**
[ɑːpərtúːnəti]

a chance to do something good
명 기회 = chance

a rare **opportunity** 드문 기회
Don't miss this **opportunity** to show your talents.
당신의 재능을 보여 줄 이번 기회를 놓치지 마세요.

082 **seize**
[siːz]

to take hold of something suddenly and violently
동 1. 와락 붙잡다, 꽉 움켜잡다 = grab 2. 장악하다

Suddenly, he **seized** my arm. 갑자기 그가 내 팔을 붙잡았다.
Don't hesitate to **seize** the opportunity. 주저하지 말고 기회를 잡으세요.
The military **seized** the city. 군대가 그 도시를 장악했다.

083 **opt**
[ɑpt]
option 명 선택권, 선택(할 수 있는 것)

to make a choice from a range of options
동 (~하기로) 택하다 ((for/to)) 유 choose, pick, select 선택하다

She **opted for** a career in music. 그녀는 음악 분야의 직업을 택했다.
She **opted to** participate in the event. 그녀는 그 행사에 참여하기로 했다.

084 **optimist**
[ɑ́ptəmist]
optimistic 형 낙관적인
optimism 명 낙관론, 낙관주의

a person who always believes that good things will happen
명 낙관론자, 낙천주의자 반 pessimist 비관주의자

She's an **optimist**. 그녀는 낙천주의자이다.

085 **survey**
[sə́ːrvei]

an examination of people's opinions made by asking people questions
명 설문 조사 동 [sərvéi] 설문 조사하다

do a **survey** 설문 조사를 하다
They **surveyed** 500 customers about the issue.
그들은 그 문제에 대해 500명의 고객에게 설문 조사를 했다.

086 **random**
[rǽndəm]
randomly 부 무작위로

done or chosen without any plan or system
형 무작위의, 닥치는 대로 하는

The survey used a **random** sample of 500 people.
그 설문 조사는 500명의 무작위 표본을 사용했다.
Pick a **random** number between 1 and 100. 1과 100 사이의 임의의 수를 고르시오.

087 **precise**
[prisáis]
precision 명 정확(성), 정밀(성)

exact, clear, and correct
형 정확한, 명확한, 정밀한

precise details 정확한 세부 내용
It was difficult to get **precise** information. 정확한 정보를 얻기는 어려웠다.

088 **accurate**
[ǽkjərət]
accuracy 명 정확(도)

correct and true in every detail
형 정확한, 틀림없는 반 inaccurate 부정확한

an **accurate** calculation 정확한 계산
The data was not **accurate**. 그 데이터는 정확하지 않았다.

089 **evaluate**
[ivǽljuèit]
evaluation 명 평가

to judge or calculate the amount, value, or quality of something
동 (양·가치 등을) 평가하다, 감정하다 *measure (수치 등을) 측정하다

We will **evaluate** how accurate the survey was.
우리는 그 설문 조사가 얼마나 정확했는지 평가할 것이다.

090 **assess**
[əsés]
assessment 명 평가; 평가 액

to make a judgment about something
동 (특성·가치 등을) 재다, 평가하다, 산정하다 ((at)) *estimate 추산하다

The teacher will **assess** the students' work. 선생님은 학생들의 작업을 평가할 것이다.
His house is **assessed at** one million dollars. 그의 집은 100만 달러로 감정된다.

091 **moderate**
[mádərət]

average in size or amount; neither too much nor too little
형 1. 보통의, 중간의 유 intermediate 중간의, 중급의 2. 적당한, 온건한

a student of **moderate** ability 중간 정도의 능력을 지닌 학생
I enjoy **moderate** exercise like walking. 나는 걷기와 같은 적당한 운동을 즐긴다.

092 **profound**
[prəfáund]
profoundly 부 깊이, 극심하게

very great or intense; felt or experienced very strongly
형 깊은, 심오한 유 deep 깊은

The book had a **profound** impact on her. 그 책은 그녀에게 깊은 영향을 미쳤다.
a **profound** question 심오한 질문

093 **endure**
[indjúər]
endurable 형 참을 수 있는

to experience (pain or suffering) for a long time
동 1. 견디다, 참다 = stand, bear 2. 오래가다, 지속되다 = last

She learned to **endure** difficult situations. 그녀는 어려운 상황을 견디는 법을 배웠다.
This tradition has **endured** for centuries. 이 전통은 수세기 동안 지속되어 왔다.

094 **durable**
[djúərəbl]
durability 명 내구성

able to last and be used for a long time (without becoming damaged)
형 내구성이 있는, 오래가는 = long-lasting

This suitcase is made of **durable** plastic. 이 여행 가방은 내구성이 있는 플라스틱으로 만들어졌다.
a **durable** battery 오래가는 건전지

095 **length**
[leŋkθ]
long 형 긴

the size or measurement of something from one end to the other
명 1. (사물의) 길이 2. (지속되는) 시간, 기간 *width 넓이

measure the **length** and width of a box 상자의 길이와 넓이를 재다
during the **length** of stay 체류 기간 동안

096 **depth**
[depθ]
deep 형 깊은

the distance from the top of something to the bottom
명 깊이 *height 높이

measure the **depth** of a hole 구멍의 깊이를 재다
We discussed the topic **in depth**. 우리는 그 주제에 대해 깊이 있게 논의했다.

097 **maximum**
[mǽksəməm]

being the largest amount that is allowed or possible

형 최대의, 최고의 명 최대, 최대량[수] 반 minimum 최소, 최저

What's the **maximum** weight limit? 최대 중량 한도는 얼마인가요?
You can carry **a maximum of** two bags. 당신은 최대 두 개의 가방을 휴대할 수 있다.

098 **mass**
[mæs]

massive 형 거대한

a large amount of something that has no particular shape

명 1. 덩어리 2. 다수, 다량 ((of)) 형 대량의, 대규모의; 대중의

It looked like **a mass of** rock. 그것은 바위 덩어리처럼 보였다.
The garden was **a mass of** roses. 정원은 장미로 가득했다.
mass production 대량 생산
mass media 대중 매체

099 **at random**

without deciding in advance what is going to happen

무작위로, 임의로 = randomly

Participants were selected **at random.** 참가자들은 무작위로 선정되었다.
Winners will be chosen **at random.** 우승자는 무작위로 선정된다.

100 **put up with**

to endure something unpleasant without complaining

~을 참다[참고 견디다] = stand, bear, endure

She **put up with** the pain. 그녀는 고통을 참았다.
I can't **put up with** this noise anymore. 나는 더 이상 이 소음을 참을 수 없다.

Check Up

A 우리말에 맞게 빈칸에 알맞은 말을 넣으세요.

1. 드문 기회 — a rare ________________
2. 설문 조사를 하다 — do a ________________
3. 심오한 질문 — a ________________ question
4. 대량 생산 — ________________ production
5. 무작위로 선정되다 — be selected ________________
6. 고통을 참다 — ________________ with the pain

B 우리말에 알맞은 말을 골라 문장을 완성하세요.

1. She (**opted to** / **opted for**) a career in music. 그녀는 음악 분야의 직업을 택했다.
2. The teacher will (**accurate** / **assess**) the students' work. 선생님은 학생들의 작업을 평가할 것이다.
3. I enjoy (**moderate** / **precise**) exercise like walking. 나는 걷기와 같은 적당한 운동을 즐긴다.
4. She learned to (**endure** / **evaluate**) difficult situations. 그녀는 어려운 상황을 견디는 법을 배웠다.
5. We discussed the topic (**in length** / **in depth**). 우리는 그 주제에 대해 깊이 있게 논의했다.

Build Up

A Write the correct word for each definition.

opt	seize	durable	evaluate	moderate	precise

1. 

to take hold of something suddenly

____

2. 

to make a choice

____

3. 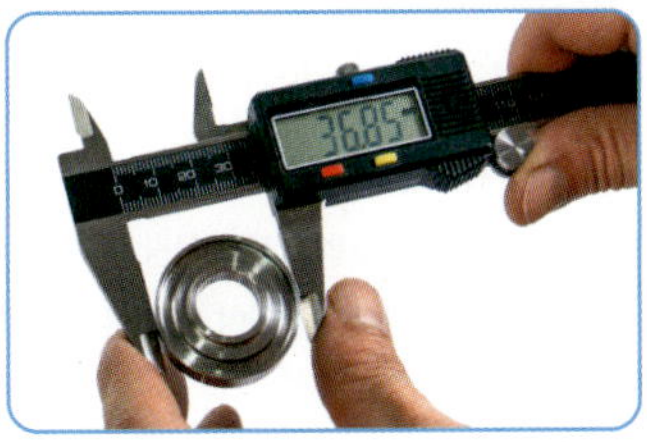

exact, clear, and correct

____

4. 

to judge or calculate

____

5. 

average in size or amount

____

6. 

able to last and be used for a long time

____

B Write the correct word or phrase next to each definition.

endure	length	optimist	random	put up with	maximum

1. a person who always believes that good things will happen ______________________
2. done or chosen without any plan or system ______________________
3. to experience (pain or suffering) for a long time ______________________
4. the size or measurement of something from one end to the other ______________________
5. being the largest amount that is allowed or possible ______________________
6. to endure something unpleasant without complaining ______________________

DAY 06

101 **affair**
[əféər]

an event or set of related events, especially impressive or shocking ones
명 (관심사가 되는) 일, 문제, 사건 = event, matter

an expert on foreign **affairs** 외교 전문가
a 24-hour news and current **affairs** channel 24시간 뉴스 및 시사 채널

102 **series**
[síəriːz]

a number of things or events that happen one after the other
명 1. 연속, 일련 2. (TV·책 등의) 연속물, 시리즈 ((on))

There have been **a series of** accidents recently. 최근에 일련의 사고가 있었다.
a new TV **series on** artificial intelligence 인공 지능(AI)에 관한 새 TV 시리즈

103 **benefit**
[bénəfit]

beneficial 형 유익한, 이로운

an advantage or help that you get from something
명 1. 혜택, 이득 2. (회사 등의) 복리후생 동 이익이 되다 *advantage 유리한 점, 이점

We enjoy the **benefits** of modern science. 우리는 현대 과학의 혜택을 누린다.
employee **benefits**, such as health insurance 건강 보험과 같은 직원 복지
The new policy will **benefit** everyone. 그 새 정책은 모두에게 이익이 될 것이다.

104 **burden**
[bə́ːrdn]

a heavy load; something difficult that you are responsible for
명 (무거운) 짐, 부담 동 ~에게 짐[부담]을 지우다

carry a heavy **burden** 무거운 짐을 지다
I don't want to **burden** you with my problems. 나는 내 문제로 네게 부담을 지우고 싶지 않다.

105 **cheat**
[tʃiːt]

cheating 명 부정행위

to behave in a dishonest way in order to gain an advantage
동 1. 부정행위를 하다 ((on/at)) 2. 속이다

He **cheated on** the exam. 그는 시험에서 부정행위를 했다.
I realized I was **cheated** by him. 나는 그에게 속았다는 것을 깨달았다.

106 **deceive**
[disíːv]

deception 명 속임(수), 기만, 사기
= deceit

to make someone believe something that is not true
동 속이다, 기만하다 *lie 거짓말을 하다; 거짓말

I was completely **deceived** by his lies. 나는 그의 거짓말에 완전히 속았다.
They **deceived** customers by false advertising. 그들은 거짓 광고로 고객들을 속였다.

107 **protest**
[prətést]

to come together to publicly express opposition to something
동 항의하다, 시위하다 ((against/at/about)) 명 [próutest] 항의, 시위

They **protested against** the policy. 그들은 그 정책에 항의하여 시위를 했다.
hold a **protest** march 시위 행진을 벌이다

108 **participate**
[pɑːrtísəpèit]

participation 명 참가, 참여
participant 명 참가자

to take part in or become involved in an activity
동 참가하다, 참여하다 ((in))

Many people **participated in** the protest. 많은 사람들이 그 시위에 참가했다.
She **participated in** the cooking competition. 그녀는 요리 대회에 참가했다.

109 **brand**
[brænd]

a type of product made by a particular company
명 상표, 브랜드 동 낙인을 찍다 ((as))

a well-known **brand** 잘 알려진 브랜드
He was **branded as** a liar. 그는 거짓말쟁이로 낙인 찍혔다.

110 **trend**
[trend]
trendy 형 최신 유행의

a general direction in which a situation is changing or developing
명 동향, 추세; 유행

the latest fashion **trends** 최신 패션 동향
There is a growing **trend** toward online shopping. 온라인 쇼핑이 늘어나는 추세이다.
Blue jeans are always **on trend**. 청바지는 항상 유행이다.

111 **fabric**
[fǽbrik]

cloth used for making clothes, curtains, etc.
명 직물, 천

This shirt is made of cotton **fabric**. 이 셔츠는 면직물로 만들어졌다.

112 **leather**
[léðər]

the skin of animals that is used to make things, such as shoes and bags
명 가죽

genuine **leather** 진짜 가죽
Leather jackets are trendy this season. 이번 시즌에는 가죽 재킷이 유행이다.

113 **slight**
[slait]
slightly 부 약간, 조금

very small in degree
형 약간의, 조금의

There has been a **slight** change in trends this year. 올해 트렌드에 약간의 변화가 있었다.

114 **bubble**
[bʌ́bl]

a ball of air or gas in liquid
명 거품, 비눗방울 동 거품이 일다, 보글보글 끓다

soap **bubbles** 비누 거품
the **bubble** bursts 거품이 꺼지다(좋던 상황이 갑자기 끝나다)
Heat the cheese until it **bubbles**. 거품이 생길 때까지 치즈를 가열하세요.

115 **excess**
[iksés]

an amount that is more than necessary or acceptable
명 초과, 과잉, 과도 형 초과한, 과도한 *access 접근; 접근하다

suffer from **an excess of** stress 과도한 스트레스를 겪다
Excess sugar consumption is bad for your health. 과도한 설탕 섭취는 건강에 해롭다.

116 **exceed**
[iksíːd]

to be more than a particular number or amount
동 초과하다, 넘어서다

The total cost should not **exceed** $500. 총 비용은 500달러를 초과해서는 안 된다.
Don't **exceed** the speed limit. 제한 속도를 초과하지 마세요.

117 **efficient**

[ifíʃənt]

efficiently 부 효율적으로
efficiency 명 효율성, 능률

working or operating quickly and effectively

형 1. 효율적인, 능률적인 ((for)) 2. 유능한 *effective 효과적인

The new plan is **efficient for** reducing costs. 그 새 계획은 비용 절감에 효율적이다.
a very **efficient** secretary 아주 유능한 비서

118 **sufficient**

[səfíʃənt]

sufficiently 부 충분히

enough for a particular purpose; as much as you need

형 충분한, (~하기에) 족한 ((to/for)) = enough

We have **sufficient** time **to** complete the task. 우리는 그 일을 끝낼 충분한 시간이 있다.

119 **take part (in)**

to participate in something

(~에) 참가하다, 참여하다

Nearly 200 teams **took part in** the competition. 거의 200팀이 그 경연에 참가했다.
Anyone who is over 18 can **take part.** 18세 이상이면 누구나 참가할 수 있다.

120 **stand out**

to be easily seen; to be much better than someone or something

눈에 띄다, 두드러지다, 돋보이다

His red shirt made him **stand out** in the crowd.
그의 빨간 셔츠는 그를 군중 속에서 눈에 띄게 했다.
Her talent really **stood out** in the competition. 그녀의 재능은 그 경연에서 정말 돋보였다.

Check Up

A 우리말에 맞게 빈칸에 알맞은 말을 넣으세요.

1. 뉴스 및 시사 채널 — news and current ________________ channel
2. 일련의 사고 — a ________________ accidents
3. 현대 과학의 혜택 — the ________________ of modern science
4. 시험에서 부정행위를 하다 — ________________ an exam
5. 시위에 참가하다 — ________________ in a protest
6. 과도한 스트레스를 겪다 — suffer from an ________________ stress

B 우리말에 알맞은 말을 골라 문장을 완성하세요.

1. Blue jeans are always (**trend** / **on trend**). 청바지는 항상 유행이다.
2. I was completely (**deceived by** / **deceived on**) his lies. 나는 그의 거짓말에 완전히 속았다.
3. Don't (**excess** / **exceed**) the speed limit. 제한 속도를 초과하지 마세요.
4. We have (**efficient** / **sufficient**) time to complete the task. 우리는 그 일을 끝낼 충분한 시간이 있다.
5. His red shirt made him (**stand out** / **stood out**) in the crowd.
그의 빨간 셔츠는 그를 군중 속에서 눈에 띄게 했다.

Build Up

A Write the correct word for each definition.

fabric	leather	participate	burden	bubble	slight

1. 

a heavy load

____

2. 

to take part in

____

3. 

cloth used for making clothes

____

4. 

the skin of animals used to make things

____

5. 

very small in degree

____

6. 

a ball of air or gas in liquid

____

B Write the correct word or phrase next to each definition.

protest	efficient	brand	stand out	affair	deceive

1. to make someone believe something that is not true ______________
2. to come together to publicly express opposition to something ______________
3. a type of product made by a particular company ______________
4. working or operating quickly and effectively ______________
5. to be easily seen; to be much better than someone or something ______________
6. an event or set of related events, especially impressive or shocking ones ______________

DAY 07

121 **entrance**
[éntrəns]
enter 동 들어가다, 입장하다

a door or gate used for entering a building or place
명 1. (출)입구, 문 2. 입장 3. 입학, 입시 ((to))

the main **entrance to** the museum 박물관 정문
Entrance to the museum is free today. 오늘은 박물관 입장이 무료이다.
an **entrance** exam 입학 시험

122 **exit**
[égzit]

a way out of a public building or large vehicle
명 출구 동 나가다, 퇴장하다 = leave

Use the emergency **exit** in case of fire. 화재 발생 시 비상 출구를 사용하세요.
They **exited** through the back door. 그들은 뒷문을 통해 나갔다.

123 **guard**
[gɑːrd]

a person whose job is to protect a place or people
명 1. 경비원, 경호원 2. 보초, 감시 동 보호하다, 지키다

The **guards** were blocking the exit. 경비원들이 출구를 막고 있었다.
stand[keep] **guard** 보초를 서다
They **guarded** the entrance to the embassy. 그들은 대사관 입구를 지켰다.

124 **security**
[sikjúərəti]
secure 형 안전한, 위험 없는

things that are done to keep someone or something safe
명 1. 보안, 경비 2. (미래를 위한) 보장, 보증

The building was under tight **security**. 그 건물은 엄격한 보안 아래 있었다.
The thief was caught on a **security** camera. 그 도둑은 보안 카메라(CCTV)에 찍혔다.
job **security** 직업 안정성

125 **approach**
[əpróutʃ]

to come close in distance or time
동 접근하다, 다가가다[오다] 명 접근법 ((to))

A stranger **approached** us. 낯선 사람이 우리에게 다가왔다.
take a new **approach to** the problem 그 문제에 대해 새로운 접근 방식을 취하다

126 **while**
[hwail]

during the time that something is happening
접 1. ~하는 동안 2. ~하는 반면에 명 잠깐, 잠시

The phone rang **while** I was waiting. 내가 기다리는 동안 전화가 울렸다.
While I like summer, he enjoys winter. 나는 여름을 좋아하는 반면, 그는 겨울을 즐긴다.
for a **while** 잠시 동안

127 **since**
[sins]

from a particular time in the past until now
전 [시점] ~ 이후 접 1. [시점] ~한 이후로 (쭉) 2. [이유] ~이기 때문에

We've been waiting here **since** two o'clock. 우리는 2시부터 여기서 기다리고 있다.
I haven't seen her **since** we graduated. 졸업한 이후로 나는 그녀를 보지 못했다.
Since a storm was approaching, we stayed inside. 폭풍이 다가오고 있었으므로 우리는 안에 머물렀다.

128 **as**
[æz]

to the same degree or amount
접 1. [때] ~하는 동안 = while 2. [이유] ~이기 때문에 = because, since
부 …만큼 ~한 ((as ~ as))

We talked a lot **as** we walked in the park. 우리는 공원을 걸으면서 많은 이야기를 나눴다.
As it was raining, we stayed indoors. 비가 오고 있어서 우리는 실내에 머물렀다.
She plays the piano **as** well **as** a pianist. 그녀는 피아니스트만큼 피아노를 잘 친다.

129 **exclude**
[iksklúːd]
exclusion 명 제외, 배제
exclusive 형 독점적인, 전용의

to intentionally not include something; to keep out
동 1. 제외하다, 배제하다 반 include 포함시키다 2. 쫓아내다, 추방하다 ((from))

He was **excluded from** the invitation list. 그는 초대 목록에서 제외되었다.
The price **excludes** tax. 그 가격은 세금을 포함시키지 않은 것이다.
They **excluded** him **from** the club. 그들은 그를 클럽에서 제명했다(추방했다).

130 **unless**
[ənlés]

except if
접 ~하지 않으면, ~이 아닌 한 *except ~을 제외하고, ~ 외에는

You can't enter **unless** you're a member. 회원이 아니면 들어갈 수 없다.

131 **restrict**
[ristríkt]
restricted 형 제한된, 한정된
restriction 명 제한

to limit or control something
동 제한하다, 통제하다 ((to)) *limit 한도; 제한하다

Access to the club is **restricted to** members only. 그 클럽 출입은 회원들로만 제한된다.
Smoking is **restricted** in public places. 공공장소에서의 흡연은 제한된다.

132 **regulate**
[régjulèit]
regulated 형 규제된, 통제된
regulation 명 규제, 통제

to control something, especially by using rules
동 1. (법 등으로) 규제하다, 통제하다 2. 조절하다, 조정하다

The use of drones is **regulated** by law. 드론의 사용은 법에 의해 규제된다.
regulate the temperature of a room 방의 온도를 조절하다

133 **bar**
[baːr]
barred 형 빗장을 지른, 가둔; 금지된

to close and lock a door or gate
동 1. 빗장을 지르다 2. 막다, 금지하다 명 막대기 (모양의 것), 빗장

All the doors and windows were **barred**. 모든 문과 창문에는 빗장이 채워져 있었다.
The security guards were **barring** the entrance. 경비원들[보안 요원들]이 입구를 막고 있었다.
an iron **bar** 쇠막대기

134 **ban**
[bæn]
banned 형 (공식적으로) 금지된, 금지당한

to decide or say officially that something is not allowed
동 금지하다 ((from)) 반 allow, permit 허락하다 명 금지(법) ((on))

Using cell phones is **banned** here. 여기서 휴대폰 사용은 금지되어 있다.
He was **banned from** the meeting. 그는 회의 참석을 금지당했다.
a **ban on** the use of plastic bags 비닐봉지 사용 금지

135 **prohibit**
[prouhíbit]
prohibited 형 (법으로) 금지된
prohibition 명 금지

to stop someone from doing something by law or by an order
동 1. (법 등으로) 금지하다 = ban, forbid 2. ~하지 못하게 하다 ((from)) = prevent

Smoking is strictly **prohibited** in this area. 이 구역에서 흡연은 엄격히 금지되어 있다.
His injury **prohibited** him **from** running. 부상 때문에 그는 달리지 못했다(그의 부상이 그를 달리지 못하게 했다).

136 **forbid**
[fərbíd]
forbidden 형 금지된, 허용되지 않는

to order someone not to do something (forbade-forbidden)
동 금하다, 금지하다 ((from))

Their religion **forbids** the eating of pork. 그들의 종교는 돼지고기 섭취를 금한다.
The coach **forbade** him **from** going out. 코치는 그가 외출하는 것을 금지했다.

137 **violate**
[váiəlèit]
violation 명 위반; 침해, 방해

to break or not obey a law, rule, or agreement
동 1. (법 등을) 위반하다, 어기다 2. 침해하다

violate traffic laws 교통 법규를 위반하다
He was punished for **violating** school rules. 그는 학교 규칙을 어겨 처벌을 받았다.
violate one's privacy (~의) 사생활을 침해하다

138 **penalty**
[pénəlti]

a punishment for breaking a law, rule, or contract
명 처벌, 형벌, 벌금 ((for))

The **penalty for** speeding is a fine. 과속에 대한 처벌은 벌금이다(과속하면 벌금을 내야 한다).
pay a **penalty** 처벌을 받다, 벌금을 내다

139 **keep A from V-ing**

to prevent A from doing something
A가 ~하는 것을 막다[못하게 하다]

The security guards **kept** us **from** entering the building.
경비원들이 우리가 그 건물에 들어가는 것을 막았다.
The heavy rain **kept** us **from** going out. 폭우 때문에 우리는 나가지 못했다.

140 **as soon as**

immediately after something happens; without delay
~하자마자, ~하는 대로 곧

As soon as it stopped raining, we went outside. 비가 그치자마자 우리는 밖으로 나갔다.
I will call you **as soon as** I arrive. 도착하는 대로 네게 전화할게.

Check Up

A 우리말에 맞게 빈칸에 알맞은 말을 넣으세요.

1. 입학 시험 — an ________________ exam
2. 비상 출구 — an emergency ________________
3. 보안 카메라 — a ________________ camera
4. 잠시 동안 — for ________________
5. 방의 온도를 조절하다 — ________________ the temperature of a room
6. 처벌을 받다, 벌금을 내다 — pay a ________________

B 우리말에 알맞은 말을 골라 문장을 완성하세요.

1. The phone rang (**while** / **since**) I was waiting. 내가 기다리는 동안 전화가 울렸다.
2. We've been waiting here (**as** / **since**) two o'clock. 우리는 2시부터 여기서 기다리고 있다.
3. The price (**includes** / **excludes**) tax. 그 가격은 세금을 포함시키지 않은 것이다.
4. You can't enter (**as** / **unless**) you're a member. 회원이 아니면 들어갈 수 없다.
5. Smoking is (**restricted** / **violated**) in public places. 공공장소에서의 흡연은 제한된다.

Build Up

A Write the correct word for each definition.

violate	approach	exit	penalty	bar	prohibit

1. 

a way out of a public building

____

2. 

to come close in distance

____

3. 

to close and lock a door

____

4. 

to stop someone from doing something by law

____

5. 

to break or not obey a law

____

6. 

a punishment for breaking a law

____

B Write the correct word or phrase next to each definition.

since	exclude	security	forbid	as soon as	regulate

1. things that are done to keep someone or something safe ______________________
2. from a particular time in the past until now ______________________
3. to intentionally not include something; to keep out ______________________
4. to control something, especially by using rules ______________________
5. to order someone not to do something ______________________
6. immediately after something happens; without delay ______________________

DAY 08

141 **neighborhood** [néibərhùd]

an area or community within a town or city

명 1. (도시의) 지역, 구역 2. 인근, 이웃 *neighbor 이웃 사람

We grew up in the same **neighborhood**. 우리는 같은 지역[동네]에서 자랐다.
Neighbors live together in a **neighborhood**. 이웃 사람들은 이웃에서[한 동네에서] 함께 산다.

142 **facility** [fəsíləti]

a building or equipment used for a particular purpose or activity

명 시설, 설비

There is a good sports **facility** in my neighborhood. 우리 동네에는 좋은 스포츠 시설이 있다.

143 **internal** [intə́ːrnl]

connected with the inside of something

형 1. 내부의 2. 체내의 반 external 외부의 *interior 내부의, 실내의

The building has a unique **internal** structure. 그 건물은 독특한 내부 구조를 가지고 있다.
medicine for **internal** use 내복약

144 **passage** [pǽsidʒ]

a long, narrow space that connects one place to another

명 1. 통로, 복도 2. (책 등의) 구절 *aisle 통로

It has a secret underground **passage**. 그곳에는 비밀 지하 통로가 있다.
She read a **passage** from the novel. 그녀는 그 소설의 한 구절을 읽었다.

145 **polish** [pɑ́liʃ]

polished 형 (잘 닦아서) 윤이 나는

to make something smooth and shiny by rubbing it

동 (윤이 나도록) 닦다, 광을 내다 명 광택(제)

They **polished** the floor and window. 그들은 바닥과 창문을 닦았다.
floor **polish** / shoe **polish** 바닥 광택제 / 구두 광택제[약]

146 **sparkle** [spɑ́ːrkl]

spark 명 불꽃 동 불꽃을 일으키다
sparkling 형 반짝거리는; 거품이 이는

to shine brightly with small flashes of light

동 1. 반짝이다 2. 생기가 넘치다 ((with)) 명 반짝거림, 광채

The window glass **sparkled** like diamonds. 창문 유리가 다이아몬드처럼 반짝였다.
Her eyes **sparkled with** excitement. 그녀의 눈은 흥분으로 반짝였다.
the **sparkle** of a diamond 다이아몬드의 광채

147 **cease** [siːs]

to stop happening; to stop doing something

동 중단되다, 그치다; 중단하다 = stop 반 continue 계속되다; 계속하다

The rain has **ceased**. 비가 그쳤다.
The sports center has **ceased** operations for maintenance.
그 스포츠 센터는 유지 보수를 위해 운영을 중단했다.

148 **neglect** [niglékt]

neglected 형 방치된

to fail to take care of someone or something

동 1. (돌보지 않고) 방치하다 2. 소홀히 하다, 등한시하다 *abandon 버리다, 포기하다

The building has been **neglected** for years. 그 건물은 수년간 방치되었다.
They have **neglected** their duties. 그들은 그들의 의무를 소홀히 했다.

149 **flame**
[fleim]

hot, bright, burning gas produced by something on fire

명 불꽃, 불길, 화염 동 활활 타오르다

The building was **in flames**. 그 건물은 화염에 휩싸여 있었다.
The fire was **flaming** high. 불길이 높이 타오르고 있었다.

150 **flash**
[flæʃ]

to shine very brightly for a short time

동 번쩍이다; 비추다 명 섬광, 번쩍임

Fire trucks' lights **flashed** in the dark. 어둠 속에서 소방차의 불빛들이 번쩍였다.
a **flash** of lightning 번갯불의 섬광[번쩍임]

151 **explode**
[iksplóud]

explosion 명 폭발, 폭파

to burst, or to make something burst, loudly and violently

동 폭발하다, 터지다; 폭발시키다

The gas pipeline **exploded**. 가스 파이프라인이 폭발했다.
explode a bomb 폭탄을 폭발시키다[터뜨리다]

152 **trap**
[træp]

to prevent someone from escaping from somewhere

동 1. 가두다 2. 덫을 놓다 명 덫; 함정

They were **trapped** in the burning building. 그들은 불타는 건물 안에 갇혀 있었다.
set a **trap** 덫을 놓다

153 **rescue**
[réskjuː]

to save someone from a dangerous or harmful situation

동 구하다, 구조[구출]하다 명 구조, 구출

Firefighters **rescued** people from the fire. 소방관들이 화재에서 사람들을 구했다.
rescue abandoned pets 버려진 애완동물들을 구조하다
a **rescue** team 구조대

154 **approximately**
[əprάksəmətli]

approximate 형 거의 정확한, 근사치인

more or less than a number or amount

부 대략, ~ 가까이, 약 유 about 약, roughly 대략, 거의

The rescue took **approximately** 5 hours. 구조 작업은 거의 5시간이 걸렸다.
The repairs will cost **approximately** $100,000. 수리비는 대략 10만 달러가 들 것이다.

155 **drown**
[draun]

to die because you are under water and cannot breathe

동 물에 빠져 죽다, 익사하다; 익사시키다

Two people **drowned** in a boating accident. 보트 사고로 두 사람이 익사했다.

156 **nightmare**
[náitmɛər]

a dream that is very frightening or unpleasant

명 1. 악몽 2. 악몽 (같은 일), 끔찍한 일

She still has **nightmares** about the accident. 그녀는 아직도 그 사건에 대한 악몽을 꾼다.
The trip turned into a **nightmare**. 그 여행은 악몽으로 변했다.

157 **pale**
[peil]

having skin that is almost white

형 1. (얼굴이) 창백한 2. (색이) 옅은, 연한 반 dark, deep 짙은, 어두운

She became **pale** with fear. 그녀는 두려움에 얼굴이 창백해졌다.
pale blue eyes 연한 파란색 눈

158 **faint**
[feint]

not clearly seen, heard, or smelled

형 (빛·소리 등이) 희미한, 약한 반 vivid 선명한, 강렬한 동 실신하다, 기절하다

a **faint** light 희미한 빛
The shocking news made her **faint**. 충격적인 소식에 그녀는 기절했다.

159 **at the time**

at a particular moment or period when something happened

그때, 그 당시에 = at that time

At the time, I was 9 years old. 그때 나는 9살이었다.
He was living in New York **at the time**. 그 당시 그는 뉴욕에 살고 있었다.

160 **as long as**

only if

~하기만 하면, ~하는 한

We'll go **as long as** the weather is good. 날씨가 좋기만 하면 우리는 갈 거야.
I'll stay with you **as long as** you need me. 네가 나를 필요로 하는 한 네 곁에 있을게.

Check Up

A 우리말에 맞게 빈칸에 알맞은 말을 넣으세요.

1. 비밀 지하 통로 — a secret underground ______________
2. 번갯불의 섬광[번쩍임] — a ______________ of lightning
3. 폭탄을 폭발시키다[터뜨리다] — ______________ a bomb
4. 버려진 애완동물들을 구조하다 — ______________ abandoned pets
5. 악몽을 꾸다 — have a ______________
6. 희미한 빛 — a ______________ light

B 우리말에 알맞은 말을 골라 문장을 완성하세요.

1. We grew up in the same (**neighbors / neighborhood**). 우리는 같은 지역[동네]에서 자랐다.
2. They (**polished / sparkled**) the floor and window. 그들은 바닥과 창문을 닦았다.
3. The building (**has neglected / has been neglected**) for years. 그 건물은 수년간 방치되었다.
4. They (**trapped / were trapped**) in the burning building. 그들은 불타는 건물 안에 갇혀 있었다.
5. We'll go (**as soon as / as long as**) the weather is good. 날씨가 좋기만 하면 우리는 갈 거야.

Build Up

A Write the correct word for each definition.

rescue
nightmare
facility
explode
internal
sparkle

1. 

a building or equipment used for a particular purpose

____

2. 

connected with the inside of something

____

3. 

to shine brightly with small flashes

____

4. 

a dream that is very frightening

____

5. 

to burst loudly and violently

____

6. 

to save someone from a dangerous situation

____

B Write the correct word or phrase next to each definition.

polish	flame	drown	approximately	cease	neglect

1. to make something smooth and shiny by rubbing it ______________________
2. to stop happening; to stop doing something ______________________
3. to fail to take care of someone or something ______________________
4. hot, bright, burning gas produced by something on fire ______________________
5. more or less than a number or amount ______________________
6. to die because you are under water and cannot breathe ______________________

Review Test 02 DAY 05-08

A 그림을 보고, 빈칸에 알맞은 단어를 넣으세요.

approach　　bar　　durable　　explode　　faint　　neighborhood

1. 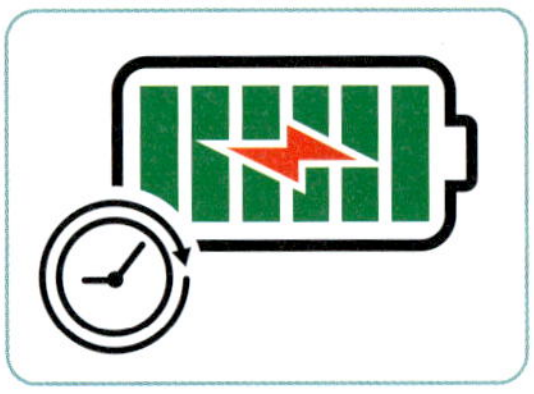

____

2. 

____

3. 

____

4. 

____

5. 

____

6. 

____

B 그림에 맞게 빈칸에 알맞은 단어를 고르세요.

1. 

We discussed the topic ______________________.
(in depth / in length)

2. 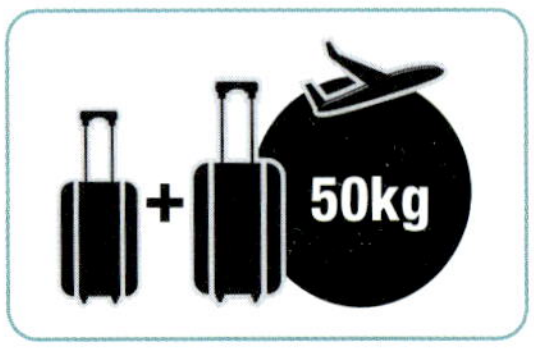

You can carry ______________________ two bags.
(a mass of / a maximum of)

3. 

Don't ______________________ the speed limit.
(excess / exceed)

4. 

Smoking is ______________________ in this place.
(prohibited / permitted)

C 우리말 뜻에 맞게 빈칸에 알맞은 말을 넣으세요.

opt for	opportunity	at random	a series of
penalty	burden	stand out	an excess of

1. a rare ______________ 드문 기회
2. ______________ a career in music 음악 분야의 직업을 택하다
3. select ______________ 무작위로 선정하다
4. ______________ accidents 일련의 사고
5. carry a heavy ______________ 무거운 짐을 지다
6. suffer from ______________ stress 과도한 스트레스를 겪다
7. ______________ in the crowd 군중 속에서 눈에 띄다
8. pay a ______________ 처벌을 받다, 벌금을 내다

D 우리말 뜻에 맞게 빈칸에 알맞은 말을 넣으세요.

benefits of	protested against	cheated on
as long as	efficient for	as soon as

1. We enjoy the ______________ modern science. 우리는 현대 과학의 혜택을 누린다.
2. He ______________ the exam. 그는 시험에서 부정행위를 했다.
3. They ______________ the policy. 그들은 그 정책에 항의하여 시위를 했다.
4. The new plan is ______________ reducing costs. 그 새 계획은 비용 절감에 효율적이다.
5. I will call you ______________ I arrive. 도착하는 대로 네게 전화할게.
6. I'll stay with you ______________ you need me. 네가 나를 필요로 하는 한 네 곁에 있을게.

E 밑줄 친 단어와 비슷한 뜻을 가진 단어를 고르세요.

1. The book had a <u>profound</u> impact on her.

   a. dark b. deep c. sufficient

2. She <u>put up with</u> the pain.

   a. made up with b. opted for c. endured

3. The heavy rain <u>kept</u> us from going out.

   a. prevented b. allowed c. regulated

4. Nearly 200 teams <u>took part</u> in the competition.

   a. competed b. assessed c. participated

F 밑줄 친 단어와 반대의 뜻을 가진 단어를 고르세요.

1. This suitcase is made of <u>durable</u> plastic.

   a. fragile b. efficient c. moderate

2. The price <u>excludes</u> tax.

   a. forbids b. decreases c. includes

3. Using cell phones is <u>banned</u> here.

   a. allowed b. protested c. prohibited

4. You should not <u>violate</u> traffic laws.

   a. regulate b. obey c. break

G 주어진 영영풀이에 알맞은 단어를 고르세요.

1. to judge or calculate the amount, value, or quality of something

   a. evaluate b. measure c. regulate

2. average in size or amount; neither too much nor too little

   a. accurate b. moderate c. humble

3. to make someone believe something that is not true

   a. deceive b. exceed c. offend

4. enough for a particular purpose; as much as you need

   a. efficient b. sufficient c. precise

5. things that are done to keep someone or something safe

   a. guard b. entrance c. security

6. to stop someone from doing something by law or by an order

   a. prohibit b. violate c. seize

H 빈칸에 알맞은 동사 형태를 넣어 문장을 완성하세요.

1. He was punished for ________________ school rules. (violate)
2. The sports center has ________________ operations for maintenance. (cease)
3. The building has been ________________ for years. (neglect)
4. The use of drones is ________________ by law. (regulate)

DAY 09

161 **suffer**
[sʌ́fər]
suffering 명 고통

to experience physical or mental pain
동 1. (병 등에) 시달리다, 고통받다 ((from)) 2. (부상 등을) 겪다, 당하다

She **suffers from** allergies in the spring. 그녀는 봄철에 알레르기로 고생한다.
suffer a heart attack 심장 마비를 겪다[일으키다]

162 **struggle**
[strʌgl]

to try very hard to do something difficult
동 1. 애쓰다, 발버둥치다 2. 싸우다, 분투하다 명 투쟁, 분투 ((to/against/for))

struggle to survive 살아남기 위해 발버둥치다
She is **struggling against** cancer. 그녀는 암과 싸우고 있다.
a **struggle for** survival 생존을 위한 투쟁

163 **stroke**
[strouk]
strike 동 치다, 때리다
명 치기, 공격; 파업

a sudden serious illness that makes you unable to move part of your body
명 1. 뇌졸중 2. 타격, 일격, 한 번 치기

He suffered a **stroke** last year. 그는 작년에 뇌졸중을 일으켰다[겪었다].
a stroke of lightning 낙뢰, 벼락

164 **symptom**
[símptəm]

a physical feeling or problem that shows that you have a disease
명 1. 증상 2. (불길한) 징후, 조짐 ((of)) = sign

the typical **symptoms of** a stroke 뇌졸중의 전형적인 증상들
Headaches may be **a symptom of** stress. 두통은 스트레스의 한 징후일 수 있다.

165 **stiff**
[stif]

hard and difficult to bend or move
형 1. 뻣뻣한, 딱딱한 2. (근육이) 뻐근한

a **stiff** collar (셔츠 등의) 뻣뻣한 칼라
My leg muscles are **stiff**. 내 다리 근육이 뻐근하다.
I've got a **stiff** neck. 목이 뻐근해요.

166 **paralyze**
[pǽrəlàiz]
paralysis 명 마비

to make someone unable to move all or part of their body
동 마비시키다 = (영) paralyse

Her legs were **paralyzed** from the accident. 그녀의 다리는 그 사고로 마비되었다.
The strike **paralyzed** the whole city. 그 파업은 도시 전체를 마비시켰다.

167 **critical**
[krítikəl]
criticize 동 비판하다, 비평하다
criticism 명 비판, 비평

expressing criticism or disapproval
형 1. 비판적인 2. 중대한 3. 위태로운, 위독한 *fatal 치명적인

a **critical** comment 비판적인 논평
face a **critical** situation 중대한 국면[상황]에 처하다
He is in **critical** condition. 그는 위독한 상태이다.

168 **crucial**
[krúːʃəl]

extremely important or necessary
형 중대한, 결정적인 ((for/to)) = vital, essential

make a **crucial** decision 중대한 결정을 내리다
Vitamins are **crucial for** good health. 비타민은 건강을 위해 필수적이다.

169 **therefore**
[ðέərfɔ̀ːr]

for that reason; because of that; so

부 그러므로, 따라서, 그 결과

The test results were positive; **therefore**, he needs treatment.
검사 결과가 양성이므로 그는 치료가 필요하다.

I think; **therefore** I am. 나는 생각한다. 고로 나는 존재한다.

170 **nevertheless**
[nèvərðəlés]

in spite of that; however; nonetheless

부 그럼에도 불구하고, 그렇기는 하지만

He was feeling sick, but **nevertheless**, he went to work.
그는 아팠지만 그럼에도 불구하고 일을 하러 갔다.

Nevertheless, we will do our best. 그럼에도 불구하고 우리는 최선을 다할 것이다.

171 **surgery**
[sə́ːrdʒəri]

surgical 형 외과의, 수술의
surgeon 명 외과 의사

medical treatment in which a doctor cuts into someone's body in order to repair something

명 수술 ((on)) = operation

He had **surgery on** his left knee. 그는 왼쪽 무릎 수술을 받았다.

172 **recovery**
[rikʌ́vəri]

recover 동 회복하다

the process of becoming well again after an illness or injury

명 회복, 완쾌 ((from))

He made a full **recovery from** the surgery. 그는 수술에서 완전히 회복되었다.

an economy **recovery** 경제 회복

173 **patient**
[péiʃənt]

patiently 부 참을성 있게
patience 명 참을성, 인내심

a person who is receiving medical treatment, especially in a hospital

명 환자 형 참을성 있는, 인내심이 있는

a cancer **patient** 암 환자

Please be **patient** and wait for your turn. 인내심을 가지고 당신의 차례를 기다려 주세요.

174 **await**
[əwéit]

to wait for someone or something

동 기다리다, 대기하다

She is anxiously **awaiting** her test results. 그녀는 초조하게 검사 결과를 기다리고 있다.

A warm welcome **awaits** you. 따뜻한 환영이 당신을 기다리고 있어요.

175 **relieve**
[rilíːv]

to remove or reduce pain or an unpleasant feeling

동 1. (고통 등을) 없애 주다, 덜다 = ease 2. 안도하게 하다 3. (심각성을) 줄이다

The medicine will **relieve** the symptoms. 이 약이 그 증상을 없애[덜어] 줄 것이다.

I was **relieved** at the news. 나는 그 소식을 듣고 안도했다.

Try to **relieve** your stress. 스트레스를 줄이려고 노력하세요.

176 **relief**
[rilíːf]

a feeling of happiness that something unpleasant has ended

명 1. 안도, 안심 2. (통증·증상의) 완화, 경감

She breathed a sigh of **relief**. 그녀는 안도의 한숨을 내쉬었다.

pain **relief** 통증 완화

177 **remarkable**

[rimá:rkəbl]

remark 명 언급; 주목(할 만함)
동 언급하다, 논평하다

very unusual or surprising and therefore deserving attention or praise

형 놀랄 만한, 주목할 만한, 두드러진 = outstanding

He made a **remarkable** recovery after the surgery. 그는 수술 후 놀라운 회복을 보였다.
bring a **remarkable** change 놀라운 변화를 가져오다

178 **rational**

[rǽʃənl]

rationally 부 이성적으로, 합리적으로

based on facts or reason rather than emotions

형 합리적인, 이성적인 반 irrational 비이성적인 유 reasonable 합리적인

make a **rational** decision 합리적인[이성적인] 결정을 하다
Humans are **rational** beings. 인간은 이성적인 존재이다.

179 **undergo surgery**

to have or experience surgery

수술을 받다 = undergo an operation

He **underwent surgery** for lung cancer. 그는 폐암 수술을 받았다.
She **underwent** plastic **surgery** on her nose. 그녀는 코 성형 수술을 받았다.

180 **keep (something) in mind**

to remember and take into consideration later; to make sure

(~을) 명심하다, 잊지 않고 기억하다

Please **keep in mind** that you need regular checkups.
정기 검진이 필요하다는 것을 잊지 마세요.
Okay. I'll **keep** that **in mind**. 알겠어요. 그것을 명심할게요.

Check Up

A 우리말에 맞게 빈칸에 알맞은 말을 넣으세요.

1. 알레르기로 고생하다 ________________ from allergies
2. 살아남기 위해 발버둥치다 ________________ to survive
3. 뇌졸중의 전형적인 증상들 the typical ________________ of a stroke
4. 비판적인 논평 a ________________ comment
5. 안도의 한숨을 내쉬다 breathe a sigh of ________________
6. 수술을 받다 undergo ________________

B 우리말에 알맞은 말을 골라 문장을 완성하세요.

1. Her legs (**paralyzed** / **were paralyzed**) from the accident. 그녀의 다리는 그 사고로 마비되었다.
2. He is in (**critical** / **crucial**) condition. 그는 위독한 상태이다.
3. Vitamins are (**crucial** / **rational**) for good health. 비타민은 건강을 위해 필수적이다.
4. He made a full (**recover** / **recovery**) from the surgery. 그는 수술에서 완전히 회복되었다.
5. The medicine will (**relieve** / **relief**) the symptoms. 이 약이 그 증상을 없애[덜어] 줄 것이다.

Build Up

A Write the correct word for each definition.

paralyze	stiff	relieve	remarkable	await	crucial

1. 

hard and difficult to bend or move

____

2. 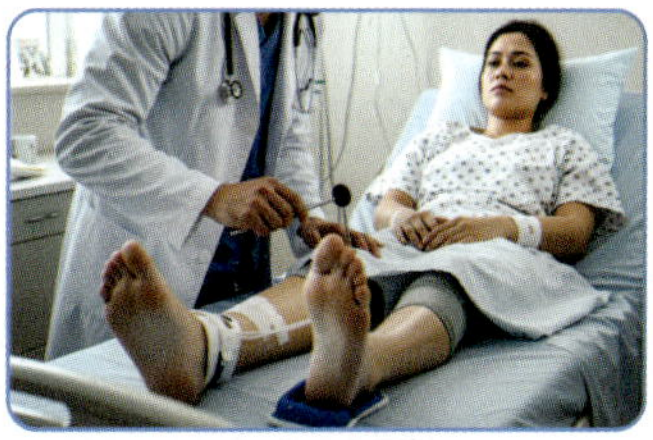

to make someone unable to move

____

3. 

extremely important or necessary

____

4. 

to wait for someone or something

____

5. 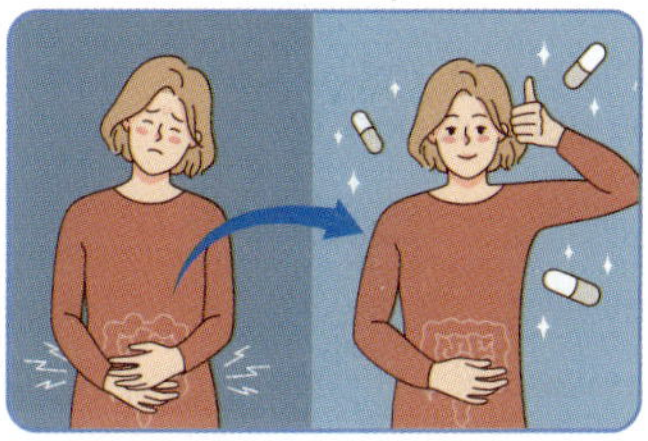

to remove or reduce pain

____

6. 

very unusual or surprising

____

B Write the correct word or phrase next to each definition.

therefore	patient	symptom	rational	nevertheless	keep (something) in mind

1. a physical feeling or problem that shows that you have a disease ______________________
2. for that reason; because of that; so ______________________
3. in spite of that; however; nonetheless ______________________
4. based on facts or reason rather than emotions ______________________
5. to remember and take into consideration later; to make sure ______________________
6. a person who is receiving medical treatment, especially in a hospital ______________________

DAY 10

181 **virus**
[váiərəs]

a very small living thing that causes disease
명 1. 바이러스, (전염성) 병원체 2. (컴퓨터) 바이러스 *bacteria 박테리아, 세균

The flu **virus** spreads easily. 독감 바이러스는 쉽게 전파된다.
The computer has a **virus**. 컴퓨터가 바이러스에 감염되었다.

182 **vaccine**
[væksí:n]

a substance that you take into your body to avoid getting a disease
명 (예방) 백신

I need to **get a vaccine** for the flu. 나는 독감 예방 주사[백신]를 맞아야 해.
develop a new **vaccine** for COVID-19 코로나19를 위한 새로운 백신을 개발하다

183 **infect**
[infékt]
infected 형 감염된
infectious 형 전염되는, 전염성의

to pass a disease to a person, animal, or plant
동 감염시키다, 병을 옮기다 ((with)) *spread 퍼지다; 퍼뜨리다

The virus has **infected** many people. 그 바이러스는 많은 사람들을 감염시켰다.
Thousands of people were **infected with** the virus.
수천 명의 사람들이 그 바이러스에 감염되었다.

184 **infection**
[infékʃən]

the act or process of causing or getting a disease
명 전염, 감염

The vaccine helps prevent **infections**. 백신은 감염을 막는 데 도움을 준다.

185 **inject**
[indʒékt]
injection 명 주사

to put a drug into someone's body by using a needle
동 주사하다, 주입하다 ((into/with))

The nurse **injected** the vaccine **into** my arm. 간호사가 내 팔에 백신 주사를 놓았다.
The children were **injected with** the flu vaccine. 아이들은 독감 백신을 맞았다.

186 **shot**
[ʃɑt]
shoot 동 (총을) 쏘다; (농구 등에서) 슛하다

a small amount of a drug that is put into your body by using a needle
명 1. 주사 (한 대) 2. (총기의) 발사 3. (농구 등에서) 슛

I got the flu **shot** last week. 나는 지난주에 독감 주사를 맞았다.
fire a **shot** 총을 쏘다, 슛을 쏘다
That was a good **shot**! 멋진 슛이었어!

187 **nerve**
[nə:rv]
nervous 형 긴장하는, 불안해하는

a cable-like structure within the body
명 1. (몸의) 신경 2. (-s) 긴장, 불안 3. 용기, 배짱

nerve cells 신경 세포들
She tried to calm her **nerves**. 그녀는 긴장을 풀기 위해[진정하려고] 애썼다.
It takes **nerve** to try something new. 새로운 것을 시도하는 데는 용기가 필요하다.

188 **tense**
[tens]
tension 명 긴장; 팽팽함

nervous or worried, and unable to relax
형 1. 긴장한, 긴장된 2. (줄 등이) 팽팽하게 당겨진 반 relaxed 긴장을 푼, 느긋한

She **felt tense** while waiting for her turn. 자신의 차례를 기다리면서 그녀는 긴장했다.
Every nerve in her body was **tense**. 그녀의 온몸의 신경이 곤두서 있었다.

189 **sneeze**
[sni:z]

to suddenly force air out through your nose and mouth with a loud noise
동 재채기하다 명 재채기 *cough 기침하다; 기침

If you **sneeze**, cover your mouth. 재채기를 할 때는 입을 가리세요.
hold in a **sneeze** 재채기를 참다

190 **snore**
[snɔ:r]

to breathe noisily through your nose and mouth while you are asleep
동 코를 골다 명 코 고는 소리

My father **snores** loudly when he sleeps. 우리 아버지는 주무실 때 코를 크게 곤다.
a loud **snore** 시끄럽게 코 고는 소리

191 **thumb**
[θʌm]

the short, thick finger on the side of your hand
명 엄지손가락

She accidentally cut her **thumb**. 그녀는 실수로 엄지손가락을 베었다.
If you liked our video, give it a **thumbs up**. 저희 영상이 맘에 드셨다면 '좋아요'를 눌러 주세요.

192 **bandage**
[bǽndidʒ]

a long piece of cloth that you tie around an injured part of the body
명 붕대 동 붕대를 감다 *Band-Aid 반창고 (상표 이름)

She **put a bandage** on the cut. 그녀는 (베인) 상처에 붕대를 감았다.
He wrapped a **bandage** around his knee. 그는 그의 무릎에 붕대를 감았다.
The nurse **bandaged** his ankle tightly. 간호사가 그의 발목에 단단히 붕대를 감았다.

193 **addicted**
[ədíktid]

addiction 명 중독
addict 명 중독자

unable to stop taking harmful drugs; doing something as a habit
형 (약물 등에) 중독된, 푹 빠져 있는 ((to))

become[get] **addicted to** drugs 약물에 중독되다
He is **addicted to** online games. 그는 온라인 게임에 빠져[중독되어] 있다.

194 **therapy**
[θérəpi]

therapist 명 치료사

the treatment of physical or mental illnesses
명 치료, 요법 *treatment 치료, 처치

new drug **therapies** 새로운 약물 치료법
He is now **in therapy**. 그는 지금 치료를 받고 있다.

195 **alternative**
[ɔ:ltə́:rnətiv]

something that can be chosen instead of something else
명 대안, 대체 ((to)) 형 대신하는, 대체의

This therapy can be an **alternative to** surgery. 이 치료법은 수술의 대안이 될 수 있다.
an **alternative** plan 대안

196 **ultimate**
[ʌ́ltəmət]

ultimately 부 궁극적으로, 결국

happening at the end of a long process
형 1. 궁극적인, 최종의 = final 2. 최대의, 최고의

Our **ultimate** goal is to overcome cancer. 우리의 궁극적인 목표는 암을 극복하는 것이다.
It'll be the **ultimate** challenge for us. 그것은 우리에게 최고의 도전이 될 것이다.

197 **marvel**

[mɑ́:rvəl]

marvelous 형 경이로운, 놀라운

something really surprising, exciting, or good

명 경이(로운 것), 놀라운 일 = wonder

the **marvels** of modern medicine 현대 의학의 경이로움

The Grand Canyon is a natural **marvel**. 그랜드 캐니언은 자연의 경이로움이다.

198 **heal**

[hi:l]

healing 명 (몸이나 마음의) 치유

to become healthy again; to make something healthy again

동 치유되다, 낫다; 치유하다 유 cure 치료하다, 낫게 하다

His ankle **healed** completely. 그의 발목은 완전히 나았다.

Time **heals** all wounds. 시간이 모든 상처를 낫게 해 준다(시간이 약이다).

199 **over the counter**

available to buy from a store without a prescription from a doctor

의사의 처방전 없이 (약국에서) 살 수 있는

Most vitamins are available **over the counter**.

대부분의 비타민은 처방전 없이 (약국에서) 살 수 있다.

Is this an **over-the-counter** medicine? 이것은 처방전 없이 살 수 있는 약인가요?

200 **break out**

to start suddenly

(전쟁·화재·전염병 등이) 발발하다, 발생하다 *outbreak 발발, 발생

War **broke out** in 1914. 1914년에 전쟁이 발발했다.

A new virus **broke out** last year. 작년에 새로운 바이러스가 발생했다.

Check Up

A 우리말에 맞게 빈칸에 알맞은 말을 넣으세요.

1. 독감 예방 주사[백신]를 맞다 get a ________________ for the flu
2. 독감 주사를 맞다 get the flu ________________
3. (베인) 상처에 붕대를 감다 put a ________________ on the cut
4. 약물에 중독되다 become ________________ drugs
5. 대안 an ________________ plan
6. 처방전 없이 (약국에서) 살 수 있는 약 an ________________ medicine

B 우리말에 알맞은 말을 골라 문장을 완성하세요.

1. The virus (**has infected** / **has injected**) many people. 그 바이러스는 많은 사람들을 감염시켰다.
2. Thousands of people (**infected** / **were infected**) with the virus.
   수천 명의 사람들이 그 바이러스에 감염되었다.
3. If you (**sneeze** / **snore**), cover your mouth. 재채기를 할 때는 입을 가리세요.
4. He is (**addiction** / **addicted**) to online games. 그는 온라인 게임에 빠져[중독되어] 있다.
5. A new virus (**breaks out** / **broke out**) last year. 작년에 새로운 바이러스가 발생했다.

Build Up

A Write the correct word for each definition.

1. 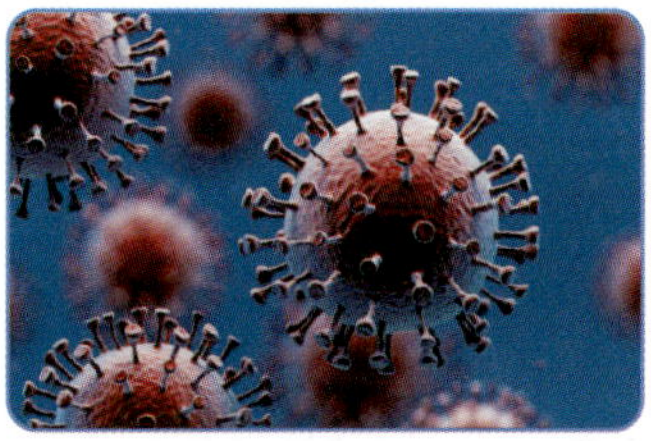

a small living thing that causes disease

____

2. 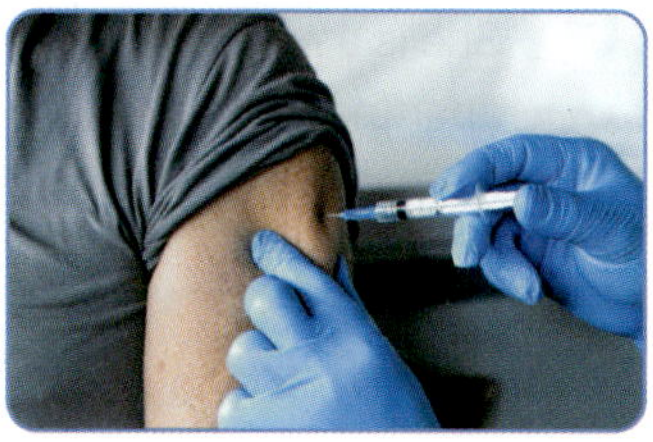

to put a drug into someone's body by using a needle

____

3. 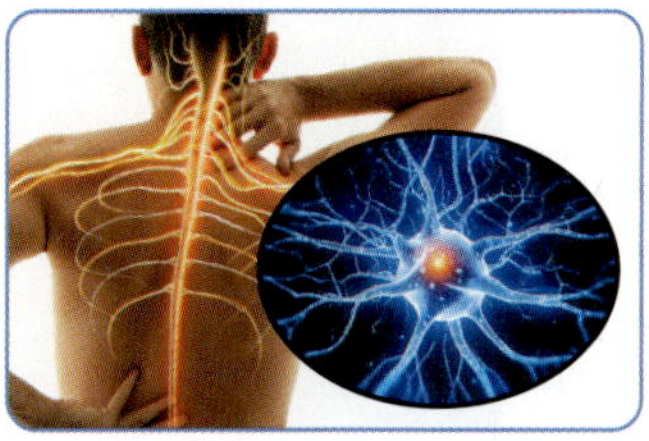

a cable-like structure within the body

____

4. 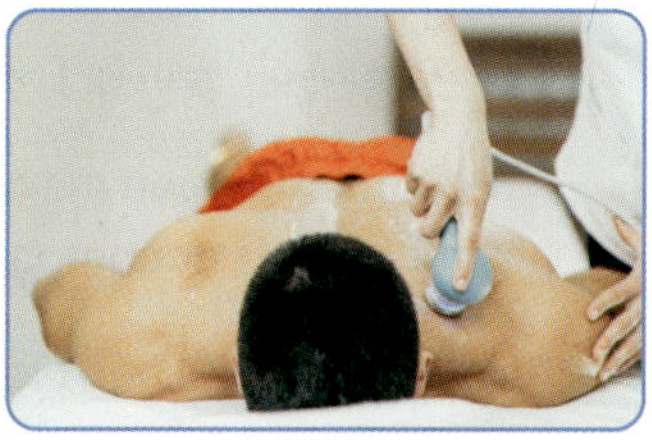

the treatment of illnesses

____

5. 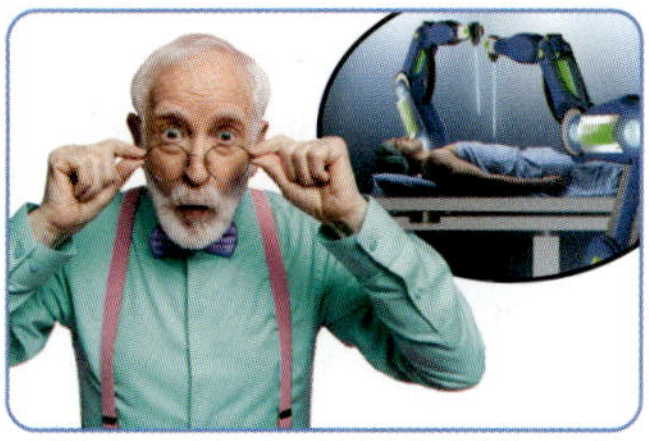

something really surprising

____

6. 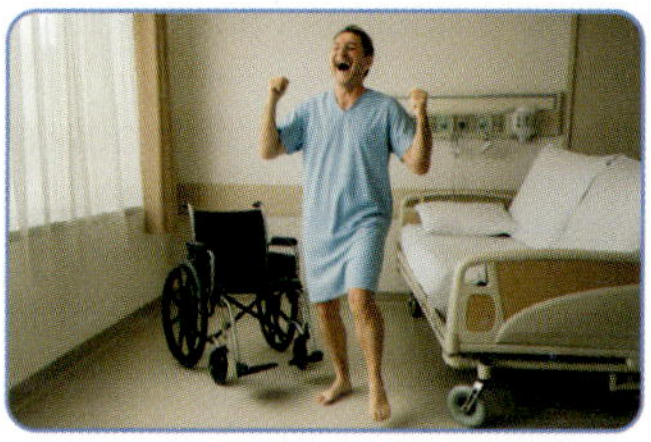

to become healthy again

____

inject | virus | nerve | heal | therapy | marvel

B Write the correct word or phrase next to each definition.

snore | thumb | infect | tense | ultimate | alternative

1. to pass a disease to a person, animal, or plant ____________________
2. nervous or worried, and unable to relax ____________________
3. the short, thick finger on the side of your hand ____________________
4. something that can be chosen instead of something else ____________________
5. happening at the end of a long process ____________________
6. to breathe noisily through your nose and mouth while you are asleep ____________________

DAY 11

201 **resident**
[rézədnt]
reside 동 거주하다
residence 명 주택, 거주지; 거주

a person who lives in a particular place
명 (특정 지역) 거주자, 주민 ((of)) 형 거주하는

She is a **resident of** New York. 그녀는 뉴욕 거주자이다.
apartment **residents** 아파트 주민들
He is **resident** in Greece. 그는 그리스에 거주하고 있다.

202 **companion**
[kəmpǽnjən]

a person or animal you spend time with or enjoy being with
명 동반자, 동행, 친구 *spouse 배우자

a traveling **companion** 여행의 동반자
a **companion** animal 반려 동물
He has been my closest **companion** since childhood. 그는 어릴 때부터 나의 가장 가까운 벗이었다.

203 **accompany**
[əkʌ́mpəni]

to go somewhere with someone; to be a companion for someone
동 1. 동행하다, 동반하다 2. (현상 등이) 동반되다 ((by))

He **accompanied** me on the trip. 그는 여행에 나와 동행했다.
strong winds **accompanied by** heavy rain 폭우가 동반된 강한 바람

204 **associate**
[əsóuʃièit]
association 명 협회; 연상(되는 것)

to relate two things or people in your mind
동 1. 연상하다, 연관 짓다 2. (~와) 어울리다 ((with)) 명 [əsóuʃiət] (사업·직장) 동료

I always **associate** the beach **with** summer. 나는 항상 해변 하면 여름이 연상된다.
Don't **associate with** those people. 그런 사람들과 어울리지 마라.
a business **associate** 사업 동료

205 **discipline**
[dísəplin]

the control of people's behavior using rules and punishments
명 규율, 훈육 동 훈육하다

He was raised with strict **discipline**. 그는 엄격한 규율 속에서 자랐다.
discipline one's child 자식을 훈육하다

206 **flexible**
[fléksəbl]

able to change to suit new conditions or situations
형 1. 융통성 있는, 탄력적인 2. 잘 구부러지는 반 inflexible 융통성 없는

We need a more **flexible** approach for the problem.
우리는 그 문제에 대해 더 유연한 접근이 필요하다.
work **flexible** hours 유연근무제[자유 근무 시간제]로 일하다
a **flexible** wire 잘 구부러지는 철사

207 **commute**
[kəmjúːt]
commuter 명 통근자

to travel regularly between work and home
동 통근하다 명 통근 (거리) ((to/from/between))

He **commutes from** Brooklyn **to** Manhattan. 그는 브루클린에서 맨해튼으로 통근한다.
It's an hour **commute to** work. 직장까지 1시간 통근 거리이다.

208 **suspend**
[səspénd]
suspension 명 정직, 정학; 중지, 유예

to officially stop something for a period of time
동 1. (일시) 중단하다 2. 정직시키다, 정학시키다 ((from)) 3. 매달다

The game was **suspended** for an hour. 그 경기는 1시간 동안 중단되었다.
He was **suspended from** work. 그는 직장에서 정직을 당했다.
A large light was **suspended from** the ceiling. 커다란 조명이 천장에 매달려 있었다.

209 **exist**
[igzíst]

to be real; to be present in a place or situation
동 존재하다, 실재하다

Do you think ghosts really **exist**? 너는 귀신이 정말 존재한다고 생각하니?
cease to **exist** 존재하지 않게 되다, 소멸하다

210 **existence**
[igzístəns]

the state of existing
명 존재, 실재

Many people believe in **the existence of** God. 많은 사람들이 신의 존재를 믿는다.

211 **destiny**
[déstəni]

the things that will happen to someone in the future; what is meant to be
명 운명, 운명의 힘

It was **destiny** that we met. 우리가 만난 것은 운명이었다.
You can't fight **destiny**. 운명에 맞서 싸울 수 없다(운명을 거역할 수 없다).

212 **fate**
[feit]
fatal 형 치명적인, 숙명적인

the things, especially bad things, that will happen to someone
명 운명(특히 좋지 않은 일), 숙명

She accepted her **fate**. 그녀는 자신의 운명[숙명]을 받아들였다.
His **fate** is now in the hands of the judge. 그의 운명은 이제 판사의 손에 달렸다.

213 **prejudice**
[prédʒudis]

an unfair feeling of dislike for a person or group because of race, religion, etc.
명 편견, 선입관 ((against)) = bias

racial **prejudice** 인종 편견
People have a **prejudice against** fat people. 사람들은 뚱뚱한 사람들에 대해 편견을 갖고 있다.

214 **spoil**
[spɔil]

to damage or ruin something
동 1. 망치다, 버려 놓다 2. (아이를) 버릇없게[응석받이로] 키우다 3. (음식이) 상하다

His prejudice **spoiled** their relationship. 그의 편견이 그들의 관계를 망쳤다.
Our picnic was **spoiled** by rain. 우리의 소풍은 비가 와서 망쳐 버렸다.
They **spoiled** their son. 그들은 아들을 버릇없게 키웠다.
I think the milk **spoiled**. 우유가 상한 것 같다.

215 **consult**
[kənsʌ́lt]
consultant 명 컨설턴트, 자문 위원

to ask for advice or information (from an expert or professional)
동 (전문가와) 상담하다, 상의하다 *counsel (전문가의) 조언, 충고; 상담을 하다

consult a lawyer 변호사에게 상담하다
If the pain continues, **consult** your doctor. 통증이 지속되면 의사와 상담하세요.

216 **divorce**
[divɔ́ːrs]
divorced 형 이혼한

the legal ending of a marriage
명 이혼 *separation 별거 동 이혼하다 *separate 헤어지다

get a **divorce** 이혼하다
Their marriage ended in **divorce**. 그들의 결혼은 이혼으로 끝이 났다.

217 **desperate**
[déspərət]

desperately 부 필사적으로; 극심하게

needing or wanting something very much

형 1. 필사적인, 절실한 ((for/to)) 2. 자포자기한, 절망적인

She was **desperate to** get a job. 그녀는 일자리를 얻기[취업을 하기] 위해 필사적이었다.
After failing the exam, she became **desperate**. 시험에 실패한 후 그녀는 절망적이 되었다.

218 **despair**
[dispέər]

the feeling of no longer having any hope

명 절망, 자포자기 동 절망하다, 체념하다 반 hope 희망; 희망하다

She cried **in despair**. 그녀는 절망하여 울었다.
Don't **despair**! Things will get better. 절망하지 마세요! 상황이 나아질 거예요.

219 **for good**

forever; permanently

영영, 영원히

They broke up **for good**. 그들은 영영 헤어졌다.
I'd like to stay here **for good**. 나는 여기에서 영원히 살고 싶다.

220 **give off**

to produce a smell, heat, light, etc.

(냄새·열·빛 등을) 내뿜다, 발산하다

The flowers **gave off** a sweet scent. 그 꽃들은 달콤한 향기를 내뿜었다.
She always **gives off** a happy vibe. 그녀는 항상 행복한 분위기를 풍긴다.

Check Up

A 우리말에 맞게 빈칸에 알맞은 말을 넣으세요.

1. 반려 동물 — a ________________ animal
2. 유연근무제[자유 근무 시간제]로 일하다 — work ________________ hours
3. 직장에서 정직을 당하다 — be ________________ from work
4. 엄격한 규율 속에서 자라다 — be raised with strict ________________
5. 변호사에게 상담하다 — ________________ a lawyer
6. 달콤한 향기를 내뿜다 — ________________ a sweet scent

B 우리말에 알맞은 말을 골라 문장을 완성하세요.

1. Don't (**accompany** / **associate**) with those people. 그런 사람들과 어울리지 마라.
2. Many people believe in the (**exist** / **existence**) of God. 많은 사람들이 신의 존재를 믿는다.
3. People have a (**prejudice** / **discipline**) against fat people. 사람들은 뚱뚱한 사람들에 대해 편견을 갖고 있다.
4. His prejudice (**suspended** / **spoiled**) their relationship. 그의 편견이 그들의 관계를 망쳤다.
5. She was (**desperate** / **despaired**) to get a job. 그녀는 일자리를 얻기[취업을 하기] 위해 필사적이었다.

Build Up

A Write the correct word for each definition.

resident	destiny	divorce	accompany	commute	spoil

1. 

a person who lives in a particular place

____

2. 

to go somewhere with someone

____

3. 

to travel regularly between work and home

____

4. 

what is meant to be

____

5. 

to damage or ruin something

____

6. 

the legal ending of a marriage

____

B Write the correct word or phrase next to each definition.

fate	discipline	suspend	companion	despair	for good

1. a person or animal you spend time with or enjoy being with __________
2. the control of people's behavior using rules and punishments __________
3. to officially stop something for a period of time __________
4. the things, especially bad things, that will happen to someone __________
5. the feeling of no longer having any hope __________
6. forever; permanently __________

DAY 12

221 **bunch**
[bʌntʃ]

a group of things that are fastened or growing together

명 다발, 송이, 묶음 ((of))

I bought **a bunch of** bananas. 나는 바나나 한 다발을 샀다.
a bunch of grapes 포도 한 송이

222 **ingredient**
[ingríːdiənt]

one of the items used in a recipe

명 1. (요리 등의) 재료, 성분 2. 구성 요소 *recipe 조리법

Mix all the **ingredients** in a bowl. 모든 재료를 그릇에 넣고 섞어라.
the essential **ingredients** for success 성공을 위한 필수 구성 요소들

223 **blend**
[blend]

blender 명 믹서기

to mix two or more things together completely

동 섞다, 혼합하다; 섞이다 ((with))

Blend the sugar and butter till smooth. 설탕과 버터를 부드러워질 때까지 잘 섞어라.
Oil does not **blend with** water. 기름은 물과 섞이지 않는다.

224 **squeeze**
[skwiːz]

squeezer 명 압착기

to press something firmly, especially with your fingers or hand

동 1. 짜다, 짜내다 2. 꽉 쥐다[잡다]

Squeeze the lemon to get the juice. 레몬을 짜서 즙을 내라.
He **squeezed** her hand. 그는 그녀의 손을 꽉 쥐었다.

225 **smash**
[smæʃ]

to break something, or to be broken into many pieces

동 때려 부수다, 깨뜨리다; 부서지다, 산산조각이 나다 ((into))

Smash garlic with a knife. 칼로 마늘을 으깨라.
smash a mirror **into** pieces 거울을 박살 내다
The vase fell and **smashed into** pieces. 꽃병이 떨어져 산산조각이 났다.

226 **seal**
[siːl]

to close something tightly so that air or liquid cannot get in or out

동 봉하다, 밀폐하다 명 봉인, 봉함

Don't forget to **seal** the jar tightly. 병을 단단히 밀봉하는 것을 잊지 마세요.
seal an envelope (편지) 봉투를 봉하다
break a **seal** 봉인을 뜯다, 개봉하다

227 **core**
[kɔːr]

the most important or central part of something

명 핵심, 중심부 형 핵심적인, 가장 중요한

Crispy chips are the **core** of the recipe. 바삭한 감자칩이 이 요리법의 핵심이다.
core skills 핵심 기술

228 **mild**
[maild]

not severe or strong

형 1. (정도가) 가벼운, 순한 2. (날씨가) 온화한, 포근한

a **mild** curry 순한 카레
a **mild** case of food poisoning 경미한 식중독
We had a **mild** winter last year. 우리는 작년에 온화한 겨울을 보냈다.

229 **electric**
[iléktrik]
electricity 명 전기, 전력

connected with electricity; using electricity for power
형 전기의, 전기를 이용하는 *electronic 전자의; 전자 장비와 관련된

an **electric** kettle 전기 주전자
Electric cars are becoming popular. 전기 차가 인기를 얻고 있다.

230 **generate**
[dʒénərèit]
generation 명 (전기 등의) 발생; 세대, 대(代)

to produce or create something, especially power, money, or ideas
동 (동력·아이디어 등을) 발생시키다, 만들어 내다 유 create 창조하다, 만들어 내다

generate electricity 전기를 생성하다, 발전을 하다
The advertisement has **generated** a lot of interest. 그 광고는 많은 관심을 불러일으켰다.

231 **fuel**
[fjúːəl]

any material that produces heat or power, usually when it is burned
명 연료 동 연료를 공급하다, 기름을 넣다

run out of **fuel** 연료가 다 떨어지다
We'd better **fuel up** at the next gas station. 다음 주유소에서 주유를 하는 것이 좋겠다.
The power plant is **fueled** by natural gas. 그 발전소는 천연가스를 연료로 사용한다.

232 **coal**
[koul]

a hard black mineral that is found below the ground and used as a fuel
명 석탄

Coal is a traditional fuel used in power plants. 석탄은 발전소에서 사용되는 전통적인 연료이다.

233 **microwave**
[máikrəweiv]

an electric oven that uses waves of energy to cook or heat food
명 전자레인지 동 전자레인지로 조리하다[데우다]

reheat the pizza in the **microwave** 피자를 전자레인지에 다시 데우다
Microwave the popcorn for 3 minutes. 팝콘을 3분간 전자레인지에 돌려 주세요.

234 **refrigerator**
[rifrídʒərèitər]

a large container that uses electricity to keep food cold
명 냉장고 = fridge *freezer 냉동고, 냉동실

You should keep leftovers in the **refrigerator**. 남은 음식은 냉장고에 보관해야 한다.
Refrigerators keep food from spoiling. 냉장고는 음식이 상하는 것을 막아 준다.

235 **utilize**
[júːtəlàiz]
utilization 명 이용, 활용

to use something for a particular purpose
동 활용하다, 이용하다 ((as)) = use

You can **utilize** the microwave **as** a cooking oven.
전자레인지를 조리용 오븐으로 활용할 수 있다.

236 **function**
[fʌ́ŋkʃən]
functional 형 기능의, 기능적인; 실용적인

the special purpose or activity for which a thing exists or is used
명 기능 동 기능하다, 작용하다

What is the **function** of this button? 이 버튼의 기능은 무엇인가요?
The button does not **function** properly. 버튼이 제대로 작동하지 않아요.

237 **dairy**
[dέəri]

made from milk; relating to foods made from milk
형 유제품의, 낙농(업)의

dairy products 유제품

238 **preserve**
[prizə́ːrv]

preserved 형 보존된
preservation 명 보존, 보호

to keep something in its original state or in good condition
동 1. 보존하다, 보호하다 2. (식품 등을) 저장하다 명 (-s) 설탕 절임

preserve the environment 환경을 보존하다
Salt is often used to **preserve** food. 소금은 흔히 음식을 보존하기 위해 사용된다.
strawberry **preserves** 딸기 설탕 절임[딸기청] *잼보다 알갱이가 더 큼

239 **be short of**

to not have enough of something
~이 부족하다[모자라다]

We may **be short of** electricity during the summer. 여름에는 전력이 부족할 수 있다.
We **are short of** bread and milk. 우리는 빵과 우유가 부족하다[모자란다].

240 **make use of**

to use something or someone, especially in order to get an advantage
~을 활용하다[이용하다] = use, utilize

You can **make use of** leftovers for lunch. 남은 음식을 점심으로 활용할 수 있다.
Try to **make** good **use of** your free time. 여가 시간을 잘 활용하도록 해라.

Check Up

A 우리말에 맞게 빈칸에 알맞은 말을 넣으세요.

1. 거울을 박살 내다 ________________ a mirror into pieces
2. (편지) 봉투를 봉하다 ________________ an envelope
3. 순한 카레 a ________________ curry
4. 전기를 생성하다, 발전을 하다 ________________ electricity
5. 연료가 다 떨어지다 run out of ________________
6. 전력이 부족하다 be ________________ electricity

B 우리말에 알맞은 말을 골라 문장을 완성하세요.

1. (**Electric** / **Electronic**) cars are becoming popular. 전기 차가 인기를 얻고 있다.
2. Oil does not (**blend from** / **blend with**) water. 기름은 물과 섞이지 않는다.
3. You should keep leftovers in the (**microwave** / **refrigerator**). 남은 음식은 냉장고에 보관해야 한다.
4. The button does not (**utilize** / **function**) properly. 버튼이 제대로 작동하지 않아요.
5. Salt is often used to (**preserve** / **protect**) food. 소금은 흔히 음식을 보존하기 위해 사용된다.

Build Up

A Write the correct word for each definition.

ingredient	squeeze	blend	bunch	dairy	smash

1. 

a group of things fastened together

____

2. 

one of the items used in a recipe

____

3. 

to mix two or more things together

____

4. 

to press something firmly

____

5. 

to break something

____

6. 

made from milk

____

B Write the correct word or phrase next to each definition.

fuel	generate	utilize	core	electric	preserve

1. the most important or central part of something ________________
2. connected with electricity; using electricity for power ________________
3. to use something for a particular purpose ________________
4. to keep something in its original state or in good condition ________________
5. to produce or create something, especially power, money, or ideas ________________
6. any material that produces heat or power, usually when it is burned ________________

Review Test 03 DAY 09-12

A 그림을 보고, 빈칸에 알맞은 단어를 넣으세요.

inject	patient	destiny	bunch	shot	nerve

1. 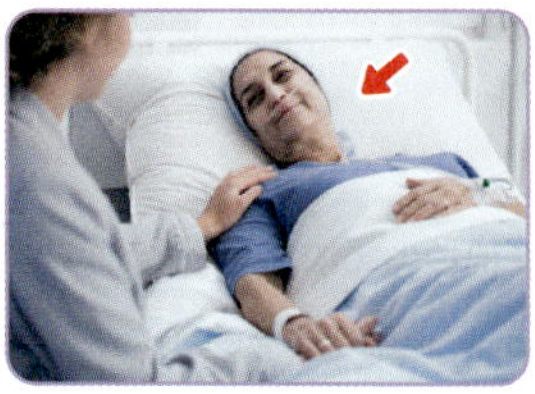 ____________

2. 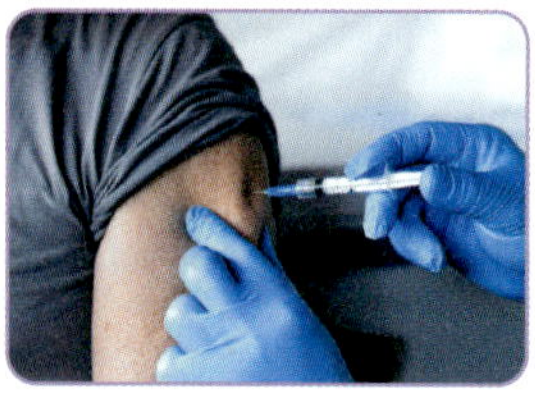 ____________

3. 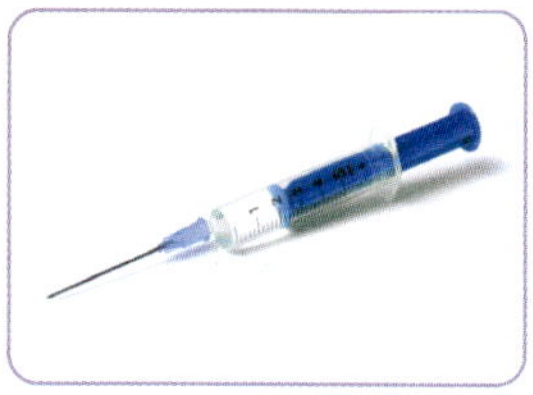 ____________

4. 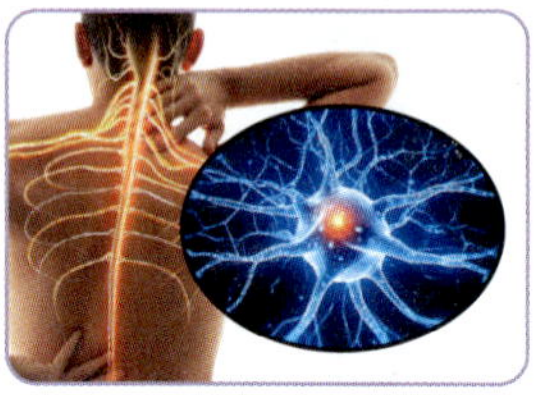 ____________

5.  ____________

6.  ____________

B 그림에 맞게 빈칸에 알맞은 단어를 고르세요.

1. 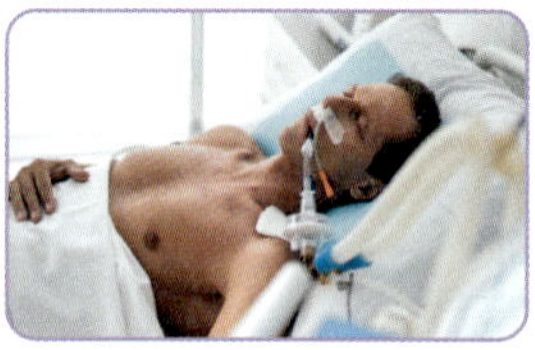

He is in ____________ condition.

(crucial / critical)

2. 

The virus ____________ many people.

(has infected / has injected)

3. 

The flowers ____________ a sweet scent.

(break out / give off)

4. 

____________ cars are becoming popular.

(Electric / Electronic)

C 우리말 뜻에 맞게 빈칸에 알맞은 말을 넣으세요.

struggle	suffer	rational	a sigh of relief
divorce	fuel	alternative	over-the-counter

1. ________________ from allergies 알레르기를 겪다, 알레르기로 고생하다
2. ________________ against cancer 암과 싸우다
3. breathe ________________ 안도의 한숨을 내쉬다
4. make a ________________ decision 합리적인[이성적인] 결정을 하다
5. an ________________ plan 대안
6. an ________________ medicine 처방전 없이 (약국에서) 살 수 있는 약
7. get a ________________ 이혼하다
8. run out of ________________ 연료가 다 떨어지다

D 우리말 뜻에 맞게 빈칸에 알맞은 말을 넣으세요.

get a vaccine	addicted to	be patient
suspended for	alternative to	desperate to

1. Please ________________ and wait for your turn. 인내심을 가지고 당신의 차례를 기다려 주세요.
2. I need to ________________ for the flu. 나는 독감 예방 주사[백신]를 맞아야 해.
3. He is ________________ online games. 그는 온라인 게임에 빠져[중독되어] 있다.
4. This therapy can be an ________________ surgery. 이 치료법은 수술의 대안이 될 수 있다.
5. The game was ________________ an hour. 그 경기는 1시간 동안 중단되었다.
6. She was ________________ get a job. 그녀는 일자리를 얻기[취업을 하기] 위해 필사적이었다.

E 밑줄 친 단어와 비슷한 뜻을 가진 단어를 고르세요.

1. Vitamins are <u>crucial</u> for good health.

   a. rational　　b. alternative　　c. vital

2. The medicine will <u>relieve</u> the symptoms.

   a. ease　　b. recover　　c. suspend

3. Please <u>keep in mind</u> that you need regular checkups.

   a. make use　　b. make a decision　　c. make sure

4. Our <u>ultimate</u> goal is to overcome cancer.

   a. permanent　　b. final　　c. essential

F 밑줄 친 단어와 반대의 뜻을 가진 단어를 고르세요.

1. She felt <u>tense</u> while waiting for her turn.

   a. severe　　b. flexible　　c. relaxed

2. I'd like to stay here <u>for good</u>.

   a. forever　　b. temporarily　　c. permanently

3. She cried in <u>despair</u>.

   a. alternative　　b. fate　　c. hope

4. We had a <u>mild</u> winter last year.

   a. harsh　　b. strong　　c. pleasant

G 주어진 영영풀이에 알맞은 단어를 고르세요.

1. a physical feeling or problem that shows that you have a disease

   a. stroke　　b. surgery　　c. symptom

2. in spite of that; however; nonetheless

   a. therefore　　b. nevertheless　　c. unless

3. to pass a disease to a person, animal, or plant

   a. inject　　b. prevent　　c. infect

4. to travel regularly between work and home

   a. commute　　b. accompany　　c. associate

5. an unfair feeling of dislike for a person or group because of race, religion, etc.

   a. nerve　　b. sympathy　　c. prejudice

6. to produce or create something, especially power, money, or ideas

   a. generate　　b. function　　c. preserve

H 빈칸에 알맞은 동사 형태를 넣어 문장을 완성하세요.

1. Her legs were ________________ from the accident. (paralyze)
2. He ______________________ for lung cancer last year. (undergo surgery)
3. War ________________ in 1914. (break out)
4. Our picnic was ________________ by rain. (spoil)

241 **wealth**
[welθ]
wealthy 형 부유한

the state of being rich; a large amount of money or property
명 부, 부유함; (많은) 재산 *property 재산; 부동산

gain **wealth** and fame 부와 명성을 얻다
She built her **wealth** through hard work. 그녀는 열심히 노력하여 부를 쌓았다.

242 **poverty**
[pávərti]
poor 형 가난한

the state of being poor
명 빈곤, 가난

fight **poverty** 가난과 싸우다, 빈곤을 퇴치하다
Many elderly people live **in poverty**. 많은 노인들이 빈곤하게 산다.

243 **rent**
[rent]
rental 명 임대, 대여; 임대물

the money that someone pays regularly to use a room, house, etc.
명 집세, 임차료 동 세내다; 세놓다 *borrow 빌리다 *lend 빌려주다

pay high **rent** 높은 집세를 내다
He **rented** an apartment for a year. 그는 1년 동안 아파트를 임대했다.
rent a car 차를 렌트하다[빌리다]

244 **deposit**
[dipázit]

a sum of money that is given as the first part of a larger payment
명 보증금, 착수금 동 (돈을) 맡기다, 예금하다 ((in/with))

pay a $100 **deposit** 100달러의 보증금을 내다
He regularly **deposits** money **in** the bank. 그는 정기적으로 은행에 돈을 예금한다.

245 **credit**
[krédit]

a way of buying something in which you arrange to pay for it at a later time
명 1. 신용 (거래) 2. 칭찬, 인정 ((to/for))

Cash or **credit** (card)? 현금으로 하시겠어요, 카드로 하시겠어요? (상점에서)
buy **on credit** 외상으로[신용거래로/신용카드로] 사다
He gave **credit to** his parents **for** his success. 그는 자신의 성공에 대해 부모님에게 공을 돌렸다.

246 **owe**
[ou]

to need to pay back money to a person, bank, business, etc.
동 1. (돈을) 빚지고 있다 2. ~은 … 덕분이다, ~을 …에게 신세지고 있다 ((to)) *debt 빚

He **owes** about $5,000 **to** the bank. 그는 은행에 약 5,000달러의 빚을 지고 있다.
I **owe** my success **to** you. 나의 성공은 당신 덕분이다.

247 **inquire**
[inkwáiər]

to ask for information about something
동 문의하다, 알아보다 ((about)) = (영) enquire

I would like to **inquire about** the job. 그 일자리에 대해 문의하고 싶습니다.
Please **inquire** at the front desk for more information.
자세한 정보는 안내 데스크에 문의하세요.

248 **inquiry**
[inkwáiəri]

a request for information about someone or something
명 1. 질문, 문의 ((about)) 2. 조사, 수사

We received a lot of **inquiries about** the job. 우리는 그 일자리에 관해 많은 문의를 받았다.
conduct an **inquiry** 조사를 실시하다, 조사하다

249 **temporary**
[témpərèri]
temporarily 🅟 일시적으로

existing or happening only for a short time
형 일시적인, 임시의

get a **temporary** job 임시직을 얻다
A **temporary** identity card will be issued to him. 그에게 임시 신분증이 발급될 것이다.

250 **permanent**
[pə́ːrmənənt]
permanently 부 영구적으로

continuing always or for a long time
형 영구적인, 영속하는

Luckily, he got a **permanent** job. 운 좋게도 그는 정규직을 얻었다[정규직으로 취업했다].

251 **frequent**
[fríːkwənt]
frequently 부 자주, 빈번히

happening or doing something often
형 자주 일어나는, 빈번한

a **frequent** customer 단골 손님
Thank you for your **frequent** visits. 자주 방문해 주셔서 감사합니다.

252 **client**
[kláiənt]

a person who uses the services of a professional person or organization
명 (전문가의 서비스를 받는) 의뢰인, 고객 *customer 손님, 고객 *consumer 소비자

I have a meeting with an important **client**. 나는 중요한 의뢰인과의 회의가 있다.

253 **disrupt**
[disrʌ́pt]
disruption 명 방해, 지장

to prevent something from continuing in its usual way
동 방해하다, 지장을 주다 유 interrupt 방해하다, 중단시키다

Protesters **disrupted** the meeting. 시위자들이 회의를 방해했다.
Traffic was **disrupted** by heavy snow. 폭설로 인해 교통에 지장이 생겼다.

254 **interfere**
[ìntərfíər]
interference 명 간섭, 참견

to try to get involved in a situation where you are not wanted or needed
동 간섭하다, 개입하다, 참견하다 ((in/with))

Don't **interfere in** other people's business. 다른 사람의 일에 간섭하지 마세요.

255 **input**
[ínpùt]

ideas, advice, money, or effort that you put into a job or activity
명 1. 조언, 의견 2. 입력, 투입 동 (컴퓨터에) 입력하다 ((into/to))

I need your **input** on this matter. 나는 이 문제에 대해 네 조언이 필요하다.
a significant **input** of money 상당한 자금의 투입
input data **into** a computer 컴퓨터에 데이터를 입력하다

256 **output**
[áutpùt]

the amount of something that is produced
명 1. 생산량, 산출량 2. 출력 동 출력하다

The factory's daily **output** has increased. 그 공장의 일일 생산량이 증가했다.
an **output** device 출력 장치
This printer can **output** high-resolution images.
이 프린터는 고해상도 이미지를 출력할 수 있다.

257 **spare**
[spɛər]

not being used or kept for emergency use

형 1. 남는, 쓰지 않는, 예비의 = extra 2. 여가의 동 할애하다, 내주다

a **spare** key / a **spare** tire 여분의 열쇠 / 예비 타이어
What do you do in your **spare** time? 여가 시간에는 무엇을 하세요?
Can you **spare** me a few minutes? 제게 몇 분만 시간을 내주실 수 있나요?

258 **waterproof**
[wɔ́tərprùf]

not allowing water to go through

형 방수의

I need a **waterproof** camera. 나는 방수 카메라가 필요하다.
The new smartphone is **waterproof.** 그 새 스마트폰은 방수가 된다.

259 **be used to N [V-ing] / get used to N [V-ing]**

to become familiar with something or someone

~에 익숙하다 / ~에 익숙해지다

I'm not **used to** getting up early. 나는 일찍 일어나는 것에 익숙하지 않다.
He **got used to** his new job quickly. 그는 새 직장에 곧 익숙해졌다.

260 **make sure (to/that)**

to take special care to do something

반드시 ~하도록 하다, 확실히 ~하다

Make sure to update your software regularly. 정기적으로 소프트웨어를 꼭 업데이트하세요.
Make sure that the window is closed. 창문이 닫혔는지 확인해라.

Check Up

A 우리말에 맞게 빈칸에 알맞은 말을 넣으세요.

1. 부와 명성을 얻다 gain ________________ and fame
2. 차를 렌트하다[빌리다] ________________ a car
3. 100달러의 보증금을 내다 pay a $100 ________________
4. 임시직을 얻다 get a ________________ job
5. 단골 손님 a ________________ customer
6. 컴퓨터에 데이터를 입력하다 ________________ data into a computer

B 우리말에 알맞은 말을 골라 문장을 완성하세요.

1. Many elderly people live (**in poor / in poverty**). 많은 노인들이 빈곤하게 산다.
2. He (**credits / owes**) about $5,000 to the bank. 그는 은행에 약 5,000달러의 빚을 지고 있다.
3. I would like to (**inquire / inquiry**) about the job. 그 일자리에 대해 문의하고 싶습니다.
4. Traffic was (**interfered / disrupted**) by heavy snow. 폭설로 인해 교통에 지장이 생겼다.
5. I'm not used to (**get up / getting up**) early. 나는 일찍 일어나는 것에 익숙하지 않다.

Build Up

A Write the correct word for each definition.

spare	poverty	temporary	wealth	waterproof	permanent

1. 

the state of being rich

____

2. 

the state of being poor

____

3. 

existing only for a short time

____

4. 

continuing always or for a long time

____

5. 

not being used or kept for emergency use

____

6. 

not allowing water to go through

____

B Write the correct word or phrase next to each definition.

frequent	rent	interfere	credit	disrupt	owe

1. the money that someone pays regularly to use a room, house, etc. ______________________
2. to need to pay back money to a person, bank, business, etc. ______________________
3. happening or doing something often ______________________
4. to prevent something from continuing in its usual way ______________________
5. to try to get involved in a situation where you are not wanted or needed ______________________
6. a way of buying something in which you arrange to pay for it at a later time ______________________

DAY 14

261 **journal**
[dʒə́ːrnl]

a newspaper or magazine that deals with a particular subject
명 1. 잡지, 학술지 2. 일기, 일지 유 diary 일기

His paper was published in a science **journal**. 그의 논문은 과학 저널에 게재되었다.
keep a **journal** 일기[일지]를 쓰다

262 **institute**
[ínstətjùːt]

an organization created for a particular purpose (such as research or education)
명 (학술·교육 등과 관련된) 기관, 협회, 연구소 *institution (대규모) 기관, 단체

a research **institute** 연구 기관, 연구소
The **institute** publishes a journal every month. 그 기관은 매달 학술잡지를 발행한다.

263 **subscribe**
[səbskráib]
subscription 명 구독(료)

to pay money to get a publication or service regularly
동 (신문 등을) 구독하다, (유료 채널 등에) 가입하다 ((to))

subscribe to a magazine 잡지를 구독하다
I **subscribe to** Netflix. 나는 넷플릭스에 가입했다[넷플릭스를 구독하고 있다].

264 **submit**
[səbmít]

to give a document, proposal, etc. to someone in authority
동 1. 제출하다 = turn in 2. 굴복하다, 복종하다 ((to)) = give in

Please **submit** your application by Friday. 금요일까지 신청서[지원서]를 제출해 주세요.
She didn't **submit to** the pressure of her boss. 그녀는 상사의 압력에 굴복하지 않았다.

265 **recruit**
[rikrúːt]

to find new people to join a company, an organization, the armed forces, etc.
동 (신입 사원·회원·신병 등을) 모집하다, 뽑다

The company is **recruiting** new employees. 그 회사는 새로운 직원을 모집하고 있다.

266 **agent**
[éidʒənt]
agency 명 대행사; (정부) 기관, ~국

a person who does business for another person
명 1. 대리인, 중개상; 에이전트 2. 스파이, 첩보원

They recruited talented players through a sports **agent**.
그들은 스포츠 에이전트를 통해 재능 있는 선수들을 모집했다.
a secret **agent** 비밀 요원, 첩보원

267 **acquire**
[əkwáiər]
acquisition 명 습득; 취득

to get or obtain something
동 1. 얻다, 획득하다 2. 습득하다, 배우다

The team **acquired** three new players this year. 그 팀은 올해 새로운 선수 세 명을 영입했다.
Children **acquire** foreign languages easily. 아이들은 외국어를 쉽게 습득한다.

268 **outcome**
[áutkʌ̀m]

the final result of an action or event
명 (어떤 행동·과정의) 결과, 결론 ((of)) 유 result (직접적인) 결과

What was the **outcome of** the game last night? 어젯밤 경기 결과는 어땠나요?
watch the **outcome of** the affair 사건의 결과를 지켜보다

269 **forecast**
[fɔ́rkæ̀st]

a statement about what will happen in the future
(forecast/forecasted–forecast/forecasted)
명 예보, 예측 동 예보하다, 예측하다

a weather **forecast** 일기 예보
Snow is **forecast** for tomorrow. 내일 눈이 내릴 것으로 예보되고 있다.
Experts **forecast** that the economy will slow. 전문가들은 경제가 둔화될 것이라고 예측한다.

270 **predict**
[pridíkt]
prediction 명 예측, 예견
predictable 형 예측[예견]할 수 있는

to say that something will happen in the future
동 예측하다, 예견하다

predict the future 미래를 예측하다
He **predicted** that our team would win. 그는 우리 팀이 이길 것이라고 예견했다.

271 **reform**
[rifɔ́ːrm]

to change a system, organization, or law in order to improve it
동 개혁하다, 개선하다 명 개혁, 개선

They plan to **reform** the old system. 그들은 오래된 시스템을 개혁할 계획이다.
a **reform** of the legal system 법률 제도의 개선

272 **refine**
[rifáin]
refinement 명 개선(된 것)

to remove the unwanted substances in something
동 1. 정제하다 2. (작은 변화를 주어) 개선하다, 다듬다

refine oil 석유를 정제하다
We need to **refine** our strategy further. 우리는 우리의 전략을 더 다듬어야 한다.

273 **revive**
[riváiv]
revival 명 회복, 부활; 재유행; 재공연

to become, or to make (someone or something) healthy and strong again
동 1. 활기를 되찾다, 회복하다; 회복시키다 2. 부활시키다, 재공연하다

The economy is beginning to **revive**. 경제가 회복되기 시작하고 있다.
revive an old tradition 오래된 전통을 되살리다
They decided to **revive** the musical *Cats*. 그들은 뮤지컬 〈캣츠〉를 재공연하기로 결정했다.

274 **restore**
[ristɔ́ːr]
restoration 명 복원, 복구

to bring back a situation or feeling that existed before
동 1. (질서·건강 등을) 회복시키다 2. (건물 등을) 복구하다, 복원하다
*recover (건강 등이) 회복되다; (손실 등을) 되찾다

restore law and order 법과 질서(치안)를 회복시키다
The museum was **restored** after the fire. 그 박물관은 화재 후 복구되었다.
restore old paintings 오래된 그림들을 복원하다

275 **assemble**
[əsémbl]
assembly 명 집회; 조립

to come together or bring (people or things) together in one place
동 1. 모이다; 모으다, 집합시키다 2. 조립하다 *gather 모이다; 모으다

All the volunteers **assembled** at the park. 모든 자원봉사자들이 공원에 모였다.
assemble a model airplane 모형 비행기를 조립하다

276 **reproduce**
[rìprədúːs]
reproduction 명 생식, 번식; 복사, 복제

to make a copy of something
동 1. 복사하다, 복제하다 2. 번식하다

Do not **reproduce** without permission. 허가 없이 복제하지 마시오(무단 복제 금지).
Many animals **reproduce** during the springtime. 많은 동물들은 봄철에 번식한다.

277 **risk**
[risk]

the possibility that something bad or dangerous may happen
명 위험(성) ((of)) = danger 동 위험을 무릅쓰다

There is **a risk of** injury when playing sports. 스포츠를 할 때는 부상의 위험이 있다.
The firefighter **risked** his life to save the boy. 그 소방관은 목숨을 걸고 그 소년을 구했다.

---

278 **threat**
[θret]
threaten 동 위협하다, 협박하다

an expression of intent to do harm
명 1. 위협, 협박 ((against/from)) 2. 위협적인 존재 ((to))

They made **a threat against** him. 그들은 그를 협박했다.
Terrorists are **a threat to** our society. 테러리스트는 우리 사회에 위협(적인 존재)이다.
Plastic waste is **a threat to** the environment. 플라스틱 쓰레기는 환경에 위협적인 존재이다.

---

279 **take a risk [risks]**

to do something that might be dangerous
위험을 감수하다, 모험을 하다

If I were you, I would **take a risk**. 내가 너라면 위험을 감수할 것이다.
I don't want to **take** any **risks**. 나는 어떤 위험도 감수하고 싶지 않다.

---

280 **be under threat**

to be in a situation where something harmful or dangerous is likely to happen
위협을 받고 있다, 위험에 처해 있다

Wildlife **is** often **under threat** due to habitat loss. 야생 동물은 서식지 손실로 종종 위협을 받는다.
The program **is under threat** of closure. 그 프로그램은 중단될 위기에 처해 있다.

Check Up

A 우리말에 맞게 빈칸에 알맞은 말을 넣으세요.

1. 일기[일지]를 쓰다 — keep a ________________
2. 신청서[지원서]를 제출하다 — ________________ an application
3. 비밀 요원, 첩보원 — a secret ________________
4. 일기 예보 — a weather ________________
5. 미래를 예측하다 — ________________ the future
6. 모형 비행기를 조립하다 — ________________ a model airplane

B 우리말에 알맞은 말을 골라 문장을 완성하세요.

1. I (**subscribe to** / **submit to**) Netflix. 나는 넷플릭스에 가입했다[넷플릭스를 구독하고 있다].
2. They plan to (**refine** / **reform**) the old system. 그들은 오래된 시스템을 개혁할 계획이다.
3. The museum was (**revived** / **restored**) after the fire. 그 박물관은 화재 후 복구되었다.
4. Do not (**recruit** / **reproduce**) without permission. 허가 없이 복제하지 마시오(무단 복제 금지).
5. Wildlife is often under (**threat** / **threaten**) due to habitat loss. 야생 동물은 서식지 손실로 종종 위협을 받는다.

Build Up

A Write the correct word for each definition.

assemble	outcome	subscribe	reproduce	threat	revive

1. 

to pay money to get a service regularly

____

2. 

the final result of an action or event

____

3. 

to become healthy and strong again

____

4. 

to come together in one place

____

5. 

to make a copy of something

____

6. 

an expression of intent to do harm

____

B Write the correct word or phrase next to each definition.

submit	recruit	institute	take a risk	acquire	forecast

1. an organization created for a particular purpose __________________
2. to give a document, proposal, etc. to someone in authority __________________
3. to get or obtain something __________________
4. a statement about what will happen in the future __________________
5. to do something that might be dangerous __________________
6. to find new people to join a company, an organization, the armed forces, etc. __________________

DAY 15

281 **export**
[ikspɔ́:rt]

to sell goods to another country

동 수출하다 명 [ékspɔ:rt] 수출, 수출품 ((to))

We **export** electronics **to** Europe. 우리는 유럽에 전자제품을 수출한다.
The factory produces cars **for export**. 그 공장은 수출용 자동차를 생산한다.

282 **import**
[impɔ́:rt]

to bring a product into one country from another to be sold

동 수입하다 명 [ímpɔ:rt] 수입, 수입품 ((from)) *trade 무역하다; 무역

The country **imports** most of its oil. 그 나라는 대부분의 석유를 수입한다.
luxury **imports from** Italy 이탈리아에서 온 고급 수입품들

283 **latest**
[léitist]

late 형 늦은
lately 부 최근에, 요즘
later 부 이후에, 나중에

the most recent or newest

형 (보통 the ~) 최신의, 가장 최근의 *recent 최근의

the latest fashion trend 최신 패션 트렌드
Have you heard **the latest** news? 너 최근[최신] 뉴스 들었니?

284 **up to date**
[ʌ́p tu deit]

modern, recent, or containing the latest information

형 현대식의, 최신(식)의 반 out of date 시대에 뒤떨어진, 구식의

This technology is very **up to date**. 이 기술은 매우 최신식이다.
the most **up-to-date** information 가장 최신 정보

285 **distribute**
[distríbju:t]

distribution 명 분배; 유통

to give something out to people or places

동 1. 나누어 주다, 분배하다 ((to)) = hand out 2. (상품을) 유통시키다

The books will be **distributed to** local schools. 그 책들은 지역 학교에 배포될 것이다.
The company **distributes** coffee and tea worldwide.
그 회사는 커피와 차를 전 세계에 유통시킨다.

286 **contribute**
[kəntríbju:t]

contribution 명 기부(금); 기여

to give something, (especially money or goods), to help someone

동 1. 기부하다, 기증하다 = donate 2. 기여하다, 공헌하다 ((to))

She **contributed** 100 dollars **to** the charity. 그녀는 그 자선 단체에 100달러를 기부했다.
Everyone **contributed to** the team's success. 모두가 팀의 성공에 기여했다.

287 **convert**
[kənvə́:rt]

conversion 명 전환, 개조
convertible 형 전환 가능한

to change something into a different form

동 전환시키다, 개조하다; 전환되다 ((to/into))

The apartment was **converted into** an office. 그 아파트는 사무실로 개조되었다.
a sofa that **converts into** a bed 침대로 전환되는 소파

288 **transform**
[trænsfɔ́rm]

transformation
명 변신, 탈바꿈; (곤충) 변태
transformer
명 변압기; 트랜스포머(변신 로봇)

to change something completely, usually in a good way

동 1. 완전히 바꾸다[탈바꿈시키다] 2. 변신하다 ((into))

They **transformed** the old factory **into** an art gallery.
그들은 그 오래된 공장을 미술관으로 변모시켰다[탈바꿈시켰다].
Caterpillars **transform into** butterflies. 애벌레는 나비로 변신한다.

289 **modify**
[mádəfài]
modification 명 수정, 변경

to change something slightly, usually to improve it
동 (약간) 수정하다, 조정하다, 변경하다 유 revise 수정하다, 개정하다

modify a plan 계획을 수정하다
The schedule has been **modified.** 일정이 조정되었다.

290 **adjust**
[ədʒʌ́st]
adjustment 명 수정, 조정; 적응

to change or move something slightly so that it works better
동 1. 조정하다, 조절하다 2. 적응하다 ((to)) = adapt, get used to

adjust the volume on the radio 라디오의 볼륨을 조절하다
She soon **adjusted to** the new environment. 그녀는 곧 새로운 환경에 적응했다.

291 **decline**
[dikláin]

to become less in amount, quality, or strength
동 1. 감소하다, 하락하다 = decrease 2. (정중히) 거절하다 = refuse 명 감소, 하락

Car sales have **declined** this year. 올해 자동차 판매가 감소했다.
She **declined** his offer. 그녀는 그의 제안을 거절했다.
a rapid **decline** / a gradual **decline** 급속한 감소 / 완만한 감소

292 **diminish**
[dimíniʃ]

to become less or to make something become less
동 줄어들다, 약해지다; 줄이다, 감소시키다 반 increase 증가하다; 증가시키다

His role in the company was **diminished.** 회사 내에서 그의 역할이 줄어들었다.
diminish the risk of hacking 해킹의 위험을 줄이다

293 **analyze**
[ǽnəlàiz]
analyst 명 분석가

to study or examine something in detail in order to understand it
동 분석하다 = (영) analyse

analyze a problem 문제를 분석하다
The data was **analyzed** by computer. 그 데이터는 컴퓨터로 분석되었다.

294 **analysis**
[ənǽləsis]

the detailed study or examination of something
명 분석

Further **analysis** of the data is needed. 데이터에 대한 추가 분석이 필요하다.

295 **dismiss**
[dismís]
dismissal 명 해고; 묵살, 기각

to allow or cause (someone) to leave
동 1. (사람을) 보내다, 해산시키다 2. 해고하다 ((from)) ≒ fire 3. 묵살하다, 기각하다

The meeting was **dismissed** early. 회의는 일찍 끝났다(해산되었다).
He was unfairly **dismissed from** his job. 그는 부당하게 직장에서 해고되었다.
The case was **dismissed.** 그 소송은 기각되었다.

296 **dispose**
[dispóuz]
disposal 명 처리, 처분

to throw something away; to get rid of something
동 버리다, 없애다, 처리하다 ((of)) 유 dump (쏟아) 버리다

Dispose of your garbage in the bin. 쓰레기는 쓰레기통에 버려 주세요.
The factory **disposed of** toxic waste illegally.
그 공장은 유독성 폐기물을 불법으로 처리했다[버렸다].

297 **fulfill**
[fulfíl]

fulfillment 명 이행, 수행; 달성

to do or provide what is necessary or needed

동 1. (의무·약속 등을) 이행하다, 수행하다 = perform 2. 달성하다 = achieve

He **fulfilled** his duties. 그는 자신의 의무를 다했다.

He finally **fulfilled** his childhood dream. 그는 마침내 자신의 어린 시절 꿈을 이뤘다.

298 **postpone**
[poustpóun]

to arrange for something to happen at a later time

동 미루다, 연기하다 = put off *delay 미루다, 지연시키다 *cancel 취소하다

The committee **postponed** the meeting until next week.
그 위원회는 회의를 다음 주로 연기했다.

The concert was **postponed** due to bad weather. 그 콘서트는 악천후로 인해 연기되었다.

299 **at the latest**

no later than the time or the date mentioned

(아무리) 늦어도 *at least 적어도, 최소한

It should be finished by tomorrow **at the latest.** 그것은 늦어도 내일까지는 완료되어야 한다.

Please submit your report by Friday **at the latest.** 늦어도 금요일까지는 보고서를 제출하세요.

300 **get rid of**

to throw something away; to dispose of

~을 제거하다[없애다], ~을 처리하다

We **got rid of** all the old furniture. 우리는 낡은 가구들을 다 처분했다.

Recycling is the best way to **get rid of** waste. 재활용은 쓰레기를 처리하는 가장 좋은 방법이다.

Check Up

A 우리말에 맞게 빈칸에 알맞은 말을 넣으세요.

1. 가장 최신 정보 — the most __________ information
2. 침대로 전환되는 소파 — a sofa that __________ into a bed
3. 문제를 분석하다 — __________ a problem
4. 급속한 감소 — a rapid __________
5. 의무를 다하다, 임무를 수행하다 — __________ one's duty
6. 쓰레기를 처리하다[없애다] — __________ waste

B 우리말에 알맞은 말을 골라 문장을 완성하세요.

1. The country (**exports** / **imports**) most of its oil. 그 나라는 대부분의 석유를 수입한다.
2. The books will be (**distributed** / **contributed**) to local schools. 그 책들은 지역 학교에 배포될 것이다.
3. Caterpillars (**convert** / **transform**) into butterflies. 애벌레는 나비로 변신한다.
4. She soon (**adjusted** / **dismissed**) to the new environment. 그녀는 곧 새로운 환경에 적응했다.
5. The concert was (**disposed** / **postponed**) due to bad weather. 그 콘서트는 악천후로 인해 연기되었다.

Build Up

A Write the correct word for each definition.

distribute	the latest	transform	dispose	modify	decline

1\.

the most recent or newest

____

2\.

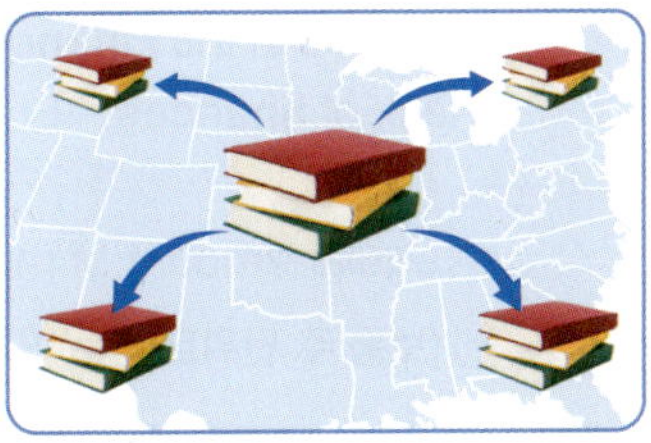

to give something out

____

3\.

to change something completely

____

4\.

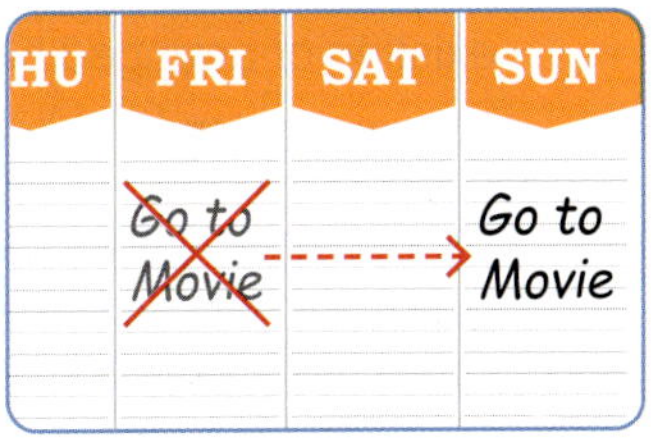

to change something slightly

____

5\.

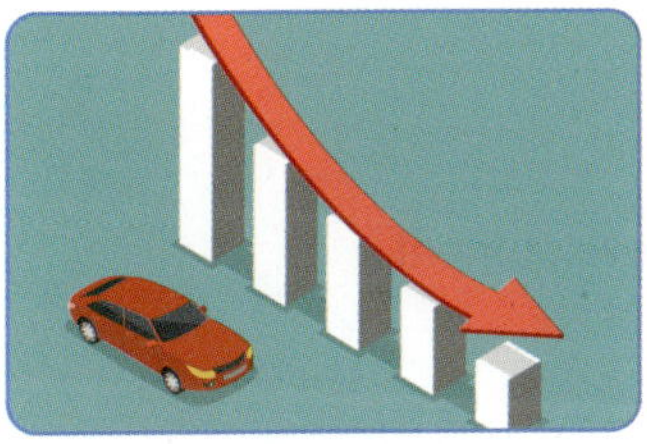

to become less; to decrease

____

6\.

to get rid of something

____

B Write the correct word or phrase next to each definition.

convert	diminish	contribute	analysis	dismiss	adjust

1. to give something, (especially money or goods), to help someone ________________
2. to change something into a different form ________________
3. to change or move something slightly so that it works better ________________
4. to become less or to make something become less ________________
5. the detailed study or examination of something ________________
6. to allow or cause (someone) to leave ________________

DAY 16

301 **finance**
[fáinæns]

financial 형 금융의, 재정의
financially 부 재정적으로

the management of money by governments or large organizations

명 1. 재정, 재무 2. (-s) 자금, 재원 *budget 예산

He works in the **Finance** Department. 그는 재무 부서에서 일한다.
a lack of **finances** 자금 부족

302 **wage**
[weidʒ]

a regular amount of money that you earn, usually every week

명 (보통 주 단위로 받는) 임금, 급료 *salary 급여, 월급 (보통 월 1회 혹은 2회)

He earns a good **wage**. 그는 좋은 급료를 받고 있다.
a weekly **wage** of $900 주급 900달러(주당 900달러의 임금)
the minimum **wage** 최저 임금

303 **prior**
[práiər]

existing or arranged before something else

형 1. 이전의, 사전의 2. (~에) 우선하는 ((to)) 유 previous 이전의, 바로 앞의

I have a **prior** engagement. 나는 선약이 있다.
give **prior** notice 사전 통보를 하다, 사전에 고지하다
Health is **prior to** money. 건강이 돈보다 우선이다.

304 **priority**
[praiɔ́ːrəti]

something that is regarded as more important or urgent than other things

명 우선 사항, 우선적으로 할 것

set **priorities** (일의) 우선순위를 정하다
Safety is the top **priority**. 안전이 최우선이다.

305 **phase**
[feiz]

a stage in a process of change or development

명 단계, 국면 유 stage 단계

The project is in the final **phase**. 그 프로젝트는 마지막 단계에 있다.
enter a new **phase** 새로운 국면에 접어들다
the **phases** of the moon 달의 위상(변하는 모습)

306 **aspect**
[æspekt]

a part of a situation, problem, or subject

명 측면

We need to consider every **aspect** of the project.
우리는 그 프로젝트의 모든 측면을 고려해야 한다.

307 **considerable**
[kənsídərəbl]

considerably 부 많이, 상당히

great in amount, size, importance, etc.

형 많은, 상당한 = significant

spend **considerable** time and money 많은 시간과 돈을 쓰다
We have made **considerable** progress. 우리는 상당한 진전을 이루었다.

308 **considerate**
[kənsídərət]

consider 동 고려하다, 숙고하다
consideration 명 사려, 배려, 숙고

caring about and respectful of others

형 사려 깊은, (남을) 배려하는 = thoughtful 반 inconsiderate 사려 깊지 못한

He is always polite and **considerate**. 그는 항상 예의 바르고 배려가 있다.

309 **conference**
[kánfərəns]

a large official meeting, usually lasting for a few days
명 회의, 회담

a peace **conference** 평화 회의[회담]
The **conference** will be held in Seoul. 그 회담은 서울에서 열릴 예정이다.

310 **convention**
[kənvénʃən]
conventional 형 관습적인; 전통적인

a large formal meeting of people with the same interest or work
명 1. (대규모) 대회, 협의회 2. 관습, 풍습 = custom

attend an annual **convention** 연례 회의[대회]에 참석하다
social **conventions** 사회적 관습

311 **cooperate**
[kouápərèit]
cooperation 명 협력, 협동
cooperative 형 협력하는, 협조하는

to work together in order to do something
동 협력하다, 협동하다 ((with))

They agreed to **cooperate with** each other. 그들은 서로 협력하기로 합의했다.

312 **collaborate**
[kəlǽbərèit]
collaboration 명 공동 작업, 협업

to work together in order to produce or achieve something
동 협력하다, 공동으로 작업하다 ((with/on/in))

They have **collaborated on** many projects. 그들은 많은 프로젝트에서 협력해 왔다.
The band **collaborated with** various artists. 그 밴드는 다양한 아티스트와 협업(콜라보)을 했다.

313 **negotiate**
[nigóuʃièit]
negotiation 명 협상, 교섭

to try to reach an agreement by formal discussion
동 협상하다, 교섭하다 ((with/for/about))

The employees are still **negotiating with** the company.
직원들은 여전히 회사와 협상 중이다.
They have been **negotiating for** more pay. 그들은 임금 인상을 위해 협상해 왔다(협상해 오는 중이다).

314 **compromise**
[kámprəmàiz]

an agreement made between two groups by giving up something
명 타협, 절충 동 타협하다, 굽히다 ((on))

make a **compromise** 타협하다, 절충하다
Both sides agreed to **compromise on** the issue. 양측은 그 문제에 대해 타협하기로 합의했다.

315 **compensate**
[kámpənsèit]
compensation 명 보상(금)

to make up for something
동 보상하다, 보상금을 주다 ((for)) *refund 환불; 환불하다

They decided to **compensate for** the loss. 그들은 손실을 보상하기로 결정했다.
The company **compensated** them **for** their extra work.
회사는 그들의 초과 근무(잔업)에 대해 보상했다.

316 **complement**
[kámpləmènt]
complementary 형 상호 보완적인

to make something else better or more attractive
동 보완하다, 보충하다 명 [kámpləmənt] 보완물 ((to))

Tom and Bob **complement** each other well. 톰과 밥은 서로를 잘 보완해 준다.
The hat is a perfect **complement to** your outfit.
그 모자는 네 옷차림에 완벽한 보완물이다(잘 어울린다).

317 **coordinate**
[kouɔ́ːrdənèit]

coordination 명 조직(화); 조화
coordinator 명 조직자, 진행자, 코디네이터

to organize or arrange activities or tasks so that they work well
동 1. 조직화하다, 조정하다 2. (옷 등을) 조화시키다; 조화되다 ((with))

coordinate the details 세부 사항을 조정하다[조율하다]
This scarf **coordinates with** your dress. 이 스카프는 당신의 드레스와 잘 어울린다.

318 **neutral**
[njúːtrəl]

not supporting any side in an argument or fight
형 중립의, 중립적인

Switzerland is known as a **neutral** nation. 스위스는 중립 국가로 알려져 있다.
neutral colors 중간 색상, (검정·흰색·회색 등의) 무채색

319 **prior to**

before a particular time or event
~에 앞서, ~ 전에

Prior to the meeting, he reviewed the report. 회의에 앞서 그는 보고서를 검토했다.
Make sure your passport is valid **prior to** going abroad.
해외로 나가기 전에 여권이 유효한지 확인해라.

320 **to one's surprise**

surprisingly or unexpectedly
놀랍게도, 뜻밖에

To my surprise, they reached a compromise. 놀랍게도 그들은 타협에 이르렀다.
Much **to our surprise**, they accepted the offer. 아주 놀랍게도 그들은 그 제안을 받아들였다.

Check Up

A 우리말에 맞게 빈칸에 알맞은 말을 넣으세요.

1. 최저 임금 the minimum ____________
2. 사전 통보를 하다, 사전에 고지하다 give ____________ notice
3. 새로운 국면에 접어들다 enter a new ____________
4. 평화 회의[회담] a peace ____________
5. 타협하다, 절충하다 make a ____________
6. 손실을 보상하다 ____________ the loss

B 우리말에 알맞은 말을 골라 문장을 완성하세요.

1. Health is (**priority** / **prior**) to money. 건강이 돈보다 우선이다.
2. We need to consider every (**aspect** / **phase**) of the project. 우리는 그 프로젝트의 모든 측면을 고려해야 한다.
3. We have made (**considerable** / **considerate**) progress. 우리는 상당한 진전을 이루었다.
4. They (**have collaborated** / **have compromised**) on many projects. 그들은 많은 프로젝트에서 협력해 왔다.
5. They have been (**negotiated** / **negotiating**) for more pay. 그들은 임금 인상을 위해 협상해 왔다(협상해 오는 중이다).

Build Up

A **Write the correct word for each definition.**

cooperate
conference
phase
complement
negotiate
neutral

1. 

a stage in a process of change

____

2. 

a large official meeting

____

3. 

to work together

____

4. 

to try to reach an agreement

____

5. 

to make something else better

____

6. 

not supporting any side in an argument

____

B **Write the correct word or phrase next to each definition.**

finance	considerable	priority	coordinate	considerate	to one's surprise

1. the management of money by governments or large organizations ______________________
2. great in amount, size, importance, etc. ______________________
3. caring about and respectful of others ______________________
4. to organize or arrange activities or tasks so that they work well ______________________
5. surprisingly or unexpectedly ______________________
6. something that is regarded as more important or urgent than other things ______________________

Review Test 04 DAY 13-16

A 그림을 보고, 빈칸에 알맞은 단어를 넣으세요.

up to date	spare	threat	conference	dispose	waterproof

1. 

____

2. 

____

3. 

____

4. 

____

5. 

____

6. 

____

B 그림에 맞게 빈칸에 알맞은 단어를 고르세요.

1. 

Traffic was ______________ by heavy snow.
(interfered / disrupted)

2. 

According to the weather ______________,
(forecast / predict)
it will rain tomorrow.

3. 

Do not ______________ without permission.
(restore / reproduce)

4. 

Caterpillars ______________ butterflies.
(transform into / convert into)

C 우리말 뜻에 맞게 빈칸에 알맞은 말을 넣으세요.

journal	predict	deposit	the latest
analyze	restore	wage	prior engagement

1. pay a $100 ____________________ 100달러의 보증금을 내다
2. keep a ____________________ 일기[일지]를 쓰다
3. ____________________ the future 미래를 예측하다
4. ____________________ old paintings 오래된 그림들을 복원하다
5. ____________________ fashion trend 최신 패션 트렌드
6. ____________________ a problem 문제를 분석하다
7. the minimum ____________________ 최저 임금
8. have a ____________________ 선약이 있다

D 우리말 뜻에 맞게 빈칸에 알맞은 말을 넣으세요.

adjusted to	owes	compensate for
a risk of	in poverty	subscribe to

1. Many elderly people live ____________________. 많은 노인들이 빈곤하게 산다.
2. He ____________________ about $5,000 to the bank. 그는 은행에 약 5,000달러의 빚을 지고 있다.
3. I ____________________ Netflix. 나는 넷플릭스에 가입했다[넷플릭스를 구독하고 있다].
4. There is ____________________ injury when playing sports. 스포츠를 할 때는 부상의 위험이 있다.
5. She soon ____________________ the new environment. 그녀는 곧 새로운 환경에 적응했다.
6. They decided to ____________________ the loss. 그들은 손실을 보상하기로 결정했다.

E 밑줄 친 단어와 비슷한 뜻을 가진 단어를 고르세요.

1. Please <u>submit</u> your application by Friday.

   a. turn in b. give in c. hand in

2. All the volunteers <u>assembled</u> at the park.

   a. interrupted b. adjusted c. gathered

3. The committee <u>postponed</u> the meeting.

   a. put off b. put on c. dismissed

4. We <u>got rid of</u> all the old furniture.

   a. distributed to b. disposed of c. contributed to

F 밑줄 친 단어와 반대의 뜻을 가진 단어를 고르세요.

1. She built her <u>wealth</u> through hard work.

   a. property b. poverty c. charity

2. Luckily, he got a <u>permanent</u> job.

   a. spare b. temporary c. particular

3. The country <u>imports</u> most of its oil.

   a. exports b. dismisses c. distributes

4. Car sales have <u>declined</u> this year.

   a. decreased b. diminished c. increased

G 주어진 영영풀이에 알맞은 단어를 고르세요.

1. a way of buying something in which you arrange to pay for it at a later time

   a. rent b. deposit c. credit

2. to ask for information about something

   a. inquiry b. inquire c. acquire

3. to change a system, organization, or law in order to improve it

   a. reform b. refine c. revive

4. the possibility that something bad or dangerous may happen

   a. threat b. risk c. priority

5. great in amount, size, importance, etc.

   a. consider b. considerate c. considerable

6. caring about and respectful of others

   a. concern b. considerate c. considerable

H 빈칸에 알맞은 동사 형태를 넣어 문장을 완성하세요.

1. The company is ______________ new employees. (recruit)
2. The data was ______________ by computer. (analyze)
3. They have ______________ on many projects. (collaborate)
4. They have been ______________ for more pay. (negotiate)

321 **historic**
[histɔ́:rik]

history 명 역사
historical 형 역사와 관련된, 역사의

important in history; likely to be important in history
형 역사적으로 중요한, 역사에 남을 만한, 역사적인

a **historic** building 역사적으로 중요한 빌딩
a **historic** moment that changed the world 세상을 바꾼 역사적인 순간

322 **era**
[érə]

a period of time in history that is special for a particular reason
명 (다른 시대들과 구별되는) 시대 ((of)) *period 기간, 시기 *age 시대, 시기

the Roman **era** 로마 시대
mark the end of **an era** 한 시대의 종말을 알리다
A new **era of** peace will open. 새로운 평화의 시대가 열릴 것이다.

323 **ancient**
[éinʃənt]

belonging to a time long ago in history, especially thousands of years ago
형 고대의, 아주 오래된

The **ancient** Egyptians built the pyramids. 고대 이집트인들은 피라미드를 건설했다.
an **ancient** oak tree 아주 오래된 떡갈나무

324 **contemporary**
[kəntémpərèri]

belonging to the present time
형 현대의, 당대의 유 modern 현대의, 근대의; 현대적인

I like **contemporary** art. 나는 현대 미술을 좋아한다.
life in **contemporary** Britain 현대 영국에서의 삶

325 **kingdom**
[kíŋdəm]

a country ruled by a king or queen
명 왕국 *palace 궁, 궁전

the **Kingdom** of Sweden 스웨덴 왕국
the United **Kingdom** 영국
Queen Elizabeth ruled the **kingdom**. 엘리자베스 여왕이 그 왕국을 다스렸다.

326 **empire**
[émpaiər]

emperor 명 황제

a group of countries that are controlled by one ruler or government
명 1. 제국 2. 기업 왕국, 거대 기업

The British **Empire** ruled the world once. 대영 제국은 한때 세계를 지배했다.
He built a media **empire**. 그는 미디어 왕국을 세웠다.

327 **dynasty**
[dáinəsti]

a period of time when a particular family ruled a country
명 왕조, 왕가

The Joseon **Dynasty** was founded in 1392. 조선 왕조는 1392년에 세워졌다.
The **dynasty** lasted for over five centuries. 그 왕조는 5세기 이상 지속되었다.

328 **crown**
[kraun]

a circular decoration for the head worn by a king or queen
명 1. 왕관 2. (the -) 왕위, 왕권 *throne 왕좌, 왕위

wear a **crown** 왕관을 쓰다, 왕위에 오르다
He refused **the crown**. 그는 왕위를 거부했다(왕이 되기를 거부했다).

329 **royal**
[rɔ́iəl]
royalty 명 왕족(들); 저작권 사용료, 인세

relating to or belonging to a king or queen
형 1. 왕실의, 왕족의 2. (보통 Royal) 왕립의, 국립의

the **royal** family 왕가, 왕실 가족
the **Royal** College of Music (영국) 왕립 음악 대학

330 **loyal**
[lɔ́iəl]
loyalty 명 충성, 충성심
loyally 부 충성스럽게

remaining faithful to someone or something and supporting them or it
형 충실한, 충성스러운 ((to)) = faithful

a **loyal** supporter 충실한[충성] 지지자
They were **loyal to** their country. 그들은 조국에 충성했다.

331 **noble**
[nóubl]
nobility 명 귀족; 고귀함

having or showing fine personal qualities that people admire
형 1. 고귀한, 고결한, 숭고한 2. 귀족의 반 humble 미천한

He was a man of **noble** character. 그는 고귀한 인품의 사람이었다.
She is from a **noble** family. 그녀는 귀족 집안 출신이다.

332 **knight**
[nait]

(in the Middle Ages) a man of high social rank who had a duty to fight for his king
명 (중세의) 기사

a black **knight** 흑기사
a **knight** in shining armor 빛나는 갑옷을 입은 기사(백마 탄 왕자, 위험에서 구해 주는 구세주)

333 **grave**
[greiv]

a place in the ground where a dead person is buried
명 무덤, 묘, 산소

dig a **grave** 무덤을 파다
We visited Grandma's **grave**. 우리는 할머니 산소에 갔다.

334 **tomb**
[tu:m]

a large grave, especially one built of stone (above or below the ground)
명 (커다란) 무덤 *흔히 중요한 인물이 묻혀 있는 석재로 만들어진 커다란 구조물을 의미

Pyramids were the **tombs** of the pharaohs. 피라미드는 파라오들의 무덤들이었다.
They found the **tomb** was empty. 그들은 무덤이 비어 있는 것을 발견했다.

335 **remains**
[riméinz]
remain 동 남아 있다, 남다

the parts of something that are left when other parts of it have gone
명 1. 남은 것, 나머지 2. 유물, 유적, 잔해 ((of))

the remains of lunch 점심 먹고 남은 것
They discovered **the remains of** an ancient temple. 그들은 고대 사원의 잔해를 발견했다.

336 **heritage**
[héritidʒ]

traditions, values, and cultural achievements passed down from previous generations
명 (국가·사회의) 유산 ((of))

the cultural **heritage of** the world 세계의 문화 유산
The building is part of our national **heritage**. 그 건물은 우리의 국가 유산의 일부이다.

337 **undergo**
[ʌ̀ndərgóu]

to experience or go through something difficult **(underwent-undergone)**
동 (변화·안 좋은 일 등을) 겪다, 경험하다

The city has **undergone** many changes. 그 도시는 많은 변화를 겪어 왔다.
She **underwent** major surgery last year. 그녀는 작년에 큰 수술을 받았다.

338 **ruin**
[rú:in]
ruined 형 폐허가 된

to spoil or destroy something completely
동 망치다, 파괴하다 명 1. 파괴, 파멸 2. (종종 ruins) 유적, 폐허 ((of))

The city has been **ruined** by a volcano. 그 도시는 화산에 의해 파괴되었다.
go to **ruin** 파멸하다; 폐허가 되다
the ruins of Pompeii 폼페이의 유적

339 **date back (to)**

to have existed since a particular time in the past
(~까지) 거슬러 올라가다

These ruins **date back to** the Roman era. 이 유적들은 로마 시대까지 거슬러 올라간다.
This festival **dates back** hundreds of years. 이 축제는 수백 년 전으로 거슬러 올라간다.

340 **look back (on)**

to think about something that happened in the past
(~을) 되돌아보다, 회상하다

He **looked back on** his childhood. 그는 자신의 어린 시절을 되돌아봤다.
Looking back, those were the best days of my life.
돌이켜보니, 그때가 내 인생에서 가장 좋은 날들이었다.

Check Up

A 우리말에 맞게 빈칸에 알맞은 말을 넣으세요.

1. 역사적으로 중요한 빌딩 — a __________ building
2. 한 시대의 종말을 알리다 — mark the end of __________
3. 왕관을 쓰다, 왕위에 오르다 — wear __________
4. 왕가, 왕실 가족 — the __________ family
5. 세계의 문화 유산 — the cultural __________ of the world
6. 폼페이의 유적 — the __________ Pompeii

B 우리말에 알맞은 말을 골라 문장을 완성하세요.

1. The Joseon (**Dynasty** / **Empire**) was founded in 1392. 조선 왕조는 1392년에 세워졌다.
2. They were (**royal to** / **loyal to**) their country. 그들은 조국에 충성했다.
3. She is from a (**noble** / **humble**) family. 그녀는 귀족 집안 출신이다.
4. The city (**has underwent** / **has undergone**) many changes. 그 도시는 많은 변화를 겪어 왔다.
5. He (**looked back** / **dated back**) on his childhood. 그는 자신의 어린 시절을 되돌아봤다.

Build Up

A Write the correct word for each definition.

remains	tomb	ancient	ruin	contemporary	kingdom

1. 

belonging to a time long ago

____

2. 

belonging to the present time

____

3. 

a country ruled by a king or queen

____

4. 

a large grave

____

5. 

the parts of something that are left

____

6. 

to spoil or destroy something completely

____

B Write the correct word or phrase next to each definition.

knight	undergo	empire	royal	date back to	crown

1. a group of countries that are controlled by one ruler or government ______________________
2. a circular decoration for the head worn by a king or queen ______________________
3. relating to or belonging to a king or queen ______________________
4. to experience or go through something difficult ______________________
5. to have existed since a particular time in the past ______________________
6. (in the Middle Ages) a man of high social rank who had a duty to fight for his king ______________________

341 **invade**
[invéid]
invasion 명 침략; 침해

to enter a country using military force in order to conquer it
동 1. (군사적으로) 침략하다, 침입하다 2. (권리 등을) 침해하다
The Spanish **invaded** the Incan Empire in 1532. 스페인은 1532년에 잉카 제국을 침략했다.
invade one's privacy (~의) 사생활을 침해하다

342 **conquer**
[káŋkər]
conquest 명 정복
conqueror 명 정복자

to take control of a country or to defeat people by force
동 1. 정복하다 2. 이기다, 물리치다 = defeat 3. (곤란 등을) 극복하다
Peru was **conquered** by the Spanish in 1532. 페루는 1532년에 스페인에 의해 정복되었다.
They **conquered** all their enemies. 그들은 모든 적들을 물리쳤다.
conquer a fear 두려움을 극복하다

343 **defense**
[diféns]
defend 동 방어하다, 지키다

the act of protecting someone or something from attack
명 1. 방어, 수비 2. 방어 시설 ((against)) = (영) defence 반 attack 공격; 공격하다
They fought **in defense of** their country. 그들은 조국을 지키기 위해 싸웠다.
The walls were built as a **defense against** enemy attacks.
그 성벽은 적의 공격에 대비한 방어 시설로 건설되었다.

344 **victory**
[víktəri]
victorious 형 승리한

a win in a battle, game, or other competition
명 승리 반 defeat 패배; 패배시키다
They won a **victory** at the battle. 그들은 그 전투에서 승리를 거두었다.
our team's 3–2 **victory** against Italy 이탈리아를 상대로 한 우리 팀의 3–2 승리

345 **capture**
[kǽptʃər]

to catch a person or an animal and keep them as a prisoner
동 1. 붙잡다, 포획하다 2. 점령하다 3. (마음·관심을) 사로잡다
Many soldiers were **captured** by the enemy. 많은 병사들이 적에게 (포로로) 잡혔다.
capture a city 도시를 점령하다
The game **captured** the attention of Gen Z. 그 게임은 Z 세대의 관심을 끌었다.

346 **occupy**
[ákjupài]
occupation 명 점유; 점령; 직업

to fill a space or period of time
동 1. (공간·시간을) 차지하다 = take up 2. 점령하다, 점거하다
The couch **occupies** too much space. 그 소파는 너무 많은 공간을 차지한다.
The issue **occupied** most of the debate. 그 문제는 토론의 대부분을 차지했다.
The Spanish army **occupied** the city. 스페인 군대가 그 도시를 점령했다.

347 **declare**
[dikléər]
declaration 명 선언(문)

to say something officially or publicly
동 선언하다, 선포하다
The two countries finally **declared** the end of the war. 두 나라는 마침내 종전을 선언했다.
declare a state of emergency 비상 사태를 선포하다

348 **descend**
[disénd]
descent 명 내려가기[오기], 하강
descendant 명 자손, 후손

to go down or come down
동 내려가다, 내려오다 반 ascend 오르다, 올라가다
The plane began to **descend**. 비행기가 하강하기 시작했다.
They **descended** the mountain slowly. 그들은 천천히 산을 내려왔다.

349 **glow**
[glou]

to produce a soft, warm light
동 (은은한 빛을 내며) 빛나다, 타다 명 (은은한) 불, 불빛 *light (해·전등 등의) 빛

The candles **glowed** in the darkness. 촛불이 어둠 속에서 빛났다.
the warm **glow** of the lamp 램프의 따뜻한 불빛

350 **glory**
[glɔ́ːri]
glorious 형 영광스러운, 영예로운

fame, praise, or honor that is given to someone
명 1. 영광, 영예 2. (하느님에 대한) 찬양, 영광 ((to))

a moment of **glory** 영광의 순간
That was the best moment of **glory** for him. 그것은 그에게 최고의 영광의 순간이었다.
give **glory to** God 신께 영광을 돌리다

351 **vanish**
[vǽniʃ]

to disappear suddenly
동 (갑자기) 사라지다, 없어지다 = disappear 반 appear 나타나다

He **vanished** without a trace. 그는 흔적도 없이 사라졌다.

352 **fade**
[feid]
faded 형 시든, 바랜, 쇠퇴한

to slowly disappear or become weaker
동 바래다, 희미해지다, 서서히 사라지다 *faint (빛·소리 등이) 희미한

Stars **fade out** as the sun rises. 태양이 떠오르면서 별들은 서서히 사라진다.
As the years passed, the memories **faded away**. 세월이 흐르면서 그 기억들은 희미해졌다.

353 **wander**
[wándər]
wanderer 명 방랑자

to walk around slowly without any clear purpose or direction
동 (정처 없이) 돌아다니다, 헤매다 ((around)) *wonder 궁금하다, 궁금해하다

He **wandered** aimlessly **around** the streets. 그는 정처 없이 거리를 돌아다녔다.
He **wandered** all over the world. 그는 전 세계를 방랑했다.

354 **withstand**
[wiðstǽnd]

to not be damaged or broken by something (withstood–withstood)
동 견뎌 내다, 이겨 내다, 버티다 유 endure 견디다, resist 저항하다; 견디다

withstand harsh weather 혹독한 날씨를 견뎌 내다
The building is designed to **withstand** earthquakes.
그 건물은 지진을 견딜 수 있도록 설계되었다.

355 **population**
[pàpjuléiʃən]

the total number of people living in a particular area or country
명 인구, (모든) 주민

What's the **population** of Seoul? 서울의 인구는 얼마인가요?
The world's **population** has increased greatly. 세계 인구는 크게 증가했다.

356 **multiply**
[mʌ́ltəplài]
multiple 형 많은, 다수의
multiplication 명 증식; 곱셈

to increase or make something increase very much in number or amount
동 1. 크게 증가하다[시키다] 2. 곱하다 ((by)) 반 divide 나누다

The city's population has **multiplied** in recent years.
최근 몇 년간 그 도시의 인구는 크게 증가했다.
If you **multiply** 4 **by** 5, you get 20. 4에 5를 곱하면 20이 된다.

357 **moreover**
[mɔːróuvər]

in addition to what has been said

㊫ 게다가, 더욱이 = besides

It was cold, and **moreover**, it was raining. 날씨가 추웠고, 게다가 비까지 오고 있었다.
The city is beautiful; **moreover**, it has a rich cultural heritage.
그 도시는 아름답고, 게다가 풍부한 문화 유산을 가지고 있다.

358 **meanwhile**
[míːnwàil]

while something else is happening

㊫ 그동안, 그사이에, 한편 = meantime

The train was delayed. **Meanwhile**, he waited in the station.
기차가 지연되었다. 그동안 그는 역에서 기다렸다.
Meanwhile, his flight was also canceled. 그사이에 그의 비행기도 취소되었다.

359 **be surrounded by**

to have a lot of people or things near you

~에 둘러싸이다[포위되다] *surround 둘러싸다 *surrender 항복하다

The castle **is surrounded by** a high stone wall. 그 성은 높은 돌담으로 둘러싸여 있다.
They **were surrounded by** the enemy. 그들은 적에게 포위되었다.

360 **be descended from**

to be related to a person or group that lived a long time ago

~의 후손[후예]이다

They **are descended from** the Vikings. 그들은 바이킹의 후손[후예]이다.
She **is descended from** royalty. 그녀는 왕족의 후손이다.

Check Up

A 우리말에 맞게 빈칸에 알맞은 말을 넣으세요.

1. 승리를 거두다 — win a ________________
2. 도시를 점령하다 — ________________ a city
3. 비상 사태를 선포하다 — ________________ a state of emergency
4. 영광의 순간 — a moment of ________________
5. 혹독한 날씨를 견뎌 내다 — ________________ harsh weather
6. 적에게 포위되다 — be ________________ by the enemy

B 우리말에 알맞은 말을 골라 문장을 완성하세요.

1. Peru was (**invaded** / **conquered**) by the Spanish in 1532. 페루는 1532년에 스페인에 의해 정복되었다.
2. Many soldiers were (**captured** / **occupied**) by the enemy. 많은 병사들이 적에게 (포로로) 잡혔다.
3. He (**vanished** / **faded out**) without a trace. 그는 흔적도 없이 사라졌다.
4. It was cold, and (**meanwhile** / **moreover**), it was raining. 날씨가 추웠고, 게다가 비까지 오고 있었다.
5. They are (**wandered** / **descended**) from the Vikings. 그들은 바이킹의 후손[후예]이다.

Build Up

A Write the correct word for each definition.

vanish | invade | fade | descend | wander | glow

1. 

to enter a country using military force

____

2. 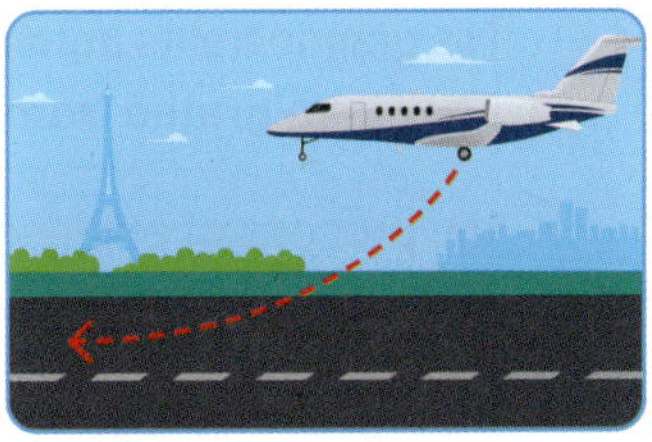

to go down or come down

____

3. 

to produce a soft, warm light

____

4. 

to walk around slowly

____

5. 

to disappear suddenly

____

6. 

to slowly disappear or become weaker

____

B Write the correct word or phrase next to each definition.

withstand | capture | population | conquer | defense | multiply

1. to take control of a country or to defeat people by force ______________________
2. the act of protecting someone or something from attack ______________________
3. to catch a person or an animal and keep them as a prisoner ______________________
4. to not be damaged or broken by something ______________________
5. the total number of people living in a particular area or country ______________________
6. to increase or make something increase very much in number or amount ______________________

361 **immigrate**
[íməgrèit]

to come to a foreign country in order to live there permanently
동 (다른 나라로) 이주해 오다, 이민을 오다 ((to/from))

His grandparents **immigrated to** America. 그의 조부모님은 미국으로 이민을 왔다.
They **immigrated from** Ireland in the 1950s. 그들은 1950년대에 아일랜드에서 이민을 왔다.

362 **immigration**
[ìməgréiʃən]
immigrant 명 이민자, 이주민

the process of entering another country to live there
명 1. 이주, 이민 2. 출입국 관리소

Immigration policies vary from country to country. 이민 정책은 나라마다 다르다.
go through **immigration** 출입국 관리소[입국 심사]를 통과하다

363 **migrate**
[máigreit]

to move from one place to another (according to the season)
동 1. (철새 등이) 이동하다 2. (다른 지역으로) 이주하다 ((to/from))

migrating birds 철새
Many birds **migrate** south for the winter. 많은 새들이 겨울을 나기 위해 남쪽으로 이동한다.
Thousands of workers **migrate to** this area each summer.
매년 여름 수천 명의 노동자들이 이 지역으로 이주한다.

364 **migration**
[maigréiʃən]
migrant 명 이주자; 철새

the movement of people, birds, or animals from one place to another
명 (대규모) 이동, 이주

seasonal **migration** 계절적 이동
The **migration** of geese usually occurs in the fall. 거위들의 이동은 보통 가을에 발생한다.

365 **race**
[reis]
racial 형 인종간의, 인종의; 민족의

a group of people who share physical characteristics, such as skin color
명 1. 인종, 종족 2. 경주

People of many different **races** immigrated to America.
다양한 인종의 사람들이 미국으로 이민을 왔다.
have a **race** 경주를 하다, 달리기 시합을 하다

366 **origin**
[ɔ́:rədʒin]
originate 동 유래하다, 비롯되다
original 형 원래의, 원본의; 독창적인

the point or place where something begins
명 1. 기원, 유래 2. 태생, 출신

the **origin** of Halloween 핼러윈의 기원
The word is French **in origin**. 그 단어는 프랑스어에서 유래했다.
She is of Irish **origin**. 그녀는 아일랜드 태생이다.

367 **tribe**
[traib]
tribal 형 부족의, 종족의

a group of people, often of related families, who live together and share the same language, culture, etc.
명 종족, 부족

the Masai **tribe** 마사이족
There are over 500 Native American **tribes** in the United States.
미국에는 500개 이상의 아메리카 원주민 부족들이 있다.

368 **ethnic**
[éθnik]

relating to a particular race of people
형 인종의, 민족의

There are various **ethnic** groups in the U.S. 미국에는 다양한 인종 집단이 있다.
a festival featuring **ethnic** food and music 민족 음식과 음악을 특징으로 하는 축제

369 **custom**
[kʌ́stəm]
customize 동 주문 제작하다

a traditional and widely accepted way of behaving in a society
명 1. 풍습, 관습 2. (-s) 관세; 세관 (통과소) *tradition 전통

the **custom** of giving presents at Christmas 크리스마스에 선물을 주는 관습
The **custom** dates back hundreds of years. 그 관습은 수백 년 전으로 거슬러 올라간다.
pass through **customs** 세관을 통과하다

370 **obey**
[oubéi]
obedience 명 순종, 복종
obedient 형 순종적인, 복종하는

to follow the commands, rules, or requests of someone or something
동 1. 복종[순종]하다 2. (명령·법 등을) 따르다, 지키다 반 disobey 불복종하다

He always **obeys** his parents. 그는 언제나 부모님께 순종한다.
Most people **obey** the law. 대부분의 사람들은 법을 지킨다.
They still **obey** their own customs. 그들은 여전히 자신들의 관습을 따른다.

371 **distant**
[dístənt]

far away in space or time
형 1. (거리가) 먼, 멀리 떨어진 2. (시간이) 먼, 아득한

Traveling to a **distant** country can be exciting. 먼 나라로 여행하는 것은 신나는 일일 수 있다.
a **distant** cousin 먼 사촌
in the **distant** past 아주 먼 옛날에

372 **distance**
[dístəns]

the amount of space between two places or things
명 1. 거리, 간격 ((from/between)) 2. 먼 곳

the **distance between** the two cities 두 도시 사이의 거리
Church bells rang **in the distance**. 멀리서 교회 종이 울렸다.
From a distance, it looks blue. 멀리서 보면 그것은 파랗게 보인다.

373 **further**
[fə́:rðər]

to a greater degree or extent; more
부 1. (거리가) 더 멀리 = farther 2. (정도가) 더 형 추가의 = additional

They walked a little **further**. 그들은 조금 더 걸었다.
Let's discuss this **further** tomorrow. 내일 이 문제에 대해 더 이야기해 보자.
We need **further** information about it. 우리는 그것에 대한 추가 정보가 필요하다.

374 **furthermore**
[fə́:rðərmɔ̀:r]

in addition to what has just been stated
부 더욱이, 게다가, 뿐만 아니라 = moreover

The weather was cold. **Furthermore**, it started to rain.
날씨가 추웠다. 게다가 비가 내리기 시작했다.

375 **dispute**
[dispjú:t]

a serious argument or disagreement between two groups
명 분쟁, 논쟁 동 분쟁을 벌이다, 논쟁하다 ((with/between))

a **dispute between** the two countries 그 두 나라 사이의 분쟁
It's no use **disputing with** them. 그들과 논쟁을 해 봐야 소용없다.

376 **settle**
[sétl]
settlement 명 해결; 정착(지)
settler 명 정착민

to end an argument or solve a disagreement
동 1. (문제 등을) 해결하다 2. 정착하다 ((in))

settle a dispute 분쟁을 해결하다
They **settled in** a small town. 그들은 작은 마을에 정착했다.

377 **independent**
[ìndipéndənt]
independence 명 독립

not controlled or ruled by another country (or others)
형 1. (국가가) 독립한 2. 독립된, 독자적인 3. 자립심이 강한 반 dependent 의존하는

India **became independent** in 1947. 인도는 1947년에 독립했다.
an **independent** movie 독립 영화, 저예산 영화
She is very **independent** for her age. 그녀는 나이에 비해 매우 자립심이 강하다.

378 **servant**
[sə́ːrvənt]
serve 동 (손님을) 시중들다, (서비스를) 제공하다; (국가 등을 위해) 복무하다

someone who works and lives in someone else's house, especially in the past
명 1. 하인, 종 2. (조직 등의) 고용인, 종업원

They treated him like a **servant**. 그들은 그를 마치 하인처럼 대했다.
a public **servant** 공무원

379 **be involved in / get involved in**

to be a part of something; to have a connection with a situation
~에 연루되다[관련되다] / ~에 개입하다[엮이다]

He **was involved in** a dispute with his neighbor. 그는 이웃과의 분쟁에 휘말렸다.
Don't **get involved in** their problems. 그들의 문제에 개입하지 마라.

380 **settle down**

to start living in a place where you will stay for a long time
1. (한곳에 자리 잡고) 정착하다 2. 진정되다; 진정시키다

I want to **settle down** and have a family someday. 나는 언젠가 정착하여 가족을 갖고 싶다.
She quickly **settled down** in her new job. 그녀는 새 직장에 빠르게 적응했다.
All right, **settle down**, everyone. 자, 모두들 진정해 주세요(조용히 해 주세요).

Check Up

A 우리말에 맞게 빈칸에 알맞은 말을 넣으세요.

1. 출입국 관리소[입국 심사]를 통과하다 — go through ________________
2. 철새 — ________________ birds
3. 핼러윈의 기원 — the ________________ of Halloween
4. 마사이족 — the Masai ________________
5. 세관을 통과하다 — pass through ________________
6. 분쟁에 휘말리다 — be ________________ a dispute

B 우리말에 알맞은 말을 골라 문장을 완성하세요.

1. His grandparents (**immigrated** / **migrated**) to America. 그의 조부모님은 미국으로 이민을 왔다.
2. Many birds (**immigrate** / **migrate**) south for the winter. 많은 새들이 겨울을 나기 위해 남쪽으로 이동한다.
3. There are various (**ethnic** / **race**) groups in the U.S. 미국에는 다양한 인종 집단이 있다.
4. Church bells rang in the (**distant** / **distance**). 멀리서 교회 종이 울렸다.
5. India became (**dependent** / **independent**) in 1947. 인도는 1947년에 독립했다.

Build Up

A Write the correct word for each definition.

obey | distant | migrate | immigrate | independent | dispute

1. 

to come to a foreign country to live there

____

2. 
to move from one place to another

____

3. 
to follow the commands, rules, or requests of someone

____

4. 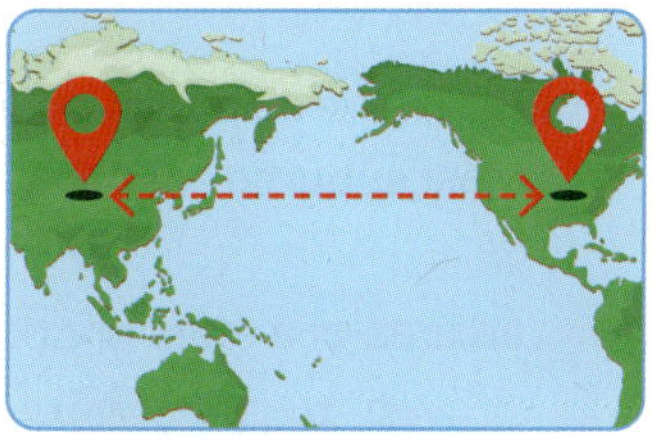
far away in space or time

____

5. 
a serious argument or disagreement

____

6. 

not controlled by another country

____

B Write the correct word or phrase next to each definition.

migration | immigration | servant | settle down | race | custom

1. the process of entering another country to live there _______________
2. the movement of people, birds, or animals from one place to another _______________
3. a traditional and widely accepted way of behaving in a society _______________
4. to start living in a place where you will stay for a long time _______________
5. a group of people who share physical characteristics, such as skin color _______________
6. someone who works and lives in someone else's house, especially in the past _______________

DAY 20

381 **urban**
[ə́:rbən]
urbanization 명 도시화

belonging or relating to a city or town
형 도시의, 도회지의 *city 도시

Most **urban** areas have traffic problems. 대부분의 도시 지역은 교통 문제를 겪고 있다.
urban life 도시 생활

382 **rural**
[rúərəl]

relating to the countryside
형 시골의, 지방의 *countryside 시골, 지방

She grew up in a **rural** area. 그녀는 시골 지역에서 자랐다.

383 **suburb**
[sʌ́bə:rb]
suburban 형 교외의

an area where people live that is outside the center of a city
명 교외, 근교

He lives in a **suburb** of Seoul. 그는 서울 교외에 살고 있다.
Most **suburbs** are not as busy as cities. 대부분의 교외 지역은 도시만큼 바쁘지 않다.

384 **county**
[káunti]

an area of a state or country that has its own government
명 군(郡), 자치주 *미국에서는 주(州) 바로 밑의 행정구역, 영국에서는 자치주를 의미

Orange **County** is located in southern California.
오렌지 카운티는 남부 캘리포니아에 위치해 있다.
Texas is divided into 254 **counties**. 텍사스는 254개의 카운티로 나뉘어 있다.

385 **region**
[rí:dʒən]
regional 형 지역의, 지방의

a large area of a country or of the world, usually without exact limits
명 지역, 지방

The **region** is famous for its beautiful beaches. 그 지역은 아름다운 해변으로 유명하다.

386 **province**
[právins]
provincial 형 주의, 도의; 지방의

one of the large areas that some countries are divided into
명 1. (행정 단위) 주(州), 성(省), 도(道) 2. (the provinces) (수도 이외의) 지방, 시골

Canada has ten **provinces**. 캐나다에는 10개의 주가 있다.
a shy young man from **the provinces** 지방 출신의 수줍음 많은 청년

387 **district**
[dístrikt]

an area of a country or city, especially one that has particular features
명 (특정한 특징이 있는) 지구, 지역, 구역

He works in New York's financial **district**. 그는 뉴욕의 금융 지구에서 일한다.
the Broadway theater **district** 브로드웨이 극장가

388 **zone**
[zoun]

an area that is different from other areas in a particular way
명 (큰 구역을 나눈) 구역, 지대 *area 지역, 구역

It's a no-parking **zone**. 여기는 주차 금지 구역이다.
The city is located in an earthquake **zone**. 그 도시는 지진 지대에 위치해 있다.

389 **border**
[bɔ́ːrdər]

the official line that separates two countries or areas
명 1. 국경, 경계선 2. 가장자리, 테두리 동 (국경·경계를) 접하다

the **border** between the U.S. and Mexico 미국과 멕시코 사이의 국경
cross the **border** 국경을 넘다
Canada **borders** the U.S. 캐나다는 미국과 국경을 접하고 있다.

390 **boundary**
[báundəri]

a real or imaginary line that marks the edges of a place
명 (한 지역을 다른 지역과 구분하는) 경계(선)

The **boundary** between the two farms is marked by a fence.
두 농장 사이의 경계는 담장으로 표시되어 있다.
the **boundary** between fact and opinion 사실과 의견의 경계

391 **govern**
[gʌ́vərn]

government 명 정부
governor 명 주지사

to officially control a country
동 1. 다스리다, 통치하다 = rule, control 2. 좌우하다, 결정하다

A president **governs** the country and represents the people.
대통령은 나라를 통치하고 국민을 대표한다.
Prices are **governed** by market demand. 가격은 시장의 수요에 의해 좌우된다.

392 **authority**
[əθɔ́ːrəti]

authorize 동 재가하다, 권위를 부여하다
authoritative 형 권위적인, 권위 있는

the official power to make decisions or control people
명 1. 권한 ((to)) 2. 권위, 권력 3. (법적) 기관, 당국

The mayor has the **authority to** declare a state of emergency.
시장은 비상 사태를 선언할 권한이 있다.
speak **with authority** 권위 있게[권위를 가지고] 말하다
according to health **authorities** 보건 당국에 따르면

393 **democracy**
[dimákrəsi]

democratic 형 민주주의의, 민주적인
democrat 명 민주주의자

a system of government in which people elect their leaders or a country with this system
명 민주주의; 민주(주의) 국가

the principles of **democracy** 민주주의 원칙
In a **democracy**, every citizen has the right to vote. 민주 국가에서 모든 시민은 투표권을 가진다.

394 **republic**
[ripʌ́blik]

republican 명 공화주의자

a country with no king or queen but with an elected government
명 공화국

The **Republic** of Korea is a democratic country. 대한민국은 민주주의 국가이다.
In a **republic**, citizens have the right to vote. 공화국에서 시민은 투표권을 가진다.

395 **ambassador**
[æmbǽsədər]

a high-ranking official who represents their government in a foreign country
명 1. 대사 ((to)) 2. 사절, 대표

She became the U.S. **ambassador to** Japan. 그녀는 주일 미국 대사가 되었다.
an **ambassador** of peace 평화의 사절

396 **embassy**
[émbəsi]

a group of officials led by an ambassador who represent their government in a foreign country
명 대사관; 대사관저

the British **Embassy** in Seoul 서울 주재 영국 대사관

397 **diplomat**
[díplǝmæt]

diplomatic 형 외교의; 외교적 수완이 있는

a person whose job is to represent his or her country in a foreign country

명 외교관

She is a skilled **diplomat.** 그녀는 숙련된[유능한] 외교관이다.

398 **welfare**
[wélfɛǝr]

the state of being happy, healthy, or successful

명 1. 복지, 안녕, 행복 = well-being 2. 복지 혜택, 보조금

a social **welfare** program 사회 복지 프로그램
Child **welfare** is important. 아동 복지는 중요하다.
His family is **on welfare.** 그의 가족은 생활 보조금(복지 수당)을 받고 있다.

399 **be (well) known for**

to be famous for something

~로 (잘) 알려져 있다, ~로 유명하다

The country **is known for** its good welfare system.
그 나라는 좋은 복지 시스템으로 잘 알려져 있다.
The region **is well known for** its fine wines. 그 지역은 고급 와인으로 매우 유명하다.

400 **be known to N / be known as**

to be widely recognized to a specified group of people

~에 알려져 있다 / ~로 알려져 있다

The author **is** well **known to** Korean readers. 그 작가는 한국 독자들에게 잘 알려져 있다.
She **is known as** an expert in her field. 그녀는 자신의 분야에서 전문가로 알려져 있다.

Check Up

A 우리말에 맞게 빈칸에 알맞은 말을 넣으세요.

1. 뉴욕의 금융 지구 — New York's financial ________________
2. 미국과 멕시코 사이의 국경 — the ________________ between the U.S. and Mexico
3. 두 농장 사이의 경계 — the ________________ between the two farms
4. 민주주의 원칙 — the principles of ________________
5. 서울 주재 영국 대사관 — the British ________________ in Seoul
6. 사회 복지 프로그램 — a social ________________ program

B 우리말에 알맞은 말을 골라 문장을 완성하세요.

1. He lives in a (**rural** / **suburb**) of Seoul. 그는 서울 교외에 살고 있다.
2. Texas is divided into 254 (**counties** / **countries**). 텍사스는 254개의 카운티로 나뉘어 있다.
3. Canada has ten (**provinces** / **regions**). 캐나다에는 10개의 주가 있다.
4. The city is located in an earthquake (**province** / **zone**). 그 도시는 지진 지대에 위치해 있다.
5. The country is (**known to** / **known for**) its good welfare system.
그 나라는 좋은 복지 시스템으로 잘 알려져 있다.

Build Up

A Write the correct word for each definition.

govern
border
embassy
rural
urban
county

1. 

relating to a city or town

____

2. 

relating to the countryside

____

3. 

an area of a state or country

____

4. 

the official line that separates two countries

____

5. 

to officially control a country

____

6. 

a group of officials led by an ambassador

____

B Write the correct word or phrase next to each definition.

province suburb ambassador diplomat authority republic

1. an area where people live that is outside the center of a city ______________________
2. one of the large areas that some countries are divided into ______________________
3. the official power to make decisions or control people ______________________
4. a country with no king or queen but with an elected government ______________________
5. a high-ranking official who represents their government in a foreign country ______________________
6. a person whose job is to represent his or her country in a foreign country ______________________

Review Test 05 DAY 17-20

A 그림을 보고, 빈칸에 알맞은 단어를 넣으세요.

district knight crown border boundary remains

1. 
______

2. 
______

3. 
______

4. 
______

5. 

______

6. 
______

B 그림에 맞게 빈칸에 알맞은 단어를 고르세요.

1. 
They were ______ their country.
(loyal to / royal to)

2. 
The city has been ______ by a volcano.
(remained / ruined)

3. 
The castle is ______ by a high stone wall.
(surrounded / located)

4. 
The ______ of geese usually occurs in the fall.
(immigration / migration)

C 우리말 뜻에 맞게 빈칸에 알맞은 말을 넣으세요.

dispute	ruins	declare	cultural heritage
historic	zone	origin of	ambassador to

1. a ________________ moment 역사적인 순간
2. the ____________________ of the world 세계의 문화 유산
3. the ________________ of Pompeii 폼페이의 유적
4. ________________ a state of emergency 비상 사태를 선포하다
5. the ________________ Halloween 핼러윈의 기원
6. a ________________ between the two countries 그 두 나라 사이의 분쟁
7. a no-parking ________________ 주차 금지 구역
8. the U.S. __________________ Korea 주한 미국 대사

D 우리말 뜻에 맞게 빈칸에 알맞은 말을 넣으세요.

wandered	won a victory	descended from
in defense of	immigrated to	in the distance

1. They fought ____________________ their country. 그들은 조국을 지키기 위해 싸웠다.
2. They ____________________ at the battle. 그들은 그 전투에서 승리를 거두었다.
3. He ________________ aimlessly around the streets. 그는 정처 없이 거리를 돌아다녔다.
4. They are ____________________ the Vikings. 그들은 바이킹의 후손[후예]이다.
5. People of many different races ____________________ America.
   다양한 인종의 사람들이 미국으로 이민을 왔다.
6. Church bells rang ____________________. 멀리서 교회 종이 울렸다.

E 밑줄 친 단어와 비슷한 뜻을 가진 단어를 고르세요.

1. I like contemporary art.

   a. ancient　b. modern　c. up to date

2. The city has undergone many changes.

   a. occupied　b. transformed　c. experienced

3. The building is designed to withstand earthquakes.

   a. endure　b. defend　c. go through

4. We need further information about it.

   a. distant　b. additional　c. furthermore

F 밑줄 친 단어와 반대의 뜻을 가진 단어를 고르세요.

1. She is from a noble family.

   a. humble　b. royal　c. ethnic

2. He vanished without a trace.

   a. faded out　b. appeared　c. disappeared

3. She is very independent for her age.

   a. mature　b. loyal　c. dependent

4. She grew up in a rural area.

   a. urban　b. suburb　c. suburban

G 주어진 영영풀이에 알맞은 단어를 고르세요.

1. a period of time in history that is special for a particular reason

   a. kingdom　　b. empire　　c. era

2. belonging to a time long ago in history, especially thousands of years ago

   a. historic　　b. ancient　　c. dynasty

3. to spoil or destroy something completely

   a. ruin　　b. descend　　c. conquer

4. to enter a country using military force in order to conquer it

   a. immigrate　　b. occupy　　c. invade

5. the total number of people living in a particular area or country

   a. resident　　b. race　　c. population

6. to move from one place to another (according to the season)

   a. migrate　　b. immigrate　　c. settle down

H 빈칸에 알맞은 동사 형태를 넣어 문장을 완성하세요.

1. Peru ______________ by the Spanish in 1532. (conquer)
2. Many soldiers ______________ by the enemy. (capture)
3. The city's population has ______________ in recent years. (multiply)
4. He was ______________ a dispute with his neighbor. (involve in)

DAY 21

401 **religion**
[rilídʒən]

the belief in and worship of a god or gods
명 1. 종교 2. (특정한) ~교 *belief 믿음, 신념 *faith 믿음, 신뢰, 신앙(심)

There are many **religions** around the world. 전 세계에는 많은 종교가 있다.
freedom of **religion** 종교의 자유
the Christian **religion** 기독교

402 **religious**
[rilídʒəs]

relating to religion; having a strong belief in a religion
형 1. 종교의 2. 신앙심이 깊은

religious beliefs 종교적 신념
My grandmother is very **religious**. 우리 할머니는 아주 신앙심이 깊다.

403 **heaven**
[hévən]

the place where good people go after they die according to some religions
명 1. 천국 2. 낙원

Do you believe in **heaven**? 당신은 천국을 믿나요?
a **heaven** on earth 지상 낙원

404 **hell**
[hel]

the place where bad people go when they die according to some religions
명 지옥, 지옥 같은 곳

go to **hell** 지옥에 가다
The vacation was like **hell**. 그 휴가는 지옥 같았다.
It's been **hell** working with him. 그와 함께 일하는 것은 지옥 같았다.

405 **worship**
[wə́ːrʃip]

to show respect for God or a god, especially by praying in a religious building
동 예배하다, 숭배하다 명 예배, 숭배 *pray 기도하다

People go to church to **worship** God. 사람들은 신에게 예배를 드리기 위해 교회에 간다.
The ancient Egyptians **worshiped** many gods. 고대 이집트인들은 많은 신들을 숭배했다.
attend **worship** 예배에 참석하다

406 **bless**
[bles]
blessing 명 축복(의 기도)

to ask God to protect someone or something
동 (신의) 가호[축복]를 빌다

God **bless** you! 당신에게 신의 축복이 있기를!

407 **mercy**
[mə́ːrsi]
merciful 형 자비로운

kindness that makes you forgive someone
명 자비, 연민 ((on))

God **have mercy on** us! 하느님 저희에게 자비를 베푸소서!
He begged for **mercy**. 그는 자비를 구했다[간청했다].

408 **miracle**
[mírəkl]
miraculous 형 기적적인

a wonderful event that is believed to be caused by the power of God
명 기적, 기적 같은 일 *wonder 경이(로운 것), 불가사의

They hoped for a **miracle**. 그들은 기적을 바랐다.
It's a miracle (that) nobody was killed in the crash. 그 사고에서 아무도 죽지 않은 것은 기적이다.

409 **creation**
[kriéiʃən]
create 동 창조하다, 창작하다
creative 형 창조적인, 창의적인
creativity 명 창조성, 창의력
creator 명 창조자

the act of creating something
명 1. 창조, 창작 2. 창조물, 창작품

the **creation** of the universe 우주의 창조[생성]
The artist was very proud of his **creation**. 그 예술가는 자신의 창작물에 매우 자부심을 느꼈다.

410 **creature**
[kríːtʃər]

anything that is living, such as an animal, but not a plant
명 생물, 생명체

all the living **creatures** in the sea 바다의 모든 살아 있는 생물들
The movie is about **creatures** from outer space. 그 영화는 외계에서 온 생명체에 관한 것이다.

411 **holy**
[hóuli]
holiness 명 신성함

relating to a god or religion
형 신성한, 성스러운 반 unholy 불경스러운

the **Holy** Bible 성서 (= the Bible)
the **holy** city of Mecca 성스러운 도시 메카

412 **sacred**
[séikrid]

relating to a religion or considered to be holy
형 성스러운, 종교적인, 신성시되는 ((to))

sacred music 종교 음악
Cows are **sacred to** Hindus. 소는 힌두교도들에게 신성시된다.

413 **sacrifice**
[sǽkrəfàis]

to give up something in order to achieve something else
동 희생하다, 희생시키다 ((for)) 명 희생, 제물

She **sacrificed** everything **for** her children. 그녀는 자녀를 위해 모든 것을 희생했다.
make a **sacrifice** 희생하다, 헌신하다
They offered **sacrifices** to the gods. 그들은 신들께 제물을 바쳤다.

414 **confess**
[kənfés]
confession 명 고백, 자백

to admit that you have done something wrong or illegal
동 1. (죄·잘못을) 자백하다 ((to)) 2. 고백하다, 인정하다 *admit 인정하다

He **confessed to** the theft. 그는 절도를 자백했다.
He **confessed** his love for her. 그는 그녀에 대한 사랑을 고백했다.
I **confess** that it was my mistake. 나는 그것은 내 실수였다고 인정한다.

415 **temple**
[témpl]

a building where people go to worship, especially in religions other than Christianity
명 신전, 사원, 사찰, 절 *church 교회

The **temple** is a holy place. 그 사원은 신성한 곳이다.
a Buddhist **temple** 절, 불교 사원

416 **silence**
[sáiləns]
silent 형 고요한, 침묵을 지키는

a complete lack of sound or noise
명 1. 고요, 정적, 적막 ((of)) = quiet 2. 침묵

the **silence** in the temple 사원 안의 고요함
A scream broke the **silence of** the night. 비명 소리가 밤의 정적을 깼다.
There was an awkward **silence** between them. 그들 사이에 어색한 침묵이 흘렀다.

417 **priest**
[priːst]

a person who is qualified to perform religious ceremonies in the Christian church
명 사제, 신부, 성직자 *minister 목사; 장관 *monk 수도자, 수도승(스님)

a Catholic **priest** 가톨릭 신부
The **priest** blessed the baby. 신부는 아기를 축복했다.

418 **meditate**
[médətèit]
meditation 명 명상, 묵상

to spend time in quiet thought for religious purposes or relaxation
동 명상하다, 묵상하다 ((on/upon))

He **meditates** for an hour every morning. 그는 매일 아침 1시간씩 명상한다.
meditate (up)on the meaning of life 인생의 의미를 묵상하다

419 **in silence**

the state of being quiet or without sound
조용히, 말 없이

We sat **in silence** in the temple. 우리는 사원에서 말 없이 앉아 있었다.
They listened to the music **in silence**. 그들은 조용히 음악을 들었다.

420 **talk to oneself**

to say one's thoughts out loud
혼잣말을 하다

She sometimes **talked to herself**. 그녀는 가끔 혼잣말을 했다.
People often **talk to themselves** when they are alone.
사람들은 혼자 있을 때 종종 혼잣말을 한다.

Check Up

A 우리말에 맞게 빈칸에 알맞은 말을 넣으세요.

1. 종교의 자유 freedom of ________________
2. 지상 낙원 a ________________ on earth
3. 자비를 구하다[간청하다] beg for ________________
4. 우주의 창조[생성] the ________________ of the universe
5. 희생하다, 헌신하다 make a ________________
6. 절, 불교 사원 a Buddhist ________________

B 우리말에 알맞은 말을 골라 문장을 완성하세요.

1. They hoped for a (**mercy** / **miracle**). 그들은 기적을 바랐다.
2. The movie is about (**creatures** / **creation**) from outer space. 그 영화는 외계에서 온 생명체에 관한 것이다.
3. Cows are (**sacrificed** / **sacred**) to Hindus. 소는 힌두교도들에게 신성시된다.
4. He (**confessed to** / **confessed for**) the theft. 그는 절도를 자백했다.
5. A scream broke the (**silent** / **silence**) of the night. 비명 소리가 밤의 정적을 깼다.

Build Up

A Write the correct word for each definition.

silence	holy	meditate	worship	bless	creature

1. 
to show respect for God
____

2. 
to ask God to protect someone
____

3. 
anything that is living but not a plant
____

4. 
relating to a god or religion
____

5. 
a complete lack of sound
____

6. 
to spend time in quiet thought
____

B Write the correct word or phrase next to each definition.

religious	hell	heaven	sacred	priest	miracle

1. relating to religion; having a strong belief in a religion ______________________
2. a wonderful event that is believed to be caused by the power of God ______________________
3. relating to a religion or considered to be holy ______________________
4. the place where good people go after they die according to some religions ______________________
5. the place where bad people go when they die according to some religions ______________________
6. a person who is qualified to perform religious ceremonies in the Christian church ______________________

DAY 22

421 **carve**
[kɑːrv]
carving 명 조각(술); 조각품

to make something by cutting into a hard material, such as wood or stone
동 1. (~에) 새기다 ((into)), 깎아서 만들다, 조각하다 ((out of/from)) 2. (글씨를) 새기다

They **carved** a star **into** the stone. 그들은 돌에 별 모양을 새겼다.
carve a toy **out of** wood 나무로 장난감을 만들다[조각하다]
carve one's name into a bench 벤치에 이름을 새기다

422 **sculpt**
[skʌlpt]
sculptor 명 조각가

to make something by carving or shaping wood, stone, metal, etc.
동 조각하다 ((out of))

He **sculpted** a beautiful woman **out of** marble. 그는 대리석으로 아름다운 여성을 조각했다.

423 **sculpture**
[skʌ́lptʃər]

a work of art made by carving or shaping wood, stone, metal, etc.
명 조각, 조각품

carve an ice **sculpture** 얼음 조각을 만들다
He carved the **sculpture** out of marble. 그는 대리석으로 그 조각품을 만들었다.

424 **statue**
[stǽtʃuː]

a figure of a person or an animal in stone, metal, etc.
명 조각상, 상 *monument (건물·동상 등의) 기념물, 기념비

The **Statue** of Liberty is a famous landmark. 자유의 여신상은 유명한 랜드마크이다.
The **statue** was made of bronze. 그 동상은 청동으로 만들어졌다.

425 **craft**
[kræft]
craftsman 명 (수)공예가

the skill of making things by hand or the objects created through such skills
명 (수)공예; 공예품 동 (손으로) 공예품을 만들다 *handcraft 수공예; 수공예품

traditional **crafts** 전통 공예(품)
These baskets were **crafted** by Native Americans.
이 바구니들은 아메리카 원주민들에 의해 만들어졌다.

426 **antique**
[æntíːk]

old and often valuable
형 (가구 등이) 골동품인, 고미술의 명 골동품, 고미술품

The room is filled with **antique** furniture. 그 방은 골동품 가구로 가득 차 있다.
My mother collects **antiques**. 우리 어머니는 골동품을 수집한다.

427 **portrait**
[pɔ́ːrtrit]

a painting, drawing, or photograph of a person
명 초상화 ((of)) *self-portrait 자화상

He painted **a portrait of** himself. 그는 자신의 초상화를 그렸다.

428 **landscape**
[lǽndskèip]

the appearance of an area of land, especially in the countryside
명 1. 풍경 2. 풍경화

a beautiful **landscape** of the countryside 시골의 아름다운 풍경
The artist is well known for his **landscapes**. 그 화가는 그의 풍경화로 잘 알려져 있다.

429 **abstract**
[æbstrǽkt]
abstraction 명 관념, 추상적 개념

existing in thought or as an idea but not having a physical reality
형 추상적인, 관념적인

abstract art 추상 미술
Your idea is too **abstract**. 너의 아이디어는 너무 추상적이다.

430 **concrete**
[kánkriːt]
concretely 부 구체적으로

made of concrete; based on facts, not on ideas or guesses
형 1. 콘크리트로 된 2. 사실에 의거한, 구체적인 명 콘크리트

a **concrete** floor 콘크리트 바닥
Can you show me a **concrete** example? 내게 구체적인 예를 보여 줄 수 있니?

431 **contrast**
[kántræst]
contrasting 형 대조적인, 대비를 이루는

an obvious difference between two or more things
명 대조, 대비 ((between/to/with)) 동 [kəntrǽst] 대조하다; 대조를 이루다 ((with))
*compare 비교하다

the **contrast between** black **and** white 검은색과 흰색의 대비
compare and **contrast** 비교 대조하다
The red roofs **contrast with** the blue sky. 빨간 지붕들이 파란 하늘과 대조를 이룬다.

432 **contrary**
[kántreri]
contrarily 부 반대로

completely different in nature or direction
형 반대의, 반대되는 ((to)) 명 (the -) (정)반대 = opposite

They have **contrary** views on the issue. 그들은 그 문제에 대해 반대되는 견해를 가지고 있다.
Contrary to popular belief, many cats dislike milk.
일반적인 믿음과는 반대로 많은 고양이들은 우유를 싫어한다.
on the contrary 그와는 반대로

433 **annual**
[ǽnjuəl]
annually 부 일 년에 한 번

happening or done once every year
형 1. 매년의, 연례의 2. 연간의, 한 해의 = yearly *biannual 연 2회의 *biennial 2년에 한 번씩의

The **annual** exhibition is held in August. 그 연례 전시회는 8월에 열린다.
an **annual** budget 연간 예산

434 **quarter**
[kwɔ́ːrtər]
quarterly 형 분기별의

one of four equal parts of something
명 1. 4분의 1 2. (매 정시 앞뒤의) 15분 3. (미국·캐나다) 25센트짜리 동전 (= 25 cents)

They cut the cake into **quarters**. 그들은 케이크를 4등분으로 잘랐다.
The budget is reviewed every **quarter**. 예산은 매 분기(1년의 4분의 1)마다 검토된다.
It's a **quarter** to seven. / It's a **quarter** past seven. 7시 15분 전이다. / 7시 15분이다.

435 **paste**
[peist]

to stick something to something else using glue
동 (풀로) 붙이다 명 반죽, 풀

She **pasted** the pictures into her scrapbook. 그녀는 그 사진들을 자신의 스크랩북에 붙였다.
tomato **paste** 토마토 페이스트

436 **attach**
[ətǽtʃ]
attachment 명 부착; 애착; 첨부 파일

to join or fix one thing to another
동 붙이다, 부착하다; 첨부하다 ((to))

She **attached** a label **to** each picture. 그녀는 각각의 사진에 라벨을 붙였다.
I **attached** the file **to** the e-mail. 나는 이메일에 그 파일을 첨부했다.

437 **pile**
[pail]

a group of things that are put on top of each other
명 (차곡차곡) 쌓아 놓은 것, 더미 ((of)) 동 (차곡차곡) 쌓다 = stack

a pile of books 책 더미
They began to **pile** the bricks in the garden. 그들은 정원에 벽돌을 쌓기 시작했다.

438 **artificial**
[àːrtəfíʃəl]

made by people; not natural or real
형 1. 인공적인, 인조의 2. 꾸민, 거짓의 반 natural 자연의; 자연스러운

To my surprise, the flowers were **artificial**. 놀랍게도, 그 꽃들은 조화였다.
This product contains no **artificial** colors. 이 제품은 인공 색소가 들어 있지 않다.
make an **artificial** smile 거짓[억지] 웃음을 짓다

439 **in contrast to**

when compared to another
~와는 대조적으로, ~에 비해

In contrast to last year, it's very cold this year. 작년에 비해 올해는 매우 춥다.
The painting is very colorful, **in contrast to** the previous one.
그 그림은 이전 그림에 비해 매우 다채롭다.

440 **on the other hand**

from another point of view
한편, 반면에

The book is entertaining, but **on the other hand**, it lacks depth.
그 책은 재미있지만, 반면에 깊이가 부족하다.
On the other hand, dogs are very loyal. 반면에 개들은 매우 충성스럽다.

Check Up

A 우리말에 맞게 빈칸에 알맞은 말을 넣으세요.

1. 얼음 조각을 만들다 — carve an ice ____________
2. 전통 공예(품) — traditional ____________
3. 추상 미술 — ____________ art
4. 검은색과 흰색의 대비 — the ____________ between black and white
5. 조화(인공적으로 만든 꽃) — ____________ flowers
6. 책 더미 — a ____________ of books

B 우리말에 알맞은 말을 골라 문장을 완성하세요.

1. They (**carved** / **crafted**) a star into the stone. 그들은 돌에 별 모양을 새겼다.
2. He (**sculpted** / **statue**) a beautiful woman. 그는 아름다운 여성을 조각했다.
3. The (**antique** / **annual**) exhibition is held in August. 그 연례 전시회는 8월에 열린다.
4. I (**pasted** / **attached**) the file to the e-mail. 나는 이메일에 그 파일을 첨부했다.
5. (**Contrary to** / **In contrast to**) last year, it's very cold this year. 작년에 비해 올해는 매우 춥다.

Build Up

A **Write the correct word for each definition.**

antique	landscape	portrait	sculpture	statue	quarter

1. 

a work of art made by carving

____

2. 

a figure of a person in stone, metal, etc.

____

3. 

old and often valuable

____

4. 

a painting of a person

____

5. 

the appearance of an area of land

____

6. 

one of four equal parts of something

____

B **Write the correct word or phrase next to each definition.**

craft	contrary	sculpt	artificial	contrast	in contrast to

1. to make something by carving or shaping wood, stone, metal, etc. ______________________
2. an obvious difference between two or more things ______________________
3. completely different in nature or direction ______________________
4. made by people; not natural or real ______________________
5. when compared to another ______________________
6. the skill of making things by hand or the objects created through such skills ______________________

441 **instrument**
[ínstrəmənt]

a tool or device used in work such as science or medicine
명 1. (정밀) 기구, 도구 2. 악기 = musical instrument

various scientific **instruments** 다양한 과학 기구들
Do you play any **instruments**? 너는 연주할 줄 아는 악기가 있니[악기를 다룰 줄 아니]?

442 **string**
[striŋ]

a very thin rope or cord that is commonly used to tie things together
명 1. 끈, 줄 2. 연속, 일련 ((of)) 3. (악기의) 현[줄]

tie up the package **with a string** 끈으로 소포를 묶다
produce **a string of** hit albums 일련의 히트 앨범을 제작하다
I like **string** instruments, such as the violin and the cello.
나는 바이올린과 첼로와 같은 현악기를 좋아한다.

443 **classical**
[klǽsikəl]

classic 명 고전, 명작
형 고전적인, 전형적인

traditional in style or idea; relating to classical music
형 1. 고전주의의, 고전적인 2. (음악이) 클래식인

classical ballet and modern ballet 고전 발레와 현대 발레
She enjoys listening to **classical** music. 그녀는 클래식 음악 듣는 것을 즐긴다.

444 **ideal**
[aidíːəl]

ideally 부 이상적으로

the best or most suitable
형 이상적인, 완벽한 ((for)) = perfect 명 이상

This program is **ideal for** beginners. 이 프로그램은 초보자에게 이상적이다.
the **ideal** and the real 이상과 현실

445 **conduct**
[kəndʌ́kt]

to carry out a particular activity or process
동 1. (특정한 활동을) 하다, 수행하다 2. 지휘하다 명 [kɑ́ndʌkt] 행위, 행동 = behavior

conduct a test to check the sound 음향을 확인하기 위해 테스트를 실시하다
The orchestra is **conducted** by John Williams. 그 오케스트라는 존 윌리엄스가 지휘한다.
bad **conduct** 나쁜 행동

446 **conductor**
[kəndʌ́ktər]

a person who conducts the performance of an orchestra or choir
명 1. 지휘자 2. (버스·기차의) 차장

The **conductor** leads the orchestra to play in harmony.
지휘자는 오케스트라가 조화롭게 연주하도록 이끈다.
the train **conductor** 기차 차장

447 **compose**
[kəmpóuz]

composition 명 작곡, 작성; 구성

to write a piece of music or writing
동 1. 작곡하다, (시·문장을) 짓다 2. 구성하다 ((of)) = make up

compose a symphony 교향곡을 작곡하다
A symphony is **composed of** four movements. 교향곡은 네 개의 악장으로 구성된다.

448 **composer**
[kəmpóuzər]

a person who writes music
명 작곡가

Mozart is one of the greatest **composers**. 모차르트는 가장 위대한 작곡가 중 한 명이다.

449 **note**
[nout]

notable 형 주목할 만한
notice 명 주목, 알아챔; 안내문

a short piece of writing to help you to remember something

명 1. 메모, 쪽지 2. 음, 음표 동 (~에) 주목하다, 주의하다

make a **note** 메모하다
The song begins with a high **note**. 그 노래는 높은 음으로 시작한다.
Please **note** the changes in the schedule. 일정의 변경 사항을 주의해서 봐 주세요.

450 **volume**
[válju:m]

the amount of sound that is produced by a television, radio, etc.

명 1. 음량, 볼륨 2. 양, 용량 ((of))

Can you turn **the volume** up? 음량[볼륨]을 높여 줄 수 있나요?
produce **a** large **volume of** products 대량의 제품을 생산하다

451 **dynamic**
[dainǽmik]

always active or changing; having or showing a lot of energy

형 역동적인; 정력적인, 활발한 *energetic 정력적인, 활기에 찬

The music features a **dynamic** rhythm. 그 음악은 역동적인 리듬을 특징으로 한다.
a **dynamic** personality 활발한 성격

452 **graceful**
[gréisfəl]

gracefully 부 우아하게, 품위 있게
grace 명 우아함, 품위; (하느님의) 은총

moving in a smooth and attractive way

형 (동작·태도 등이) 우아한, 품위를 지키는 *elegant (모습 등이) 우아한, 고상한

The dancers were all tall and **graceful**. 무용수들은 모두 키가 크고 우아했다.

453 **touched**
[tʌtʃt]

touch 동 만지다

having emotional feelings because you are grateful or pleased

형 감동한, 감동받은 ((by)) *touching 감동적인

I was deeply **touched by** his kind words. 나는 그의 친절한 말에 깊이 감동했다.
The audience was **touched by** the performance. 관객은 그 공연에 감동받았다.

454 **ever**
[évər]

at any time; in any case

부 1. [의문문·조건문] 언젠가, 지금까지 2. [부정문] 결코, 전혀

Have you **ever** seen a ballet? 너는 발레를 (한 번이라도) 본 적이 있니?
Have you **ever** been to Paris? 너는 파리에 가 본 적이 있니?
I would not **ever** lie to you. 나는 절대 너에게 거짓말을 하지 않을 것이다.

455 **clip**
[klip]

a short section or video of a movie, TV show, etc.

명 1. 클립, 짧은 영상 ((from)) 2. 핀, 클립 *video 영상, 동영상

I watched a **clip from** Spielberg's new movie. 나는 스필버그 새 영화의 클립을 봤다.
a paper **clip** 종이 클립[핀]

456 **stream**
[stri:m]

a small narrow river

명 개울, 시냇물 동 1. 줄줄[계속] 흐르다 2. (영상 등을 실시간으로) 재생하다

a shallow **stream** 얕은 개울
Tears **streamed** down her face. 눈물이 그녀의 얼굴을 타고 흘러내렸다.
I subscribe to a **streaming** service. 나는 스트리밍 서비스를 구독 중이다.
*streaming service 인터넷에서 다운로드 없이 동영상 등을 실시간으로 제공하는 YouTube, Netflix 같은 온라인 플랫폼

457 **engage**
[ingéidʒ]

engagement 명 참여, 관계함; 약혼
engaged 형 (~하느라) 바쁜; (~와) 약혼한

to attract someone's interest
동 1. (관심을) 끌다 2. 참여하다, 관여하다 ((in)) *involve 수반하다, 연루시키다

The story **engaged** his interest. 그 이야기는 그의 흥미를 끌었다.
He decided to **engage in** volunteer work. 그는 자원봉사에 참여하기로 결정했다.

458 **yet**
[jet]

still; until the present time
부 1. [부정문] 아직 2. [의문문] 벌써

I'm not ready **yet**. 나는 아직 준비가 안 됐다.
Have you seen the movie **yet**? 너 그 영화 벌써 봤니?

459 **be composed of**

to be formed from various things
~으로 이루어지다[구성되다]

The movie **is composed of** three parts. 그 영화는 세 개의 부분으로 이루어져 있다.
An orchestra **is composed of** many instruments. 오케스트라는 많은 악기로 구성되어 있다.

460 **be engaged in**

to be involved or take part in a particular activity or task
~에 관여하다[참여하다]

He **was engaged in** the project at that time. 그는 당시 그 프로젝트에 관여하고 있었다.
The students **are engaged in** a science experiment. 학생들은 과학 실험에 참여하고 있다.

Check Up

A 우리말에 맞게 빈칸에 알맞은 말을 넣으세요.

1. 현악기 ________________ instruments
2. 이상과 현실 the ________________ and the real
3. 테스트를 실시하다 ________________ a test
4. 교향곡을 작곡하다 ________________ a symphony
5. 가장 위대한 작곡가 중 한 명 one of the greatest ________________
6. 음량[볼륨]을 높이다 turn ________________ up

B 우리말에 알맞은 말을 골라 문장을 완성하세요.

1. She enjoys listening to (**classic** / **classical**) music. 그녀는 클래식 음악 듣는 것을 즐긴다.
2. I was deeply (**touching** / **touched**) by his kind words. 나는 그의 친절한 말에 깊이 감동했다.
3. Have you (**ever** / **yet**) been to Paris? 너는 파리에 가 본 적이 있니?
4. I watched a (**clip** / **stream**) from Spielberg's new movie. 나는 스필버그 새 영화의 클립을 봤다.
5. The movie is (**engaged in** / **composed of**) three parts. 그 영화는 세 개의 부분으로 이루어져 있다.

Build Up

A Write the correct word for each definition.

conductor	instrument	string	clip	stream	composer

1. 

a tool or device used in work

____

2. 

a very thin rope or cord

____

3. 

a person who conducts an orchestra

____

4. 

a person who writes music

____

5. 

a short section of a movie, TV show, etc.

____

6. 

a small narrow river

____

B Write the correct word or phrase next to each definition.

dynamic	touched	classical	conduct	engage	be engaged in

1. traditional in style or idea; relating to classical music ______________________
2. to carry out a particular activity or process ______________________
3. always active or changing; having or showing a lot of energy ______________________
4. having emotional feelings because you are grateful or pleased ______________________
5. to attract someone's interest ______________________
6. to be involved or take part in a particular activity or task ______________________

DAY 24

461 **literature** [lítərətʃər]
literary 형 문학의

written works (such as poems and novels) that are valued as works of art
명 문학

classic **literature** 고전 문학
great works of **literature** 위대한 문학 작품들
She studied English **literature** in college. 그녀는 대학에서 영문학을 공부했다.

462 **theme** [θiːm]

the main subject or idea in a piece of writing, movie, etc.
명 주제, 테마 *subject 주제; 과목 *topic 화제, 주제

the main **theme** of the book 그 책의 주요 주제[테마]
Great works of literature often explore universal **themes**.
위대한 문학 작품은 흔히 보편적인 주제를 탐구한다.

463 **novel** [návəl]
novelist 명 소설가

a long written story, usually about imaginary characters and events
명 소설

a **novel** by Jane Austen 제인 오스틴의 소설
The movie is based on a **novel**. 그 영화는 소설을 바탕으로 하고 있다.

464 **author** [ɔ́ːθər]

a person who writes books; the person who wrote a particular book
명 작가, 저자 *writer 작가, 필자 *poet 시인

a best-selling **author** 베스트셀러 작가
Who's the **author** of the book? 그 책의 저자는 누구니?

465 **fiction** [fíkʃən]
fictional 형 허구적인, 소설의

written stories about people and events that are not real
명 1. 소설 2. 허구, 꾸며낸 이야기 반 nonfiction 논픽션, 비소설

I enjoy reading **fiction**, especially fantasy novels. 나는 소설, 특히 판타지 소설을 즐겨 읽는다.
a science-**fiction** film 공상 과학 영화 (= sci-fi film)
His explanation is pure **fiction**. 그의 설명은 순전히 허구이다(사실이 아니다).

466 **myth** [miθ]
mythical 형 신화 속에 나오는; 가공의

a traditional or legendary story, often involving supernatural beings or events
명 1. 신화 = mythology 2. 근거 없는 믿음, 사회적 통념 *legend 전설

ancient Greek **myths** 고대 그리스 신화
It's a myth that money brings happiness. 돈이 행복을 가져다준다는 것은 근거 없는 통념이다.

467 **philosophy** [filásəfi]
philosophical 형 철학의, 철학적인
philosopher 명 철학자

the study of the nature and meaning of the universe and of human life
명 철학

a **philosophy** book 철학 책
He has a unique **philosophy** of life. 그는 독특한 인생 철학을 가지고 있다.

468 **ethic** [éθik]
ethical 형 윤리적인, 도덕에 관계된

rules of behavior based on ideas about what is morally good and bad
명 1. (가치 체계로서의) 도덕, 윤리 2. (-s) (행동 규범으로서의) 윤리 *moral 도덕상의

He wrote an article about work **ethics**. 그는 직업 윤리에 관한 기사를 썼다.
The company has its own code of **ethics**. 그 회사는 자체적인 윤리 강령을 가지고 있다.

469 **paragraph**
[pǽrəgræ̀f]

a section of a piece of writing
명 단락, 절

The opening **paragraph** of the novel was unique. 그 소설의 첫 단락은 독특했다.

470 **summary**
[sʌ́məri]

summarize 동 요약하다

a short statement that gives the main points of something
명 요약, 개요 ((of)) 형 요약한, 간략한 = brief

Write a brief **summary of** the novel. 그 소설의 간단한 요약문을 작성하시오.
In summary, it was worth reading. 요약하자면[요컨대], 그것은 읽을 가치가 있었다.
a **summary** review 간략한 비평

471 **verbal**
[və́ːrbəl]

verb 명 동사

relating to words or using words
형 1. 언어의, 말의 2. (글이 아니라) 말로 된, 구두의 = oral 반 nonverbal 비언어적인

She has strong **verbal** skills. 그녀는 뛰어난 언어 능력을 가지고 있다.
a **verbal** agreement 구두 합의

472 **lyric**
[lírik]

lyrical 형 서정적인

the words of a song
명 (-s) 노래 가사 ((for/to)) 형 서정(시)의, 서정적인

She wrote the **lyrics for** most of her songs. 그녀는 자신의 노래의 대부분의 가사를 썼다.
write **lyric** poetry 서정시를 쓰다

473 **tragic**
[trǽdʒik]

tragedy 명 비극

making you feel very sad, often involving death
형 비극적인, 비극의 반 comic 희극의; 웃기는

Romeo and Juliet's **tragic** love story 로미오와 줄리엣의 비극적인 사랑 이야기

474 **trick**
[trik]

tricky 형 (다루기) 힘든, 까다로운

something you do to cheat someone or to annoy someone as a joke
명 1. 속임수, 장난 ((on)) 2. 마술 동 속임수를 쓰다

This card game has a few **tricks**. 이 카드 게임에는 몇 가지 속임수가 있다.
He **played a trick on** me. 그는 내게 장난을 쳤다.
a card **trick** 카드 마술
I was **tricked**, so I felt stupid. 나는 속아서 바보 같은 기분이 들었다.

475 **quote**
[kwout]

quotation 명 인용, 인용구[문]

to repeat the exact words that another person said or wrote
동 (남의 말·글 등을) 인용하다 명 인용구[문]

He **quoted** a passage from the Bible. 그는 성경의 한 구절을 인용했다.
His essay was full of **quotes**. 그의 에세이는 인용문 투성이였다.

476 **imply**
[implái]

implication 명 영향; 함축, 암시

to suggest or show something without saying it directly
동 1. 넌지시 비치다[나타내다] 2. 암시하다, 시사하다 *indicate 나타내다, 보여 주다

He **implied** that they were wrong. 그는 그들이 틀렸음을 넌지시 비쳤다.
The report **implies** that his death was not an accident.
그 보고서는 그의 죽음이 사고가 아니었음을 암시한다.

477 **conscience**
[kánʃəns]
conscientious 형 양심적인, 성실한

the part of your mind that tells you whether your actions are right or wrong
명 양심

I decided it according to my own **conscience**. 나는 내 양심에 따라 그것을 결정했다.
have a guilty **conscience** 양심의 가책을 느끼다, 죄책감이 들다

478 **virtue**
[və́ːrtʃuː]

behavior or attitudes that show high moral standards
명 1. 선, 선행 2. 미덕, 덕목, 장점

lead a life of **virtue** 선한 삶을(착하게) 살다
Honesty is an important **virtue**. 정직은 중요한 미덕이다.

479 **do the trick**

to solve a problem; to achieve the desired effect
문제를 해결하다, 효과가 있다

Add a bit of salt. That'll **do the trick**. 소금을 조금 추가해 봐. 그러면 될 거야.
Luckily, the medicine **did the trick**. 다행히 그 약이 효과가 있었다.

480 **take away**

to remove something; to make something disappear
~을 가져가다[데려가다], ~을 없애다, ~을 빼앗다

The waiter **took** our plates **away** from the table. 웨이터가 식탁에서 우리의 접시를 치웠다.
The pills will **take away** the pain. 그 알약이 통증을 없애 줄 것이다.
Don't **take away** my toys. 내 장난감을 빼앗지 마세요.

Check Up

A 우리말에 맞게 빈칸에 알맞은 말을 넣으세요.

1. 위대한 문학 작품들 — great works of ____________
2. 그 책의 주요 주제[테마] — the main ____________ of the book
3. 베스트셀러 작가 — a best-selling ____________
4. 공상 과학 영화 — a ____________ film
5. 철학 책 — a ____________ book
6. 양심의 가책을 느끼다, 죄책감이 들다 — have a guilty ____________

B 우리말에 알맞은 말을 골라 문장을 완성하세요.

1. It's a (**myth** / **fiction**) that money brings happiness. 돈이 행복을 가져다준다는 것은 근거 없는 통념이다.
2. Write a brief (**paragraph** / **summary**) of the novel. 그 소설의 간단한 요약문을 작성하시오.
3. She has strong (**verbal** / **virtue**) skills. 그녀는 뛰어난 언어 능력을 가지고 있다.
4. He (**quoted** / **implied**) that they were wrong. 그는 그들이 틀렸음을 넌지시 비쳤다.
5. Luckily, the medicine (**played a trick** / **did the trick**). 다행히 그 약이 효과가 있었다.

Build Up

A Write the correct word for each definition.

lyric	tragic	novel	trick	myth	paragraph

1. 

a long written story ________

2. 

a traditional or legendary story ________

3. 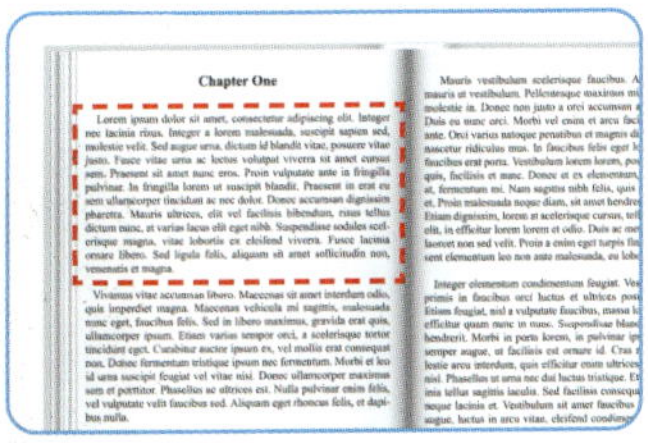

a section of a piece of writing ________

4. 

the words of a song ________

5. 

making you feel very sad ________

6. 

something you do to cheat someone ________

B Write the correct word or phrase next to each definition.

conscience	take away	ethic	quote	fiction	philosophy

1. written stories about people and events that are not real ________
2. the study of the nature and meaning of the universe and of human life ________
3. rules of behavior based on ideas about what is morally good and bad ________
4. to repeat the exact words that another person said or wrote ________
5. to remove something; to make something disappear ________
6. the part of your mind that tells you whether your actions are right or wrong ________

Review Test 06 DAY 21-24

A 그림을 보고, 빈칸에 알맞은 단어를 넣으세요.

temple   craft   carve   contrast   abstract   portrait

1. 
____

2. 
____

3. 
____

4. 
____

5. 
____

6. 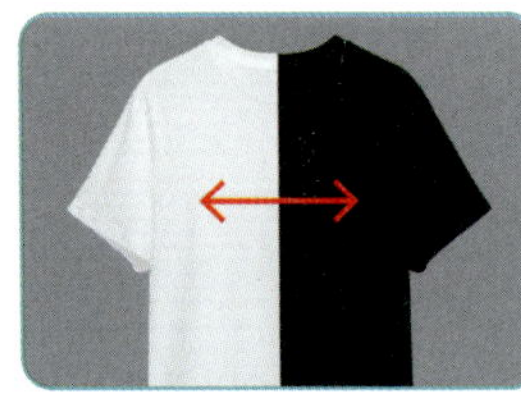
____

B 그림에 맞게 빈칸에 알맞은 단어를 고르세요.

1. 
The artist is well known for his ______________.
(landscapes / self-portraits)

2. 
The ______________ of Liberty is a famous landmark.
(Statue / Sculpture)

3. 
Mozart is one of the greatest ______________.
(conductors / composers)

4. 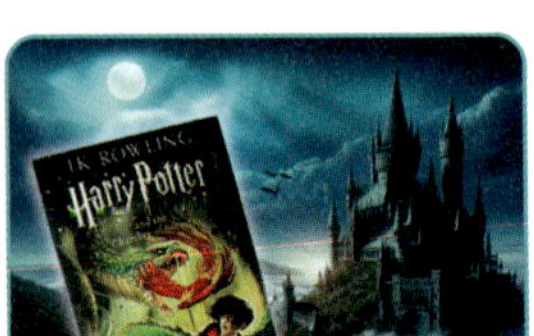

I enjoy reading ______________, especially fantasy novels.
(fiction / nonfiction)

C 우리말 뜻에 맞게 빈칸에 알맞은 말을 넣으세요.

classical	silence	contrary to	ice sculpture
religion	author	conscience	in contrast to

1. freedom of ________________ 종교의 자유
2. break the ________________ of the night 밤의 정적을 깨다
3. carve an ________________ 얼음 조각을 만들다
4. ________________ popular belief 일반적인 믿음과는 반대로
5. ________________ last year 작년에 비해
6. ________________ ballet and modern ballet 고전 발레와 현대 발레
7. a best-selling ________________ 베스트셀러 작가
8. according to my own ________________ 내 양심에 따라

D 우리말 뜻에 맞게 빈칸에 알맞은 말을 넣으세요.

confessed to	creatures	string instruments
take away	sacrificed	streaming service

1. The movie is about ________________ from outer space.
   그 영화는 외계에서 온 생명체에 관한 것이다.
2. She ________________ everything for her children. 그녀는 자녀를 위해 모든 것을 희생했다.
3. He ________________ the theft. 그는 절도를 자백했다.
4. I like ________________, such as the violin and the cello.
   나는 바이올린과 첼로와 같은 현악기를 좋아한다.
5. I subscribe to a ________________. 나는 스트리밍 서비스를 구독 중이다.
6. The pills will ________________ the pain. 그 알약이 통증을 없애 줄 것이다.

E 밑줄 친 단어와 비슷한 뜻을 가진 단어를 고르세요.

1. The temple is a <u>holy</u> place.

   a. sacred　　b. sacrificed　　c. silent

2. He <u>sculpted</u> a beautiful woman out of marble.

   a. crafted　　b. carved　　c. sketched

3. The <u>annual</u> exhibition is held in August.

   a. daily　　b. monthly　　c. yearly

4. He <u>conducted</u> a test to check the sound.

   a. carried out　　b. took away　　c. engaged in

F 밑줄 친 단어와 반대의 뜻을 가진 단어를 고르세요.

1. It's been <u>hell</u> working with him.

   a. mercy　　b. miracle　　c. heaven

2. To my surprise, the flowers were <u>artificial</u>.

   a. natural　　b. graceful　　c. instant

3. Your idea is too <u>abstract</u>.

   a. concrete　　b. real　　c. imaginary

4. It is based on Romeo and Juliet's <u>tragic</u> love story.

   a. tricky　　b. comic　　c. ideal

G 주어진 영영풀이에 알맞은 단어를 고르세요.

1. relating to religion; having a strong belief in a religion

   a. holy　　b. sacred　　c. religious

2. a wonderful event that is believed to be caused by the power of God

   a. miracle　　b. bless　　c. heaven

3. to admit that you have done something wrong or illegal

   a. talk to oneself　　b. confess　　c. approve

4. to spend time in quiet thought for religious purposes or relaxation

   a. worship　　b. pray　　c. meditate

5. an obvious difference between two or more things

   a. contrast　　b. contrary　　c. opposite

6. written works (such as poems and novels) that are valued as works of art

   a. philosophy　　b. ethic　　c. literature

H 빈칸에 알맞은 동사 형태를 넣어 문장을 완성하세요.

1. These baskets ____________________ by Native Americans. (craft)
2. A symphony ____________________ of four movements. (compose)
3. He ____________________ in the project at that time. (engage)
4. The orchestra ____________________ by John Williams. (conduct)

DAY 25

481 **grand**
[grænd]

very large and impressive
형 웅장한, 장대한, 멋진 *vast (크기 등이) 방대한, 광대한

There was a **grand** castle on the hill. 언덕 위에 웅장한 성이 있었다.
the **Grand** Canyon 그랜드 캐니언

482 **scenery**
[síːnəri]
scene 명 풍경; 장면; 현장

the natural features of an area, such as mountains, valleys, and rivers
명 (멋진) 경치, 풍경 *landscape (시골 지역의) 풍경

We stopped to enjoy the **scenery**. 우리는 경치를 즐기기 위해 멈췄다.
The **scenery** was breathtaking. 경치가 숨 막히도록 아름다웠다.

483 **pole**
[poul]

the most northern or southern point on the Earth
명 1. (지구의) 극 2. 막대기, 장대

the North **Pole** / the South **Pole** 북극 / 남극
a tent **pole** 텐트 버팀목

484 **polar**
[póulər]

relating to the North or South Pole or the region around it
형 북극[남극]의, 극지의 *Arctic 북극의; (the -) 북극 *Antarctic 남극의; (the -) 남극

Polar bears live in the Arctic. 북극곰은 북극에 산다.
Polar ice is melting fast. 극지방의 얼음이 빠르게 녹고 있다.

485 **horizon**
[həráizn]

the line in the distance where the sky seems to meet the land or sea
명 (the -) 수평선, 지평선

The sun is rising **on the horizon**. 태양이 수평선[지평선] 위로 떠오르고 있다.
The sun sank **below the horizon**. 해가 수평선[지평선] 아래로 가라앉았다(졌다).

486 **horizontal**
[hɔ̀ːrəzántl]
horizontally 부 수평으로, 가로로

flat and level; going across and parallel to the ground
형 수평(선)의, 가로의 반 vertical 수직의, 세로의 *parallel 평행한

He drew a **horizontal** line on the paper. 그는 종이에 가로로 선을(수평선을) 하나 그었다.
horizontal stripes 가로 줄무늬

487 **harsh**
[haːrʃ]

very difficult and unpleasant to live in
형 1. 혹독한 2. 가혹한, 냉혹한 = cruel, severe

a **harsh** winter 혹독한 겨울
The punishment was **harsh** and unfair. 그 처벌은 가혹하고 부당했다.

488 **fertile**
[fə́ːrtl]
fertility 명 비옥함; 생식력

producing many plants or crops
형 1. 비옥한, 기름진 = rich 2. (사람·동물이) 새끼를 가질 수 있는, 가임의

The **fertile** soil in this region is good for farming. 이 지역의 비옥한 토양은 농사에 좋다.
fertile women 가임 여성들

489 **crop**
[krɑp]

a plant that is grown by farmers and used as food
명 1. (농)작물 2. 수확량

Wheat and barley are their main **crops**. 밀과 보리가 그들의 주요 농작물이다.
a decrease in the rice **crop** 쌀 수확량의 감소

490 **grain**
[grein]

the seeds of crops (such as wheat, corn, and rice), or these crops themselves
명 1. (곡식의) 낟알 2. [집합적] 곡물

a grain of corn 옥수수 낟알(한 알)
Wheat is a type of **grain**. 밀은 곡물의 한 종류이다.

491 **cultivate**
[kʌ́ltəvèit]

cultivated 형 경작된, 재배된
cultivation 명 경작, 재배

to prepare and use land for growing plants or crops
동 1. (땅을) 경작하다, 일구다 2. (작물을) 재배하다

In spring, farmers **cultivate** the land. 봄에 농부들은 땅을 경작한다.
We **cultivate** mainly rice and beans. 우리는 주로 쌀과 콩을 재배한다.

492 **plant**
[plænt]

to put plants or seeds in the ground to grow
동 (나무·씨앗 등을) 심다, 뿌리다 *sow (씨를) 뿌리다 명 식물

plant trees 나무를 심다
Farmers **plant** seeds every spring. 농부들은 매년 봄에 씨를 뿌린다.
All **plants** need light and water. 모든 식물은 빛과 물을 필요로 한다.

493 **absorb**
[əbzɔ́:rb]

absorption 명 흡수

to take in (something, such as water) in a natural or gradual way
동 흡수하다, 빨아들이다 = take in, soak up

Plant roots **absorb** water. 식물의 뿌리는 물을 흡수한다.

494 **soak**
[souk]

soaked 형 흠뻑 젖은

to put (something) in a liquid for a period of time
동 1. (액체에) 담그다; 흠뻑 적시다 ((in/with)) 2. 빨아들이다, 흡수하다 = soak up

soak beans **in** water 콩을 물에 담그다
His shirt was **soaked with** sweat. 그의 셔츠는 땀으로 흠뻑 젖었다.
Plants **soak up** water from the soil. 식물은 토양에서 물을 빨아들인다.

495 **harvest**
[há:rvist]

the time of year when crops are gathered from the fields
명 1. 수확(기), 추수 2. 수확물 동 수확하다, 추수하다

It's **harvest** season. 수확철이다.
a good **harvest** / a poor **harvest** 풍작 / 흉작
They will **harvest** the pumpkins next week. 그들은 다음 주에 호박을 수확할 것이다.

496 **yield**
[ji:ld]

to produce or provide something, such as profit or crops
동 1. (수익 등을) 내다, 산출하다 = produce 2. 항복[굴복]하다 ((to))

yield a profit 이익을 내다
This soil always **yields** good crops. 이 토양은 늘 좋은 작물을 생산한다.
He **yielded to** their demands. 그는 그들의 요구에 굴복했다.

497 **hybrid**
[háibrid]

an animal or plant produced from parents of different breeds

명 1. (동식물의) 잡종, 교배종 ((of)) 2. 혼합물, 혼성체 = mixture

a **hybrid of** two roses 두 장미의 교배종
a **hybrid** car 하이브리드 자동차 *휘발유·전기 병용 자동차

498 **versus**
[vɔ́ːrsəs]

against; in contrast to

전 (경기 등에서) ~ 대(對), ~에 대하여 = (약어) vs.

the Italy **versus** Brazil match 이탈리아 대 브라질 경기
The report compares urban living **versus** rural living.
그 보고서는 도시 생활과 시골 생활을 비교한다.

499 **on the horizon**

likely to happen soon; coming in the near future

(어떤 일이) 곧 일어날 듯한

More storms are **on the horizon.** 더 많은 폭풍이 다가오고 있다.
Finally, success is **on the horizon.** 마침내 성공이 보인다.

500 **give in (to)**

to yield to someone else's demands, pressure, or circumstances

(~에) 굴복하다, 항복하다

They never **gave in** but kept fighting. 그들은 결코 굴복하지 않고 계속 싸웠다.
He eventually **gave in to** their pressure. 그는 결국 그들의 압력에 굴복했다.

Check Up

A 우리말에 맞게 빈칸에 알맞은 말을 넣으세요.

1. 북극 the North ______________
2. 가로로 선을(수평선을) 하나 긋다 draw a ______________ line
3. 나무를 심다 ______________ trees
4. 이익을 내다 ______________ a profit
5. 하이브리드 자동차 a ______________ car
6. 이탈리아 대 브라질 Italy ______________ Brazil

B 우리말에 알맞은 말을 골라 문장을 완성하세요.

1. The sun is rising (**below the horizon** / **on the horizon**). 태양이 수평선[지평선] 위로 떠오르고 있다.
2. The (**fertile** / **harsh**) soil in this region is good for farming. 이 지역의 비옥한 토양은 농사에 좋다.
3. In spring, farmers (**plant** / **cultivate**) the land. 봄에 농부들은 땅을 경작한다.
4. His shirt was (**soaked with** / **soaked up**) sweat. 그의 셔츠는 땀으로 흠뻑 젖었다.
5. They will (**yield** / **harvest**) the pumpkins next week. 그들은 다음 주에 호박을 수확할 것이다.

Build Up

A Write the correct word for each definition.

harsh	grand	scenery	absorb	grain	soak

1. 

very large and impressive

____

2. 

the natural features of an area

____

3. 

very difficult and unpleasant to live in

____

4. 

the seeds of crops

____

5. 

to take in; to soak up

____

6. 

to put (something) in a liquid

____

B Write the correct word or phrase next to each definition.

crop	yield	polar	horizon	give in (to)	on the horizon

1. relating to the North or South Pole or the region around it ______________________
2. the line in the distance where the sky seems to meet the land or sea ______________________
3. a plant that is grown by farmers and used as food ______________________
4. to produce or provide something, such as profit or crops ______________________
5. likely to happen soon; coming in the near future ______________________
6. to yield to someone else's demands, pressure, or circumstances ______________________

DAY 26

501 **site**
[sait]

the place where something (such as a building) is, was, or will be located

명 1. (건물 등의) 자리, 장소 2. (사건 등의) 현장, (특정) 장소 유 place 장소, spot (특정한) 곳

This is the **site** for the new airport. 여기가 새 공항 부지이다.
the **site** of the air crash 항공기 추락 현장
a camping **site** 캠프장, 야영지

502 **locate**
[lóukeit]

location 명 위치, 장소
located 형 (~에) 위치한

to find the exact position of something or someone

동 1. (위치를) 알아내다, 찾다 2. (특정 위치에) 두다, 설치하다

Can you **locate** the site on the map? 지도에서 그 장소를 찾을 수 있니?
They **located** their factory in Chicago. 그들은 그들의 공장을 시카고에 두었다.

503 **construct**
[kənstrʌ́kt]

construction 명 건설, 공사; 구성
constructive 형 건설적인

to build something such as a building, bridge, road, etc.

동 1. 건설하다 유 build 짓다, 세우다 2. (이론 등을) 구성하다, 고안해 내다

The bridge was **constructed** in 2002. 그 다리는 2002년에 건설되었다.
construct a new theory 새로운 이론을 구축하다

504 **pave**
[peiv]

pavement 명 포장 도로

to cover a surface with flat stones, bricks, concrete, etc.

동 (길·도로 등을) 포장하다 ((with))

pave the road **with** concrete 도로를 콘크리트로 포장하다
The road is **paved with** asphalt. 그 도로는 아스팔트로 포장되어 있다.

505 **architecture**
[ɑ́ːrkɪtèktʃər]

architect 명 건축가
architectural 형 건축학[술]의

the art and study of designing buildings

명 1. 건축, 건축학 2. 건축 양식

He studied **architecture** at university. 그는 대학에서 건축학을 공부했다.
Gothic **architecture** 고딕 건축 양식

506 **fountain**
[fáuntən]

a structure that forces water up into the air

명 1. 분수 2. 원천, 샘 ((of))

the Trevi **Fountain** in Rome 로마의 트레비 분수
The **fountain** is a hot spot for tourists. 그 분수는 관광객들에게 인기 있는 장소이다.
a **fountain of** wealth 부의 원천

507 **establish**
[istǽbliʃ]

establishment 명 설립; 기관, 시설

to start or create an organization, system, place, etc.

동 1. (국가·학교·기업 등을) 설립하다 2. 수립하다, 확립하다

The school was **established** in 1912. 그 학교는 1912년에 설립되었다.
establish a successful relationship 성공적인 관계를 수립하다

508 **found**
[faund]

foundation 명 토대, 기반; 재단
founder 명 창립자, 설립자

to start an organization or institution, especially by providing money

동 1. (기관 등을 돈을 대서) 설립하다 2. ~에 근거를 두다[기반을 두다] ((on))

The hospital was **founded** by Dr. Smith. 그 병원은 스미스 박사에 의해 설립되었다.
It was **founded on** charity. 그것은 자선을 기반으로 하고 있었다.
a story **founded on** facts 사실에 바탕을 둔 이야기

509 **metal** [métl]
metallic 형 금속의, 금속성인

a hard, shiny material such as iron or gold
명 금속

The gate is made of **metal**. 그 문은 금속으로 만들어져 있다.
Gold and silver are precious **metals**. 금과 은은 귀금속이다.

510 **steel** [stiːl]

a strong, hard metal made of iron and carbon
명 강철

the iron and **steel** industry 철강업
The bridge is made of **steel**. 그 다리는 강철로 만들어져 있다.

511 **complex** [kəmpléks]
complexity 명 복잡성, 복잡함

consisting of many different parts; difficult to understand
형 복잡한 = complicated 명 [kámpleks] 복합 건물, (건물) 단지

The building has a very **complex** structure. 그 건물은 매우 복잡한 구조를 가지고 있다.
a sports **complex** 스포츠 복합 건물

512 **device** [diváis]

a tool or machine designed for a specific purpose
명 (특별히 고안된) 장치, 기구, 기기 *tool 도구

A safety **device**, such as a smoke detector, is essential.
연기 감지기와 같은 안전 장치는 필수적이다.
Please turn off all electronic **devices**. 모든 전자 기기를 꺼 주세요.

513 **equipment** [ikwípmənt]

supplies or tools needed for a special purpose
명 (특정 목적을 위해 필요한) 장비, 용품 *gear 장비, 복장

camping **equipment** 캠핑 장비[용품]
Safety **equipment** is essential at construction sites. 안전 장비는 건설 현장에서 필수적이다.

514 **equip** [ikwíp]

to provide equipment or supplies
동 장비를 갖추다 ((with))

The gym is **equipped with** a variety of exercise equipment.
그 체육관에는 다양한 운동 기구가 갖추어져[구비되어] 있다.

515 **replace** [ripléis]
replacement 명 교체, 대체(물)

to be used instead of someone or something else
동 1. 대체하다, 대신하다 2. 바꾸다, 교체하다 ((with))

There's nobody who can **replace** her. 그녀를 대신할 수 있는 사람은 아무도 없다.
replace soda **with** water 탄산음료를 물로 바꾸다[대체하다]
replace the battery in the remote control 리모컨의 배터리를 교체하다

516 **substitute** [sʌ́bstətjùːt]
substitution 명 대체; 대체물, 대용품

to use someone or something instead of someone or something else (temporarily)
동 (임시로) 대신 쓰다 명 대리(인), 대용품 ((for/with)) *alternative 대안; 대신하는

You can **substitute** margarine **for** butter. 버터 대신 마가린을 사용해도 된다.
Butter can be **substituted with** margarine. 버터는 마가린으로 대체될 수 있다.
a **substitute for** meat 고기 대용품
a **substitute** player 대체 선수, 교체 선수

517 **split**
[split]

to divide, or to make something divide, into two or more parts **(split–split)**

동 1. 나누다, 쪼개다; 나뉘다, 분열되다 ((into)) = divide 2. 찢어지다 = tear

They **split** the team **into** two groups. 그들은 팀을 두 개의 그룹으로 나누었다.
Let's **split** the bill. (계산서를) 나눠서 내자. / 각자 계산하자.
His pants **split** when he bent over. 그가 몸을 숙였을 때 그의 바지가 찢어졌다.

518 **envy**
[énvi]
envious 형 부러워하는

to want something that someone else has

동 부러워하다, 질투하다 명 부러움, 선망, 질투 ((of)) 유 jealousy 질투, 시샘

I **envy** you. 나는 네가 부럽다.
Our university is **the envy of** the world. 우리 대학은 세계의 선망의 대상이다.

519 **be located in [on]**

to be in a specific place

~에 위치해 있다

The building site **is located in** Manhattan. 그 건설 현장은 맨해튼에 위치해 있다.
It **is located on** the second floor of this building. 그것은 이 건물 2층에 있다.

520 **take over**

to replace someone in a job or position; to get control of something

~을 인계받다, ~을 인수하다

The new manager **took over** the project. 새 매니저가 그 프로젝트를 넘겨받았다.
The company was **taken over** by Apple. 그 회사는 애플에 인수되었다.

Check Up

A 우리말에 맞게 빈칸에 알맞은 말을 넣으세요.

1. 도로를 콘크리트로 포장하다 ____________ the road ____________ concrete
2. 사실에 바탕을 둔 이야기 a story ________________ on facts
3. 캠핑 장비[용품] camping ________________
4. 탄산음료를 물로 바꾸다[대체하다] ________________ soda with water
5. 고기 대용품 a ________________ for meat
6. ~에 위치해 있다 be ________________ in[on]

B 우리말에 알맞은 말을 골라 문장을 완성하세요.

1. The school was (**constructed** / **established**) in 1912. 그 학교는 1912년에 설립되었다.
2. The hospital was (**found** / **founded**) by Dr. Smith. 그 병원은 스미스 박사에 의해 설립되었다.
3. Please turn off all electronic (**devices** / **equipment**). 모든 전자 기기를 꺼 주세요.
4. The gym is (**equipped** / **split**) with a variety of exercise equipment.
그 체육관에는 다양한 운동 기구가 갖추어져[구비되어] 있다.
5. You can (**substitute** / **replace**) margarine for butter. 버터 대신 마가린을 사용해도 된다.

Build Up

A Write the correct word for each definition.

fountain	metal	split	construct	complex	device

1. 

to build something

____

2. 

a structure that forces water up into the air

____

3. 

a hard, shiny material

____

4. 

consisting of many different parts

____

5. 

a tool or machine

____

6. 

to divide into two or more parts

____

B Write the correct word or phrase next to each definition.

architecture	establish	site	take over	replace	envy

1. the art and study of designing buildings ______________
2. to start or create an organization, system, place, etc. ______________
3. to be used instead of someone or something else ______________
4. to want something that someone else has ______________
5. the place where something (such as a building) is, was, or will be located ______________
6. to replace someone in a job or position; to get control of something ______________

DAY 27

521 **environment**
[inváiərənmənt]
environmental 형 환경의, 환경과 관련된

the natural world in which people, animals, and plants live
명 1. (the -) 자연 환경 2. (주위의) 환경

protect **the environment** 환경을 보호하다
We must provide a safe **environment** for children.
우리는 어린이들을 위한 안전한 환경을 제공해야 한다.

522 **circumstance**
[sə́:rkəmstæns]
circumstantial 형 상황(으로부터)의

a condition or fact that affects a situation
명 (일·사건 등을 둘러싼) 상황, 정황 *situation 상황, 처지

Under the **circumstances**, what should we do? 이런 상황에서 우리는 무엇을 해야 할까요?
Do your best in any **circumstance**. 어떤 상황에서든 최선을 다하세요.

523 **conserve**
[kənsə́:rv]
conservation 명 보존, 보호

to keep and protect something from being damaged or destroyed
동 1. 보존하다, 보호하다 = preserve 2. 아끼다, 아껴 쓰다

We must **conserve** our forests for future generations.
우리는 미래 세대를 위해 우리의 숲을 보존해야 한다.
We need to **conserve** water. 우리는 물을 아껴 써야 한다.

524 **aside**
[əsáid]

kept to be used later
부 1. (나중에 쓰려고) 따로 2. 한쪽으로 *reserve 따로 남겨 두다

set aside some money for repairs 수리를 위해 따로 돈을 좀 떼어 놓다
This area is **set aside** to preserve wildlife.
이 지역은 야생 동물을 보호하기 위해 따로 남겨 둔 것이다.
move a table **aside** 테이블을 한쪽으로 치우다

525 **bloom**
[blu:m]

to produce flowers
동 꽃이 피다, 꽃을 피우다 명 꽃 유 blossom (특히 과실수의) 꽃; 꽃이 피다

Most roses **bloom** in spring. 대부분의 장미는 봄에 핀다.
The garden is full of **blooms**. 정원은 꽃으로 가득하다.

526 **throughout**
[θru:áut]

in every part of a place; during the whole period of time
전 1. ~의 도처에 2. ~ 동안 쭉, 내내

Cherry blossoms bloomed **throughout** the park. 벚꽃이 공원 곳곳에 피었다.
The park is open to visitors **throughout** the year. 그 공원은 일 년 내내 방문객에게 개방된다.

527 **shade**
[ʃeid]
shady 형 그늘이 드리워진

an area that is dark and cool under or behind something
명 그늘

They sat down **in the shade of** a tree. 그들은 나무 그늘에 앉았다.

528 **bury**
[béri]
burial 명 매장

to put a dead body in the ground; to put something under the ground
동 (땅에) 묻다, 매장하다, 숨기다

They **buried** their pet in the backyard. 그들은 뒷마당에 그들의 애완동물을 묻었다.
The grass was **buried** under the blossoms. 잔디는 꽃에 묻혀(꽃으로 뒤덮여) 있었다.
They decided to **bury** a time capsule. 그들은 타임캡슐을 묻기로 했다.

529 **pollution**
[pəlúːʃən]
pollute 동 오염시키다
pollutant 명 오염 물질

the process of making air, water, soil, etc. dirty; the state of being dirty
명 오염, 공해

water **pollution** 수질 오염
The air **pollution** is getting worse. 대기 오염이 점점 더 심해지고 있다.

530 **mount**
[maunt]
mountainous 형 산이 많은; 산더미 같은

to increase gradually in amount or level
동 1. 증가하다 2. (계단 등을) 오르다 명 (Mount) 산 = Mt.

Concern is **mounting** over climate change. 기후 변화에 대한 우려가 커지고 있다.
mount the stairs 계단을 오르다
Mount Everest 에베레스트 산

531 **sudden**
[sʌ́dn]
suddenly 부 갑자기, 갑작스럽게

happening or done quickly and unexpectedly
형 갑작스러운

a **sudden** change in the weather 날씨의 갑작스러운 변화
His death was very **sudden**. 그의 죽음은 매우 갑작스러웠다.

532 **disaster**
[dizǽstər]
disastrous 형 처참한, 형편없는

something that happens suddenly and causes a lot of damage
명 재해, 대참사; 재앙

Natural **disasters** are increasing. 자연재해가 증가하고 있다.
Plastic waste can cause an environmental **disaster**.
플라스틱 쓰레기는 환경 재앙을 초래할 수 있다.

533 **avoid**
[əvɔ́id]
avoidance 명 회피; 방지
avoidable 형 막을[피할] 수 있는

to prevent something bad from happening
동 1. 막다, 방지하다 2. 피하다, 회피하다

We need to **avoid** further danger. 우리는 더 이상의 위험을 막아야 한다.
avoid an accident 사고를 피하다[방지하다]
He has been **avoiding** me all week. 그는 일주일 내내 나를 피하고 있다.

534 **prevent**
[privént]
prevention 명 예방, 방지
preventive 형 예방의

to stop something from happening
동 1. 막다, 예방하다 2. ~하는 것을 막다 ((from))

To **prevent** further disaster, we should take action.
더 이상의 재앙을 막기 위해 우리는 조치를 취해야 한다.
Bad weather **prevented** us **from** leaving. 악천후가 우리가 떠나는 것을 막았다.

535 **tide**
[taid]
tidal 형 조수의

a regular rise and fall in the level of the ocean
명 조수, 조류

The **tide** is coming in[going out]. 조수가 들어오고[나가고] 있다.
high **tide** / low **tide** 밀물, 만조 / 썰물, 간조

536 **flood**
[flʌd]
flooded 형 물에 잠긴, 침수된

a large amount of water covering an area that is usually dry
명 홍수 반 drought 가뭄 동 물에 잠기다, 홍수가 나다 *overflow 넘쳐흐르다

Typhoons often cause **floods**. 태풍은 종종 홍수를 일으킨다.
The river is **in flood**. 강이 범람하고 있다.
The river **flooded** after the heavy rain. 폭우가 내린 후 강이 범람했다.

537 **lightning**
[láitniŋ]

a flash of light in the sky caused by electricity

명 번개, 벼락 형 아주 빠른, 번개 같은 *thunder 천둥 *flash 번쩍임; 번쩍이다

Lightning flashed in the sky. 하늘에서 번개가 번쩍였다(쳤다).
The tree was struck by **lightning**. 그 나무는 벼락을 맞았다.
She ran **like lightning**. 그녀는 번개처럼 달렸다.

538 **secure**
[sikjúər]

security 명 안전, 안보; 안심, 안도

safe from danger

형 1. 안전한, 위험 없는 = safe 2. 안정된, 확실한

find a **secure** place 안전한 장소를 찾다
She **felt secure** when she arrived home. 그녀는 집에 도착하자 안도감을 느꼈다.
a **secure** job 안정적인 직업

539 **put A in danger**

to place someone or something in a dangerous position

A를 위험에 빠뜨리다

Plastic waste can **put** sea creatures **in danger**.
플라스틱 쓰레기는 바다 생물을 위험에 빠뜨릴 수 있다.
Careless driving can **put** others **in danger**. 부주의한 운전은 다른 사람들을 위험에 빠뜨릴 수 있다.

540 **all of a sudden**

quickly and unexpectedly

갑자기

All of a sudden, the lights went out. 갑자기 불이 나갔다(정전이 되었다).
All of a sudden, she burst into tears. 갑자기 그녀가 울음을 터뜨렸다.

Check Up

A 우리말에 맞게 빈칸에 알맞은 말을 넣으세요.

1. 환경을 보호하다 protect ________________
2. 일 년 내내 ________________ the year
3. 타임캡슐을 묻다 ________________ a time capsule
4. 수질 오염 water ________________
5. 사고를 피하다[방지하다] ________________ an accident
6. 갑자기 all of ________________

B 우리말에 알맞은 말을 골라 문장을 완성하세요.

1. Do your best in any (**circumstance** / **environment**). 어떤 상황에서든 최선을 다하세요.
2. We must (**set aside** / **conserve**) our forests. 우리는 우리의 숲을 보존해야 한다.
3. His death was very (**sudden** / **suddenly**). 그의 죽음은 매우 갑작스러웠다.
4. Bad weather (**avoided** / **prevented**) us from leaving. 악천후가 우리가 떠나는 것을 막았다.
5. Plastic waste can put sea creatures (**in flood** / **in danger**).
   플라스틱 쓰레기는 바다 생물을 위험에 빠뜨릴 수 있다.

Build Up

A Write the correct word for each definition.

mount	secure	lightning	shade	bloom	flood

1. 

to produce flowers

____

2. 

an area that is dark and cool

____

3. 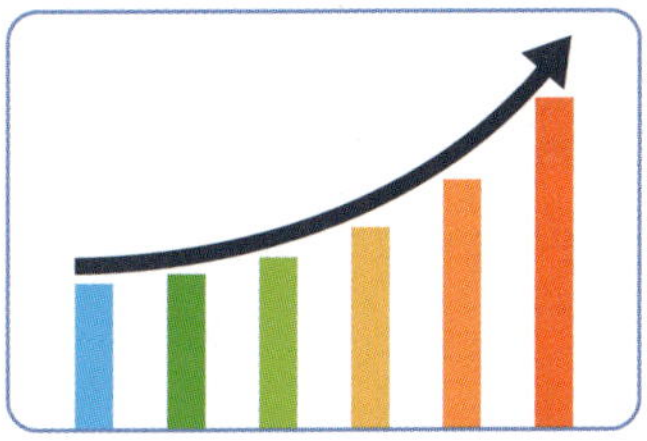

to increase gradually

____

4. 

a large amount of water covering an area

____

5. 

a flash of light in the sky

____

6. 

safe from danger

____

B Write the correct word or phrase next to each definition.

pollution	disaster	bury	tide	conserve	put A in danger

1. to keep and protect something from being damaged or destroyed ______________
2. something that happens suddenly and causes a lot of damage ______________
3. a regular rise and fall in the level of the ocean ______________
4. to place someone or something in a dangerous position ______________
5. to put a dead body in the ground; to put something under the ground ______________
6. the process of making air, water, soil, etc. dirty; the state of being dirty ______________

DAY 28

541 **summit**
[sʌ́mit]

the highest point of something, especially the top of a mountain

명 1. (산의) 정상, 꼭대기 ((of)) 2. 정상 회담

They reached the **summit of** Mount Everest. 그들은 에베레스트 산 정상에 도달했다.
hold a **summit** 정상 회담을 열다

542 **peak**
[pi:k]

the highest point of something

명 1. 절정, 정점 2. (산의) 꼭대기 동 절정에 달하다

Traffic reaches its **peak** at 8:00 AM. 교통량은 오전 8시에 최고조에 달한다.
a mountain **peak** 산꼭대기
Electricity usage **peaks** during the summer. 전기 사용량은 여름에 절정에 달한다.

543 **steep**
[sti:p]

rising or falling very sharply or quickly

형 1. 가파른, 비탈진 2. 급격한 반 gentle 완만한 *stiff 뻣뻣한

The mountain was rocky and **steep**. 그 산은 바위가 많고 가팔랐다.
a **steep** increase 급격한 증가

544 **slope**
[sloup]

a surface that rises at an angle, especially part of a hill or mountain

명 경사면, (산)비탈

They climbed the steep **slope**. 그들은 가파른 경사를 올라갔다.
a mountain **slope** 산비탈
The ski **slope** was covered with snow. 스키 슬로프는 눈으로 덮여 있었다.

545 **crack**
[kræk]

cracked 형 금이 간, 갈라진

a thin line or break in a surface

명 (갈라져 생긴) 금, 틈 동 금이 가다; 금이 가게 하다

There are **cracks** in the ice. 얼음에 금이 가 있다.
The ice **cracked** as I stepped onto it. 내가 발을 올리자 얼음이 갈라졌다.

546 **gap**
[gæp]

a space or hole in the middle of something or between two things

명 1. 틈(새), 구멍 2. (시간·공간의) 간격, 공백 3. 격차, 차이

a **gap** between two rocks 두 바위 사이의 틈
Despite the age **gap**, we became good friends. 나이 차이에도 불구하고 우리는 좋은 친구가 되었다.
the **gap** between the rich and the poor 빈부 격차(부자와 가난한 사람들 사이의 격차)

547 **earthquake**
[ə́:rθkweik]

a sudden, violent shaking of the Earth's surface

명 지진

The city is in an **earthquake** zone. 그 도시는 지진 지대에 있다.
Earthquakes often cause severe damage. 지진은 종종 심각한 피해를 초래한다.

548 **volcano**
[valkéinou]

volcanic 형 화산의, 화산 작용에 의한

a mountain with a hole at the top that sometimes explodes and produces lava

명 화산

An active **volcano** is very dangerous. 활화산은 매우 위험하다.

549 **erupt**
[irʌ́pt]
eruption 명 분출; 발발

to force out or release suddenly and violently
동 1. (화산이) 분출하다, 폭발하다 = explode 2. (갑자기) 분출되다 = break out

The volcano could **erupt** at any time. 그 화산은 언제든지 폭발할 수 있다.
Violence **erupted** in the city. 도심에서 폭력 사태가 발생했다.

550 **haste**
[heist]
hasty 형 서두른, 성급한

great speed in doing something
명 서두름, 급함 *hurry 서두름; 서두르다 *rush 바쁨; 급히 움직이다

They left the village **in haste**. 그들은 서둘러 마을을 떠났다.

551 **species**
[spíːʃiːz]

a group of animals or plants that share similar characteristics
명 (동물·식물의) 종(種) *breed (가축의) 품종

Cats and tigers are different **species**. 고양이와 호랑이는 서로 다른 종이다.
Rainforests are home to many rare **species**. 열대우림은 많은 희귀종의 서식지이다.

552 **cell**
[sel]
cellular 형 세포의

the smallest basic unit of a living thing
명 1. 세포 2. (작게 구분된) 방, 칸

All living things are made up of **cells**. 모든 생물은 세포로 구성되어 있다.
cell phone 휴대전화, 핸드폰

553 **range**
[reindʒ]

a set of different things of the same general type
명 1. (같은 종류의) 다양성 2. 범위, 폭 동 (범위가) ~에서 … 사이이다

a wide **range** of plants 다양한(광범위한) 종류의 식물들
the average age **range** 평균 연령대
The prices **range from** $500 **to** $1,000. 가격은 500달러에서 1,000달러 사이이다.

554 **chain**
[ʧein]

a line of metal rings connected together
명 1. 사슬, 체인 2. 연쇄, 연속 ((of)) 3. (상점 등의) 체인(점)

All living things are part of a food **chain**. 모든 생물은 먹이 사슬의 일부이다.
a chain of events 일련의 사건들
a supermarket **chain** 슈퍼마켓 체인점

555 **prey**
[prei]

an animal that is hunted and killed by another animal
명 (사냥 동물의) 먹이, 먹잇감, 사냥감 ((for)) 반 predator 포식자, 포식 동물

Zebras are easy **prey for** lions. 얼룩말은 사자의 손쉬운 먹잇감이다.
The food chain shows how predators and **prey** are linked.
먹이 사슬은 포식자와 먹잇감이 어떻게 연결되어 있는지를 보여 준다.

556 **evolve**
[iválv]
evolution 명 진화

to change or develop gradually over a long period of time
동 1. 진화하다; 진화시키다 ((from)) 2. (점진적으로) 발전하다 ((into))

Did humans **evolve from** chimpanzees? 인간은 침팬지에서 진화했나요?
It **evolved from** an idea **into** a theory. 그것은 하나의 아이디어에서 이론으로 발전했다.

557 **endangered**
[indéindʒərd]

endanger 동 위험에 빠뜨리다
danger 명 위험
dangerous 형 위험한

in danger of becoming extinct
형 멸종 위기에 처한 유 threatened 멸종 위험에 직면한

an **endangered** species 멸종 위기종
The sea turtle is now **endangered.** 바다거북은 현재 멸종 위기에 처해 있다.

558 **extinct**
[ikstíŋkt]

extinction 명 멸종, 소멸

no longer existing
형 1. 멸종된, 더 이상 존재하지 않는 2. (화산이) 활동을 멈춘

Dinosaurs became **extinct** approximately 65 million years ago.
공룡은 약 6,500만 년 전에 멸종되었다.
an **extinct** volcano 사화산

559 **at risk (of)**

(to be) in danger of being harmed or damaged
(~할) 위험에 처한, 위험이 있는

Many species are **at risk of** extinction. 많은 종들이 멸종 위험에 처해 있다.
He is **at risk of** losing his job. 그는 일자리를 잃을 위기에 처해 있다.

560 **as far as**

to the degree or extent that something applies
(거리·범위·정도가) ~까지, ~하는 한

As far as I know, nearly 1 million species are at risk of extinction.
내가 아는 한, 거의 100만 종이 멸종 위험에 처해 있다.
I will help you **as far as** I can. 나는 할 수 있는 한(최대한) 너를 돕겠다.

Check Up

A 우리말에 맞게 빈칸에 알맞은 말을 넣으세요.

1. 정상 회담을 열다 hold a ______________
2. 빈부 격차(부자와 가난한 사람들 사이의 격차) the ______________ between the rich and the poor
3. 지진 지대 an ______________ zone
4. 활화산 an active ______________
5. 멸종 위기종 an ______________ species
6. 멸종 위험에 처해 있는 at ______________ extinction

B 우리말에 알맞은 말을 골라 문장을 완성하세요.

1. Traffic reaches its (**summit** / **peak**) at 8:00 AM. 교통량은 오전 8시에 최고조에 달한다.
2. They left the village (**hurry** / **in haste**). 그들은 서둘러 마을을 떠났다.
3. Rainforests are home to many rare (**slopes** / **species**). 열대우림은 많은 희귀종의 서식지이다.
4. Zebras are easy (**prey** / **predator**) for lions. 얼룩말은 사자의 손쉬운 먹잇감이다.
5. Dinosaurs (**became extinct** / **became extinction**). 공룡은 멸종되었다.

Build Up

A Write the correct word for each definition.

prey	erupt	extinct	cell	summit	steep

1. 

the highest point of something; peak

____

2. 

rising or falling very sharply

____

3. 

to force out suddenly; to explode

____

4. 

the smallest basic unit of a living thing

____

5. 

an animal that is hunted by another animal

____

6. 

no longer existing

____

B Write the correct word or phrase next to each definition.

evolve	range	at risk of	slope	species	earthquake

1. a surface that rises at an angle, especially part of a hill or mountain ______________
2. a sudden, violent shaking of the Earth's surface ______________
3. a group of animals or plants that share similar characteristics ______________
4. a set of different things of the same general type ______________
5. to change or develop gradually over a long period of time ______________
6. (to be) in danger of being harmed or damaged ______________

Review Test 07 DAY 25-28

A 그림을 보고, 빈칸에 알맞은 단어를 넣으세요.

volcano earthquake food chain polar bury evolve

1. 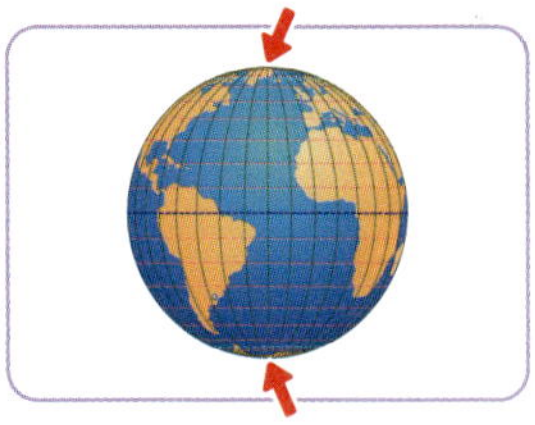

____

2. 

____

3. 

____

4. 

____

5. 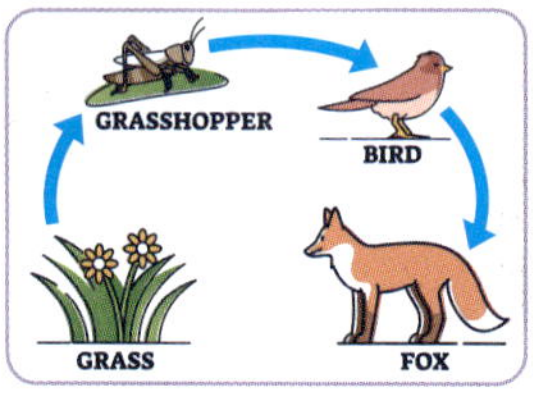

____

6. 

____

B 그림에 맞게 빈칸에 알맞은 단어를 고르세요.

1. 

The _______________ is a hot spot for tourists.
(architecture / fountain)

2. 

Please turn off all electronic _______________.
(devices / equipment)

3. 

The grass is _______________ under the blossoms.
(bloomed / buried)

4. 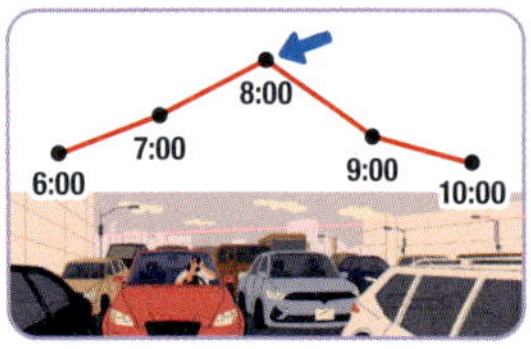

Traffic reaches its _______________ at 8:00 AM.
(peak / summit)

C 우리말 뜻에 맞게 빈칸에 알맞은 말을 넣으세요.

versus	harvest	replace ~ with	in any circumstance
split	equipment	endangered	the environment

1. have a good ________________ 풍작을 거두다
2. the Italy ________________ Brazil match 이탈리아 대 브라질 경기
3. buy camping ________________ 캠핑 장비[용품]를 사다
4. ________________ soda ________________ water 탄산음료를 물로 바꾸다[대체하다]
5. ________________ the bill (계산서를) 나눠서 내다, 각자 부담하다
6. protect ________________ 환경을 보호하다
7. do one's best ________________ 어떤 상황에서든 최선을 다하다
8. an ________________ species 멸종 위기종

D 우리말 뜻에 맞게 빈칸에 알맞은 말을 넣으세요.

on the horizon	soaked with	fertile soil
rare species	located on	in danger

1. The ________________ in this region is good for farming. 이 지역의 비옥한 토양은 농사에 좋다.
2. His shirt was ________________ sweat. 그의 셔츠는 땀으로 흠뻑 젖었다.
3. More storms are ________________. 더 많은 폭풍이 다가오고 있다.
4. It is ________________ the second floor of this building. 그것은 이 건물 2층에 (위치해) 있다.
5. Plastic waste can put sea creatures ________________.
   플라스틱 쓰레기는 바다 생물을 위험에 빠뜨릴 수 있다.
6. Rainforests are home to many ________________. 열대우림은 많은 희귀종의 서식지이다.

E 밑줄 친 단어와 비슷한 뜻을 가진 단어를 고르세요.

1. Plant roots absorb water.

a. soak up b. take up c. take over

2. He eventually yielded to their demands.

a. gave in to b. handed in to c. prior to

3. Butter can be substituted with margarine.

a. cultivated b. replaced c. made up

4. The volcano could erupt at any time.

a. evolve b. split c. explode

F 밑줄 친 단어와 반대의 뜻을 가진 단어를 고르세요.

1. He drew a horizontal line on the paper.

a. vertical b. parallel c. striped

2. We need to conserve water.

a. preserve b. pollute c. waste

3. Typhoons often cause floods.

a. disaster b. tide c. drought

4. The mountain was rocky and steep.

a. harsh b. gentle c. sudden

G 주어진 영영풀이에 알맞은 단어를 고르세요.

1. the natural features of an area, such as mountains, valleys, and rivers

   a. scenery   b. countryside   c. environment

2. an animal or plant produced from parents of different breeds

   a. species   b. crop   c. hybrid

3. the art and study of designing buildings

   a. facility   b. sculpture   c. architecture

4. to want something that someone else has

   a. envy   b. envious   c. jealousy

5. to replace someone in a job or position; to get control of something

   a. take after   b. take over   c. take part

6. the process of making air, water, soil, etc. dirty; the state of being dirty

   a. disaster   b. flood   c. pollution

H 빈칸에 알맞은 동사 형태를 넣어 문장을 완성하세요.

1. The bridge ______________________ in 2002. (construct)
2. The road ______________________ asphalt. (pave with)
3. The school ______________________ in 1912. (establish)
4. The company ______________________ by Apple last year. (take over)

DAY 29

561 **experiment**
[ikspérəmənt]

experimental 형 실험의, 실험적인

a test done in order to learn or discover something

명 실험 동 실험하다, 시험하다 ((on))

conduct an **experiment** 실험을 (실시)하다
Scientists often **experiment on** rats. 과학자들은 종종 쥐를 대상으로 실험을 한다.

562 **laboratory**
[lǽbərətɔ̀:ri]

a room or building used for scientific research or experiments

명 실험실, 연구실 = lab

They are conducting experiments in the **laboratory**. 그들은 실험실에서 실험을 진행하고 있다.
Laboratory-grown meat is getting popular. 실험실에서 배양된 고기가 인기를 얻고 있다.

563 **procedure**
[prəsí:dʒər]

a way of doing something, especially the usual or correct way

명 절차, 수순, 방법 *process 과정, 절차 *sequence 순서

a standard **procedure** 표준 절차, 정식 절차
Always follow the safety **procedures**. 항상 안전 절차를 따르세요.

564 **proceed**
[prəsí:d]

to continue doing something that has already been started

동 (계속) 진행하다, 나아가다 ((with))

Let's **proceed with** the schedule as planned. 계획대로 일정을 진행합시다.
They decided to **proceed with** the project. 그들은 프로젝트를 계속 진행하기로 결정했다.

565 **solid**
[sálid]

firm or hard; not in the form of a liquid or gas

형 단단한, 고체의 명 고체 *gas 기체, 가스

a **solid** object 단단한 물체
Ice is a **solid** form of water. 얼음은 물의 고체 형태이다.
Ice is a type of **solid**. 얼음은 고체의 일종이다.

566 **liquid**
[líkwid]

flowing freely like water; not a solid or a gas

형 액체의, 액상의 명 액체

liquid soap 액체 비누(물비누)
When ice melts, it changes from a solid to a **liquid**. 얼음이 녹으면 고체에서 액체로 변한다.

567 **substance**
[sʌ́bstəns]

material with particular physical characteristics

명 물질 *material 재료, 원료, 물질 *matter 문제; 물질

Diamond is the hardest **substance**. 다이아몬드는 가장 단단한 물질이다.
A solid is a **substance** that is not a gas or a liquid. 고체는 기체나 액체가 아닌 물질이다.

568 **magnet**
[mǽgnit]

magnetic 형 자석 같은, 자성의
magnetism 명 자성, 자력
magnetic field 명 자기장

an iron object that makes other pieces of iron move toward it

명 자석

a bar **magnet** 막대 자석
Magnets pull metal objects. 자석은 금속 물체를 끌어당긴다.

569 **evaporate**
[ivǽpərèit]

evaporation 명 증발, 발산

to change from a liquid into a gas, especially by heating

동 (액체가) 증발하다; 증발시키다

Water **evaporates** when it boils. 물은 끓으면 증발한다.
In the water cycle, the sun causes water to **evaporate**.
물 순환에서 태양은 물을 증발시킨다.

570 **upward**
[ʌ́pwərd]

toward a higher position, level, or value

부 위쪽으로 = (영) upwards 형 위를 향한; (양·가격이) 상승하는
반 downward 아래쪽으로; 하향의, 내려가는

The warm air moves **upward**. 따뜻한 공기는 위로 올라간다.
move in an **upward** direction 위쪽 방향으로 움직이다
an **upward** trend 상승 추세[경향]

571 **physics**
[fíziks]

physical 형 물질의, 물리적인; 신체의

the science that deals with matter and energy and the relationships between them

명 물리학 *biology 생물학

She majored in **physics** at college. 그녀는 대학에서 물리학을 전공했다.

572 **chemical**
[kémikəl]

chemistry 명 화학; (사람 사이의) 화학 반응

connected with chemistry

형 화학의, 화학적인 명 화학 물질

a **chemical** laboratory 화학 실험실, 화학 연구소
Burning plastic can produce toxic **chemicals**.
플라스틱을 태우면 독성 화학 물질이 생성될 수 있다.

573 **mechanical**
[məkǽnikəl]

mechanic 명 수리공, 정비사
machine 명 기계
machinery 명 기계류

relating to machinery; having or using machinery

형 1. 기계의, 기계와 관련된 2. 기계로 작동되는

The flight was canceled due to **mechanical** problems.
그 항공편은 기계적 결함으로 인해 취소되었다.
a **mechanical** toy (태엽을 감는 등의) 기계 장치로 된 장난감

574 **logical**
[lɑ́dʒikəl]

logic 명 논리, 타당성

agreeing with the rules of logic; sensible or reasonable

형 1. 논리적인 2. 타당한, 사리에 맞는

His explanation was clear and **logical**. 그의 설명은 명확하고 논리적이었다.
It was a **logical** conclusion. 그것은 타당한 결론이었다.

575 **install**
[instɔ́:l]

installation 명 설치

to put a piece of equipment somewhere and make it ready to use

동 1. (장비 등을) 설치하다 2. (프로그램을) 설치하다, 깔다

They have **installed** a security system. 그들은 보안 시스템을 설치했다.
We've **installed** new anti-virus software. 우리는 새 바이러스 검사 소프트웨어를 설치했다.

576 **insert**
[insə́:rt]

insertion 명 삽입, 끼워넣기

to put something inside or into something else

동 1. 넣다, 끼우다 2. (글 등을) 삽입하다, 끼워 넣다 ((in/into))

insert the key **into** the lock 열쇠를 자물쇠에 넣다[끼우다]
He **inserted** his card **into** the ATM. 그는 현금 자동 인출기(ATM)에 카드를 넣었다.
insert a new paragraph **in** the article 기사에 새 단락을 삽입하다

577 **innovation**
[ìnəvéiʃən]

innovate 동 혁신하다
innovative 형 혁신적인, 획기적인

a new idea or method, or the use of new ideas and methods
명 혁신, 쇄신, 획기적인 것

Technological **innovation** in AI is amazing. AI 분야의 기술 혁신은 놀랍다.
Constant **innovation** is essential for success. 끊임없는 혁신은 성공에 필수적이다.

578 **revolution**
[rèvəlúːʃən]

revolutionary 형 혁명의, 혁명적인 명 혁명가

a significant and often violent change in political power or government
명 혁명, 대변혁

The French **Revolution** began in 1789. 프랑스 혁명은 1789년에 시작되었다.
This discovery caused a **revolution** in medicine. 이 발견은 의학계에 혁명을 일으켰다.

579 **carry out**

to do and complete a task; to conduct
~을 수행하다, ~을 이행하다

We will **carry out** a survey about the matter. 우리는 그 문제에 대해 설문 조사를 실시할 것이다.
Scientists **carried out** experiments to test the theory.
과학자들은 그 이론을 검증하기 위해 실험을 했다.

580 **have good chemistry (with)**

to have a strong, positive connection with another person
(~와) 잘 통하다, 케미가 좋다

We **have** very **good chemistry**. 우리는 아주 잘 통한다.
I **have good chemistry with** my colleagues. 나는 내 동료들과 잘 맞는다.

Check Up

A 우리말에 맞게 빈칸에 알맞은 말을 넣으세요.

1. 실험을 실시하다 conduct an ________________
2. 안전 절차를 따르다 follow the safety ________________
3. 단단한 물체 a ________________ object
4. 막대 자석 a bar ________________
5. AI 분야의 기술 혁신 technological ________________ in AI
6. 프랑스 혁명 the French ________________

B 우리말에 알맞은 말을 골라 문장을 완성하세요.

1. Let's (**proceed** / **procedure**) with the schedule as planned. 계획대로 일정을 진행합시다.
2. Diamond is the hardest (**solid** / **substance**). 다이아몬드는 가장 단단한 물질이다.
3. The flight was canceled due to (**mechanical** / **logical**) problems.
그 항공편은 기계적 결함으로 인해 취소되었다.
4. They have (**inserted** / **installed**) a security system. 그들은 보안 시스템을 설치했다.
5. We have very good (**chemical** / **chemistry**). 우리는 아주 잘 통한다.

Build Up

A Write the correct word for each definition.

insert	upward	solid	laboratory	evaporate	liquid

1. 

a room used for scientific experiments

2. 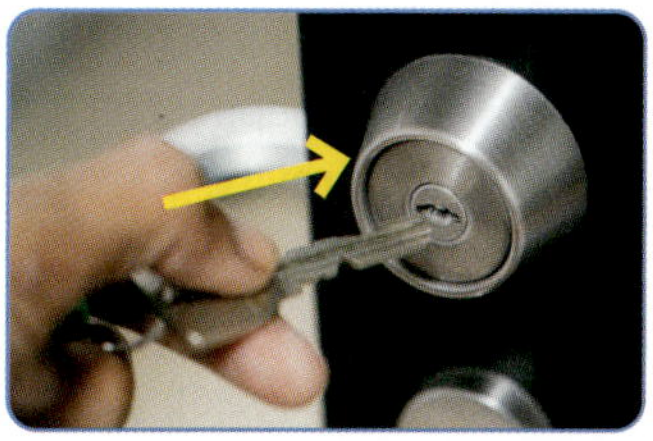

to put something inside

3. 

firm or hard

4. 

flowing freely like water

5. 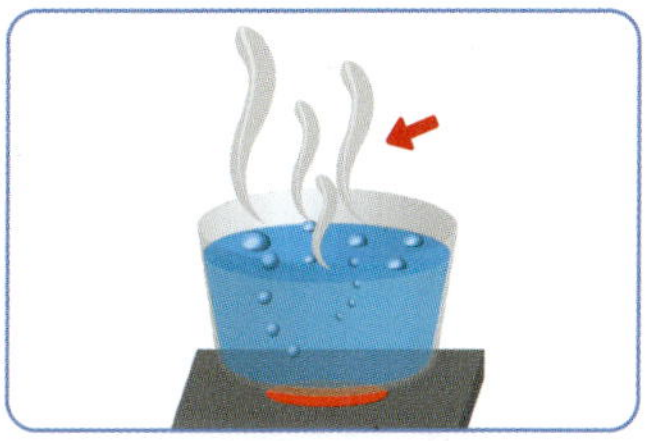

to change from a liquid into a gas

6. 

toward a higher position

B Write the correct word or phrase next to each definition.

magnet	experiment	mechanical	logical	chemical	carry out

1. a test done in order to learn or discover something
2. an iron object that makes other pieces of iron move toward it
3. connected with chemistry
4. relating to machinery; having or using machinery
5. agreeing with the rules of logic; sensible or reasonable
6. to do and complete a task; to conduct

DAY 30

581 **gravity**
[grǽvəti]

the force that causes objects to fall to the ground
명 중력, 지구 인력 *gravitation (만유)인력, 중력

Newton's law of **gravity** 뉴턴의 중력의 법칙
Gravity keeps us on the ground. 중력은 우리가 땅 위에 있도록 해 준다.
In zero **gravity**, objects float instead of falling. 무중력 상태에서 물체는 떨어지지 않고 떠다닌다.

582 **attract**
[ətrǽkt]

attraction 명 끌림, 끌어당김; (사람을 끄는) 명소, 명물; 매력
attractive 형 매력적인

to pull or draw toward oneself or itself
동 1. (자석·중력이) 끌어당기다 2. (흥미 등을) 끌다, 매혹하다

Gravity **attracts** all objects toward the center of the Earth.
중력은 모든 물체를 지구의 중심으로 끌어당긴다.
She **attracts** people like a magnet. 그녀는 자석처럼 사람들을 끌어당긴다.

583 **satellite**
[sǽtəlàit]

an object that moves around a larger object in space
명 1. (행성의) 위성 2. 인공위성

The moon is **a satellite of** Earth. 달은 지구의 위성이다.
launch a **satellite** 인공위성을 발사하다

584 **rotate**
[róuteit]

rotation 명 회전, 자전; 순환, 교대

to move or turn in a circle, especially around a fixed point
동 1. 회전하다; (천체가) 자전하다 = spin 2. (일을) 교대로 하다 *orbit 궤도를 돌다; 궤도

Earth **rotates** once every 24 hours. 지구는 24시간마다 한 번 회전한다[자전한다].
Every 30 days, we **rotate** shifts. 30일마다 우리는 교대 근무를 한다.

585 **motion**
[móuʃən]

move 동 움직이다

the act or process of moving
명 1. 운동, 움직임 2. 동작, 몸짓 = gesture *movement 움직임, 이동

Astronomers record the **motion** of the stars. 천문학자들은 별들의 움직임을 기록한다.
In sign language, different hand **motions** are used. 수화에서는 다양한 손동작[손짓]이 사용된다.

586 **object**
[ábdʒikt]

a thing that you can see or touch, but is not alive
명 1. 물건, 물체 2. 대상 3. 목적, 목표 ((of))

UFO stands for unidentified flying **object**. UFO는 '미확인(정체불명의) 비행 물체'를 나타낸다.
UFOs are interesting **objects** of study. UFO는 흥미로운 연구 대상이다.
the **object of** their research 그들의 연구 목표

587 **alien**
[éiljən]

a creature from another world
명 외계인; 외국인 형 생경한, 이질적인; 외계의

Do **aliens** exist? 외계인은 존재할까?
adjust to an **alien** environment 생경한[외계] 환경에 적응하다

588 **encounter**
[inkáuntər]

to experience something; to meet someone unexpectedly
동 맞닥뜨리다, 마주하다 명 (뜻밖의) 만남, 조우

encounter many difficulties 많은 난관에 맞닥뜨리다
In the movie, the kids **encounter** aliens. 그 영화에서 아이들은 외계인과 조우하게 된다.
an amazing **encounter** 멋진 조우

589 **parallel**
[pǽrəlèl]

extending in the same direction and not meeting

형 1. 평행의, 나란한 ((to)) 2. 유사한, 병행하는

parallel lines 평행선
The two lines are **parallel to** each other. 그 두 선은 서로 평행하다.
the **parallel** universe theory 평행 우주 이론
*하나의 우주에 병행하여 존재하는 또 다른 우주가 있다는 이론 = 다중 우주론(multiverse)

590 **vertical**
[vəːrtikəl]
vertically 부 수직으로

going straight up or down from a surface

형 수직의, 세로의 반 horizontal 수평의, 가로의

vertical line 수직선, 세로선
The cliff was almost **vertical**. 그 절벽은 거의 수직이었다.

591 **military**
[míliteri]

connected with soldiers or the armed forces

형 군의, 군사의 명 (the -) 군, 군대 *army 육군 / navy 해군 / marines 해병대 / air force 공군

military service 군 복무, 병역
join **the military** (군에) 입대하다
He served in **the military** for two years. 그는 2년간 군 복무를 했다.

592 **force**
[fɔːrs]

physical power or strength

명 1. 힘, 무력 2. (육해공군을 포함한) 군대 동 강요하다 ((to))

the **force** of the explosion 폭발의 힘, 폭발력
U.S. **forces** 미국 군대
He **forced** me **to** do it. 그는 내게 그것을 하도록 강요했다.

593 **weapon**
[wépən]

an object (such as a gun or knife) that is used for attacking someone

명 무기, 병기

carry a deadly **weapon** 흉기를 지니다
He is the secret **weapon** on our team. 그는 우리 팀의 비밀 병기이다.

594 **nuclear**
[njúːkliər]

using, producing, or resulting from nuclear energy

형 원자력의; 핵(무기)의

Nuclear energy is used to generate electricity. 원자력[핵에너지]은 전기를 생성하는 데 사용된다.
a **nuclear** power plant 원자력 발전소
nuclear weapons 핵무기

595 **gun**
[gʌn]

a weapon that is used to shoot bullets

명 총 *bullet 총알

He was carrying a **gun**. 그는 총을 소지하고 있었다.
fire a **gun** 총을 쏘다

596 **bomb**
[bɑm]

a weapon that explodes and causes damage

명 폭탄 동 폭탄으로 공격하다, 폭격하다 *missile 미사일

a **bomb** attack 폭탄 공격
A **bomb** exploded in the city center. 도심에서 폭탄이 폭발했다.
The village was **bombed** during the war. 그 마을은 전쟁 중에 폭격을 당했다.

597 **terror**

[térər]

terrorist 명 테러리스트, 테러범
terrorism 명 테러리즘, 테러 행위
terrible 형 끔찍한

a feeling of extreme fear

명 1. 두려움, 공포(심) 2. 테러 (행위) *panic 극심한 공포, 공황

People screamed **in terror.** 사람들은 겁에 질려 비명을 질렀다.
The government declared the war on **terror.** 정부는 테러와의 전쟁을 선포했다.

598 **horror**

[hɔ́ːrər]

horrible 형 끔찍한, 소름끼치는

a strong feeling of shock and fear

명 1. 공포(감), 경악 2. ~의 참상 ((of)) *fear 공포, 두려움

a **horror** movie 공포 영화
The crowd cried out **in horror.** 군중은 공포에 질려 울부짖었다[비명을 질렀다].
the horrors of war 전쟁의 참상

599 **go around**

to move around; to turn around; to orbit

~ 주위를 돌다; (여기저기) 돌아다니다; (병·소문 등이) 돌다

Earth **goes around** the sun. 지구는 태양 주위를 돈다.
He often **goes around** barefoot. 그는 종종 맨발로 돌아다닌다.
A false rumor is **going around.** 거짓 소문이 돌고 있다.

600 **run into**

to meet someone by chance; to bump into; to encounter

~와 우연히 마주치다, ~와 충돌하다[부딪치다]

Guess who I **ran into** today! 오늘 내가 누구와 마주쳤는지 알아맞혀 봐!
His car **ran into** a truck. 그의 차가 트럭과 충돌했다.

Check Up

A 우리말에 맞게 빈칸에 알맞은 말을 넣으세요.

1. 인공위성을 발사하다 launch a ________________
2. 평행선 ________________ lines
3. 미확인 비행 물체 unidentified flying ________________
4. (군에) 입대하다 join ________________
5. 핵무기 ________________ weapons
6. 공포 영화 a ________________ movie

B 우리말에 알맞은 말을 골라 문장을 완성하세요.

1. In (**gravity** / **zero gravity**), objects float instead of falling. 무중력 상태에서 물체는 떨어지지 않고 떠다닌다.
2. Gravity (**attracts** / **keeps**) all objects toward the center of the Earth.
중력은 모든 물체를 지구의 중심으로 끌어당긴다.
3. The moon is a (**satellite** / **object**) of Earth. 달은 지구의 위성이다.
4. The two lines are (**vertical** / **parallel**) to each other. 그 두 선은 서로 평행하다.
5. People screamed (**on terror** / **in terror**). 사람들은 겁에 질려 비명을 질렀다.

Build Up

A Write the correct word for each definition.

weapon	alien	attract	parallel	rotate	vertical

1. 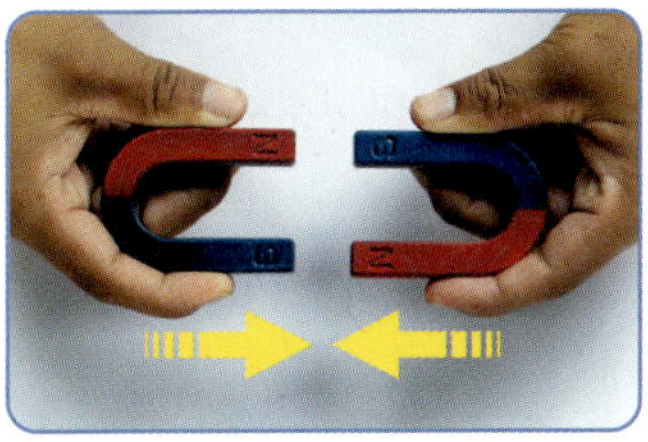

to pull or draw toward oneself

____

2. 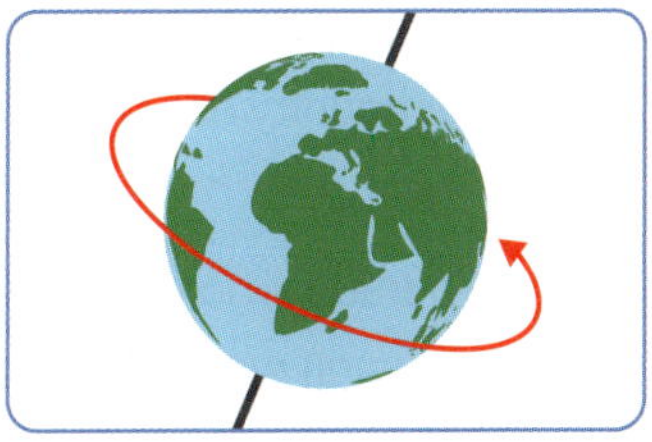

to move or turn in a circle

____

3. 

a creature from another world

____

4. 

an object such as a gun or knife

____

5. 

going straight up or down from a surface

____

6. 

extending in the same direction and not meeting

____

B Write the correct word or phrase next to each definition.

satellite	encounter	gravity	military	go around	nuclear

1. the force that causes objects to fall to the ground ______________________
2. an object that moves around a larger object in space ______________________
3. to experience something; to meet someone unexpectedly ______________________
4. connected with soldiers or the armed forces ______________________
5. using, producing, or resulting from nuclear energy ______________________
6. to move around; to turn around; to orbit ______________________

601 **political**
[pəlítikəl]
politically 부 정치적으로
politics 명 정치
politician 명 정치인

relating to politics or government
형 1. 정치의, 정치적인 2. 정당의

a sensitive **political** issue 민감한 정치적 문제
Our country has two main **political** parties. 우리나라에는 두 주요 정당이 있다.

602 **candidate**
[kǽndidèit]

a person who is trying to be elected or is applying for a job
명 (선거의) 입후보자, (일자리의) 후보자 ((for))

a presidential **candidate** 대통령 후보(자), 대통령 선거 출마자
He is a strong **candidate for** the job. 그는 그 일의 유력한 후보자이다.

603 **council**
[káunsl]

a group of people who are elected to govern an area (such as a city or county)
명 1. (지방 자치 단체의) 의회 2. 협의회, 자문 위원회

a city **council** 시의회
She's on the local **council**. 그녀는 지방 의회 의원이다.
the U.N. Security **Council** 유엔 안전 보장 이사회

604 **consist**
[kənsíst]

to be formed or made up of something
동 (~로) 구성되다, 이루어지다 ((of))

The council **consists of** ten members. 그 위원회는 10명의 위원으로 구성되어 있다.

605 **corrupt**
[kərʌ́pt]
corruption 명 부패, 오염

doing things that are dishonest or illegal
형 1. 부패한, 타락한 = rotten 2. 손상된, 오류가 생긴 동 부패하게 만들다

corrupt politicians 부패한 정치인들
corrupt data 손상된 데이터
Officials were **corrupted** by greed. 관료들[공무원들]은 탐욕으로 인해 부패했다.

606 **decay**
[dikéi]
decayed 형 부패한, 썩은

to be destroyed gradually by natural processes
동 썩다, 부패하다 = rot 명 부식, 부패

In autumn, the leaves fall and begin to **decay**. 가을에는 잎들이 떨어져 썩기 시작한다.
tooth **decay** 충치

607 **resign**
[rizáin]
resignation 명 사임, 사직

to leave a job or position in a formal or official way
동 사임하다, 사직하다, 물러나다 ((from/as))

He **resigned from** his post after the scandal. 그는 그 스캔들 이후 (그의 직에서) 사임했다.
resign as governor 주지사직에서 물러나다

608 **retire**
[ritáiər]
retired 형 은퇴한, 퇴직한
retirement 명 은퇴, 퇴직

to stop doing your job, usually because you are old
동 은퇴하다, 퇴직하다 ((from/as))

She **retired from** teaching two years ago. 그녀는 2년 전에 교직에서 은퇴했다.
retire as principal 교장으로 퇴직하다

609 **liberty**
[líbərti]
liberal 형 자유민주적인, 진보적인

the freedom to do whatever you want without asking for permission
명 (지배·억압 등으로부터의) 자유 유 freedom 자유(로운 상태)

the fight for **liberty** and equality 자유와 평등을 위한 투쟁
The Statue of **Liberty** is a symbol of freedom and democracy.
자유의 여신상은 자유와 민주주의의 상징이다.

610 **party**
[pá:rti]

a political organization with particular beliefs and aims
명 1. 정당, ~당 2. 파티

the Democratic **Party** 민주당
I have always voted for the Green **Party**. 나는 항상 녹색당에 투표해 왔다.
throw a **party** 파티를 열다

611 **civil**
[sívəl]
civilization 명 문명 (사회)

relating to the ordinary people who live in a country
형 1. 시민의, 민간의 2. 내정의, 국내의 *citizen 시민

We should protect our **civil** rights. 우리는 우리의 시민권을 보호해야 한다.
civil war 내전

612 **folk**
[fouk]

people in general
명 1. (보통 folks) 사람들 2. (친근한 호칭) 여러분 형 민속의

Folks around here are pretty friendly. 이곳 사람들은 꽤 친절하다.
All right, **folks**, let's get started. 자, 여러분, 시작합시다.
an Irish **folk** song 아일랜드 민요

613 **justice**
[dʒʌ́stis]

the fair treatment of people
명 1. 정의, 공정(성) 2. 사법; 재판

They fought for **justice** and liberty. 그들은 정의와 자유를 위해 싸웠다.
a court of **justice** 법원

614 **justify**
[dʒʌ́stəfài]

to show that someone or something is right or reasonable
동 정당화하다, 옳음을 증명하다 *judge 판단하다, 평가하다; 판사

He tried to **justify** his behavior. 그는 자신의 행동을 정당화하려고 했다.
Violence cannot be **justified** no matter what. 폭력은 어떤 상황에서도 정당화될 수 없다.

615 **legal**
[lí:gəl]
legally 부 법률상, 법적으로; 합법적으로

connected with the law; allowed by the law
형 1. 법률의 2. 합법의, 합법적인

the **legal** system 법률 제도
Is it **legal** to fish in this river? 이 강에서 낚시하는 것은 합법인가요?

616 **illegal**
[ilí:gəl]
illegally 부 불법적으로

not allowed by the law
형 불법의, 불법적인

park in **illegal** parking areas 불법 주차 구역에 주차하다
It is **illegal** to park here. 여기에 주차하는 것은 불법이다.
Driving without a license is **illegal**. 면허 없이 운전하는 것은 불법이다.

617 **incident**
[ínsədənt]

a serious or violent event, such as a crime or an accident

명 (범죄 등의) 사건, 일 *accident (우연한) 사고

There was a shooting **incident** last night. 어젯밤에 총격 사건이 있었다.
Police are investigating the **incident**. 경찰이 그 사건을 조사하고 있다.

618 **coincide**
[kòuinsáid]

coincidence 명 우연의 일치; 동시 발생

to take place at the same time

동 1. 동시에 일어나다 2. 일치하다, 아주 비슷하다 ((with))

The two incidents **coincided**. 그 두 사건은 동시에 일어났다.
His opinion **coincides with** mine. 그의 의견은 나의 의견과 일치한다.

619 **consist of**

to be made up of; to be composed of

~로 이루어지다, ~로 구성되다

A soccer team **consists of** eleven players. 축구 팀은 11명의 선수로 이루어져 있다.
Breakfast **consisted of** cereal, milk, and fruit.
아침 식사는 시리얼, 우유, 그리고 과일로 구성되어 있었다.

620 **step down (from)**

to leave your job or official position

(요직 등에서) 물러나다, 사임하다 = step aside

He has **stepped down** as chairperson. 그는 의장직에서 물러났다.
He was forced to **step down from** his post. 그는 자리[직책]에서 물러나야 했다.

Check Up

A 우리말에 맞게 빈칸에 알맞은 말을 넣으세요.

1. 민감한 정치적 문제 — a sensitive ______________ issue
2. 교장으로 퇴직하다 — ______________ as principal
3. 자유의 여신상 — the Statue of ______________
4. 민주당 — the Democratic ______________
5. 법률 제도 — the ______________ system
6. 불법 주차 구역 — ______________ parking areas

B 우리말에 알맞은 말을 골라 문장을 완성하세요.

1. The council (**consists of** / **consists from**) ten members. 그 위원회는 10명의 위원으로 구성되어 있다.
2. In autumn, the leaves fall and begin to (**corrupt** / **decay**). 가을에는 잎들이 떨어져 썩기 시작한다.
3. He (**retired** / **resigned**) from his post after the scandal. 그는 그 스캔들 이후 (그의 직에서) 사임했다.
4. He tried to (**justice** / **justify**) his behavior. 그는 자신의 행동을 정당화하려고 했다.
5. There was a shooting (**incident** / **accident**) last night. 어젯밤에 총격 사건이 있었다.

Build Up

A Write the correct word for each definition.

candidate	folk	resign	incident	illegal	party

1. 

a person who is trying to be elected

____

2. 

to leave a job or position

____

3. 

a political organization

____

4. 

people in general

____

5. 

not allowed by the law

____

6. 

a serious or violent event

____

B Write the correct word or phrase next to each definition.

consist of	corrupt	retire	justify	coincide	civil

1. doing things that are dishonest or illegal ______________
2. to stop doing your job, usually because you are old ______________
3. relating to the ordinary people who live in a country ______________
4. to show that someone or something is right or reasonable ______________
5. to take place at the same time ______________
6. to be made up of; to be composed of ______________

621 **criminal** [kríminl]
crime 명 범죄, 범행

relating to crime; involving illegal activity
형 범죄의 명 범죄자, 범인

do **criminal** behavior 범죄 행위를 하다
He is a dangerous **criminal**. 그는 위험한 범죄자이다.

622 **commit** [kəmít]

to do something illegal or something that is considered wrong
동 (범죄·잘못 등을) 저지르다, 범하다

He **committed** a serious crime. 그는 심각한 범죄를 저질렀다.

623 **rob** [rɑb]
robbery 명 강도(질)
robber 명 강도

to steal money or property from a person or place
동 (돈·재산을) 강탈하다, 강도질을 하다 *steal 훔치다

They **robbed** a bank downtown. 그들은 시내의 한 은행을 털었다.
She was **robbed** while walking home. 그녀는 집으로 걸어가던 중 강도를 당했다.

624 **murder** [mə́:rdər]
murderer 명 살인자

the crime of intentionally killing a person
명 살인 동 살인하다, 살해하다 *kill 죽이다

The man committed **murder**. 그 남자는 살인을 저질렀다.
He denies **murdering** the clerk. 그는 그 점원을 살해한 것을 부인하고 있다.

625 **evidence** [évədəns]
evident 형 분명한, 눈에 띄는
evidently 부 분명히, 눈에 띄게

facts, signs, or objects that show clearly that something is true
명 증거, 증거물 ((for)) 유 proof 증거(물), 증명

Is there any **evidence for** that? 그것에 대한 증거가 있나요?
No new **evidence** has been found. 새로운 증거는 발견되지 않았다.

626 **clue** [klu:]

a piece of evidence or information that helps you solve a crime or mystery
명 (범행의) 단서, (문제 해결의) 실마리

Finally, police have found a vital **clue**. 마침내 경찰은 결정적 단서를 찾았다.
provide a **clue** 실마리를 제공하다

627 **witness** [wítnis]

someone who sees a crime or an accident
명 (사건·사고의) 목격자 ((to)) 동 목격하다

Police are looking for **witnesses to** the shooting. 경찰은 그 총격 사건의 목격자를 찾고 있다.
Several people **witnessed** the incident. 여러 사람이 그 사건을 목격했다.

628 **emerge** [imə́:rdʒ]
emergent 형 나타나는; 신생의, 신흥의

to come out of a dark or hidden place
동 1. (어둠 등에서) 나오다, 모습을 드러내다 2. 드러나다, 알려지다 *appear 나타나다

He **emerged** from the darkness. 그가 어둠 속에서 모습을 드러냈다.
Eventually, the truth **emerged**. 결국 진실이 드러났다.

629 **suspect**
[səspékt]

to think that someone may have committed a crime or done something bad
동 의심하다, 혐의를 두다 ((of)) 명 [sʌ́spekt] 용의자 *doubt 의심하다; 의심

The police **suspect** him **of** murder. 경찰은 그를 살인 혐의로 의심하고 있다.
He is a **suspect** in the murder case. 그는 살인 사건의 용의자이다.

630 **victim**
[víktim]

a person who has been hurt or killed by a crime or an accident
명 피해자, 희생자

victims of crime 범죄 피해자들
The identity of the **victim** is not known. 피해자의 신원은 알려지지 않았다.

631 **trace**
[treis]

to find or discover something by following its evidence or marks
동 추적하다, (추적하여) 찾아내다 = track down 명 자취, 흔적

They **traced** the suspect's whereabouts. 그들은 용의자의 행방을 추적했다.
vanish **without a trace** 흔적도 없이 사라지다

632 **pursue**
[pərsúː]
pursuit 명 추구; 뒤쫓음, 추적

to follow or chase someone or something to catch them
동 1. 뒤쫓다, 추격하다 = chase, run after 2. 추구하다

The suspect is being **pursued** by police. 그 용의자는 경찰에 쫓기고 있다.
pursue a goal 목표를 추구하다

633 **arrest**
[ərést]

to seize someone by legal authority
동 체포하다, 구속하다 ((for)) 명 체포 *catch 잡다, 붙잡다

The police **arrested** the suspect. 경찰이 그 용의자를 체포했다.
He was **arrested for** robbery. 그는 강도 혐의로 체포되었다.
You are **under arrest** for theft. 당신을 절도 혐의로 체포합니다.

634 **accuse**
[əkjúːz]
accusation 명 고발, 기소; 비난

to claim that someone has done something wrong or illegal
동 1. 비난하다 = blame 2. 고발하다, 기소하다 ((of))

They **accused** him **of** cheating on the exam. 그들은 그가 시험에서 부정행위를 했다고 비난했다.
He was **accused of** murder. 그는 살인 혐의로 기소되었다.

635 **guilty**
[gílti]
guilt 명 유죄(임); 죄책감

responsible for committing a crime or doing something bad
형 1. 유죄의 ((of)) 2. 죄책감을 느끼는

The jury found him **guilty of** murder. 배심원단은 그가 살인에 대해 유죄라고 판단했다.
She **felt guilty** about lying. 그녀는 거짓말한 것에 대해 죄책감을 느꼈다.

636 **innocent**
[ínəsənt]
innocence 명 결백, 무죄; 순진

not guilty of a crime or other wrong act
형 1. 무죄의, 결백한 2. 순결한, 순진한

She thinks he is **innocent**. 그녀는 그가 무죄라고 생각한다.
an **innocent** young child 순진한 어린 아이

637 **prison**
[prízn]

prisoner 명 재소자, 죄수; 포로

a place where criminals are kept as a punishment

명 교도소

The robber was sent to **prison**. 그 강도는 교도소로 보내졌다(교도소에 수감되었다).
He is **in prison** for robbery. 그는 강도죄로 교도소에 수감되어 있다.

638 **jail**
[dʒeil]

a prison, especially a small local prison

명 감옥, 구치소 동 [주로 수동태로] 투옥하다, 수감하다 ((for))

go to **jail** 감옥에 가다
He was **jailed for** 30 years for murder. 그는 살인죄로 30년 형에 처해졌다.

639 **so far**

until now; up to this point

지금까지, 이 시점까지

How's your work? – **So far**, so good. 당신의 일은 어때요? – 지금까지는 좋아요.
So far, everything is going well as planned. 지금까지 모든 것이 계획대로 잘 진행되고 있다.

640 **not only A but also B**

B as well as A

A뿐만 아니라 B도 역시

He was accused of **not only** theft **but also** robbery.
그는 절도뿐만 아니라 강도 혐의로도 기소되었다.
She enjoys **not only** hiking **but also** camping. 그녀는 하이킹뿐만 아니라 캠핑도 즐긴다.
She **not only** wrote the text **but also** drew the illustrations.
그녀는 글을 썼을 뿐만 아니라 삽화도 그렸다.

Check Up

A 우리말에 맞게 빈칸에 알맞은 말을 넣으세요.

1. 범죄 행위를 하다 — do ______________ behavior
2. 결정적 단서를 찾다 — find a vital ______________
3. 목격자를 찾다[구하다] — look for ______________
4. 흔적도 없이 사라지다 — vanish without ______________
5. 감옥에 가다 — go to ______________
6. 순진한 어린 아이 — an ______________ young child

B 우리말에 알맞은 말을 골라 문장을 완성하세요.

1. He is a (victim / suspect) in the murder case. 그는 살인 사건의 용의자이다.
2. He was (arrested / accused) for robbery. 그는 강도 혐의로 체포되었다.
3. He was (arrested / accused) of murder. 그는 살인 혐의로 기소되었다.
4. She thinks he is (guilty / innocent). 그녀는 그가 유죄라고 생각한다.
5. He is (under prison / in prison) for robbery. 그는 강도죄로 교도소에 수감되어 있다.

Build Up

A Write the correct word for each definition.

trace	witness	rob	arrest	prison	pursue

1. 

to steal money or property

____

2. 

someone who sees a crime or an accident

____

3. 

to track down

____

4. 

to follow or chase someone

____

5. 

to seize someone by legal authority

____

6. 

a place where criminals are kept

____

B Write the correct word or phrase next to each definition.

victim	murder	evidence	guilty	commit	not only A but also B

1. to do something illegal or something that is considered wrong ________________
2. the crime of intentionally killing a person ________________
3. facts, signs, or objects that show clearly that something is true ________________
4. a person who has been hurt or killed by a crime or an accident ________________
5. responsible for committing a crime or doing something bad ________________
6. B as well as A ________________

Review Test 08 DAY 29-32

A 그림을 보고, 빈칸에 알맞은 단어를 넣으세요.

magnet horror laboratory witness evaporate candidate

1. 

____

2. 

____

3. 

____

4. 

____

5. 

____

6. 

____

B 그림에 맞게 빈칸에 알맞은 단어를 고르세요.

1. 

Ice is ______________________ form of water.
(a solid / a liquid)

2. 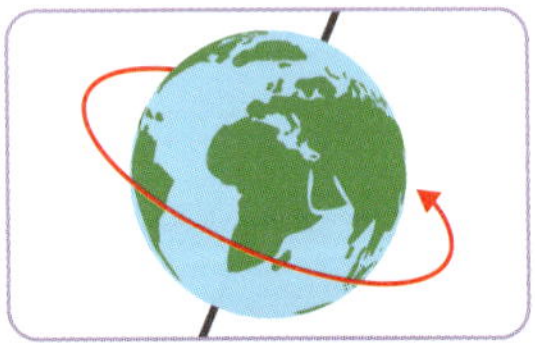

Earth ______________________ once every 24 hours.
(orbits / rotates)

3. 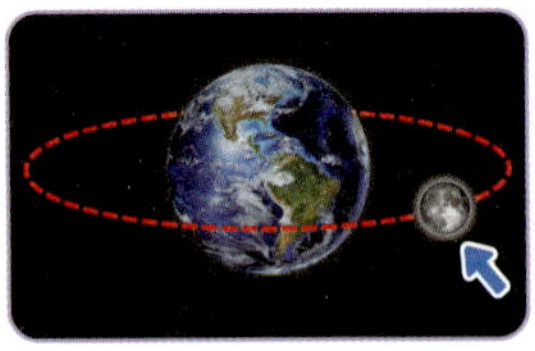

The moon is a ______________________ of Earth.
(planet / satellite)

4. 

In autumn, the leaves fall and begin to ______________________.
(decay / corrupt)

C 우리말 뜻에 맞게 빈칸에 알맞은 말을 넣으세요.

chemicals	innovation	experiment	carry out
weapon	satellite	victims	the military

1. conduct an ____________________ 실험을 (실시)하다
2. produce toxic ____________________ 독성 화학 물질을 생성하다
3. technological ____________________ in AI AI 분야의 기술 혁신
4. ____________________ a survey 설문 조사를 실시하다
5. launch a ____________________ 인공위성을 발사하다
6. join ____________________ (군에) 입대하다
7. carry a deadly ____________________ 흉기를 지니다
8. ____________________ of crime 범죄 피해자들

D 우리말 뜻에 맞게 빈칸에 알맞은 말을 넣으세요.

zero gravity	consisted of	so far
proceed with	flying object	good chemistry

1. Let's ____________________ the schedule as planned. 계획대로 일정을 진행합시다.
2. We have very ____________________. 우리는 아주 잘 통한다.
3. In ____________________, objects float instead of falling.
   무중력 상태에서 물체는 떨어지지 않고 떠다닌다.
4. UFO stands for unidentified ____________________. UFO는 '미확인(정체불명의) 비행 물체'를 나타낸다.
5. Breakfast ____________________ cereal, milk, and fruit.
   아침 식사는 시리얼, 우유, 그리고 과일로 구성되어 있었다.
6. ____________________, everything is going well as planned.
   지금까지 모든 것이 계획대로 잘 진행되고 있다.

E 밑줄 친 단어와 비슷한 뜻을 가진 단어를 고르세요.

1. Diamond is the hardest substance.

   a. material b. solid c. liquid

2. Gravity attracts all objects toward the center of the Earth.

   a. pushes b. pulls c. floats

3. Earth goes around the sun.

   a. rotates b. spins c. orbits

4. He was forced to step down from his post.

   a. retire b. emerge c. resign

F 밑줄 친 단어와 반대의 뜻을 가진 단어를 고르세요.

1. They have installed a security system.

   a. refused b. rejected c. removed

2. The cliff was almost vertical.

   a. horizontal b. parallel c. circle

3. Driving without a license is illegal.

   a. fair b. justice c. legal

4. She thinks he is innocent.

   a. responsible b. guilty c. criminal

G 주어진 영영풀이에 알맞은 단어를 고르세요.

1. relating to machinery; having or using machinery

   a. mechanical　　b. physical　　c. logical

2. a significant and often violent change in political power or government

   a. innovation　　b. revolution　　c. operation

3. the force that causes objects to fall to the ground

   a. nuclear　　b. motion　　c. gravity

4. doing things that are dishonest or illegal

   a. decay　　b. corrupt　　c. commit

5. the freedom to do whatever you want without asking for permission

   a. liberty　　b. party　　c. democracy

6. facts, signs, or objects that show clearly that something is true

   a. clue　　b. witness　　c. evidence

H 빈칸에 알맞은 동사 형태를 넣어 문장을 완성하세요.

1. We have ____________ new anti-virus software. (install)
2. Violence cannot be ____________ no matter what. (justify)
3. The suspect is being ____________ by police. (pursue)
4. She ____________ while walking home. (rob)

ANSWER KEY

DAY 01

Check Up .... p. 8

A 1. virtual 2. memorable 3. selfie
4. pose for 5. edit 6. immediate / instant

B 1. revised 2. brilliant 3. imitate
4. on her own 5. impact

Build Up .... p. 9

A 1. virtual 2. selfie 3. immediate
4. incredible 5. resemble 6. imitate

B 1. unrealistic 2. imaginary 3. snap
4. technique 5. unbelievable 6. on one's own

DAY 02

Check Up .... p. 12

A 1. broadcast 2. fame 3. celebrity
4. profile 5. pity 6. twist

B 1. have been rivals 2. by instinct 3. offended
4. sympathy for 5. showing off

Build Up .... p. 13

A 1. channel 2. celebrity 3. applaud
4. profile 5. supervise 6. insult

B 1. broadcast 2. passion 3. cast
4. sympathy 5. be scheduled to 6. interview

DAY 03

Check Up .... p. 16

A 1. weird 2. spell 3. insight
4. fragile / delicate 5. delicate 6. caution

B 1. enabled 2. distinguish 3. perspective
4. sensible 5. make up for

Build Up .... p. 17

A 1. wicked 2. distinct 3. fragile
4. cautious 5. sensitive 6. humble

B 1. enable 2. distinguish 3. modest
4. dedicate 5. make up with 6. insight

DAY 04

Check Up .... p. 20

A 1. fake 2. genuine 3. ashamed
4. a state of 5. certificate 6. valid

B 1. identified 2. swear to 3. ensure
4. get permission 5. approve of

Build Up .... p. 21

A 1. recognize 2. genuine 3. swear
4. shameful 5. certificate 6. consent

B 1. ensure 2. status 3. permit
4. approve 5. qualify 6. identify A with B

DAY 01-04

Review Test 01 pp. 22-25

A 1. virtual 2. applaud 3. profile
4. certificate 5. wicked 6. fragile

B 1. resembles 2. imitate 3. celebrity
4. swear to

C 1. pose for 2. take after 3. on my own
4. broadcast 5. sympathy for 6. a spell
7. distinguish 8. make up for

D 1. impact on 2. by instinct 3. show off
4. in a state of 5. get permission
6. identify, with

E 1. c 2. b 3. c 4. b

F 1. b 2. a 3. b 4. c

G 1. b 2. c 3. a 4. a 5. c 6. b

H 1. imitated 2. broadcast 3. dedicated to
4. recognized as

DAY 05

Check Up .... p. 28

A 1. opportunity 2. survey 3. profound
4. mass 5. at random / randomly 6. put up

B 1. opted for 2. assess 3. moderate
4. endure 5. in depth

Build Up .... p. 29

A 1. seize 2. opt 3. precise
4. evaluate 5. moderate 6. durable

B 1. optimist 2. random 3. endure
4. length 5. maximum 6. put up with

DAY 06

Check Up .... p. 32

A 1. affairs 2. series of 3. benefits
4. cheat on 5. participate / take part
6. excess of

B 1. on trend 2. deceived by 3. exceed
4. sufficient 5. stand out

Build Up .... p. 33

A 1. burden 2. participate 3. fabric
4. leather 5. slight 6. bubble

B 1. deceive 2. protest 3. brand
4. efficient 5. stand out 6. affair

DAY 07

Check Up .... p. 36

A 1. entrance 2. exit 3. security
4. a while 5. regulate 6. penalty

B 1. while 2. since 3. excludes
4. unless 5. restricted

Build Up .... p. 37

A 1. exit 2. approach 3. bar
4. prohibit 5. violate 6. penalty

B 1. security 2. since 3. exclude
4. regulate 5. forbid 6. as soon as

DAY 08

Check Up .... p. 40

A 1. passage 2. flash 3. explode
4. rescue 5. nightmare 6. faint

B 1. neighborhood 2. polished
3. has been neglected 4. were trapped
5. as long as

Build Up .... p. 41

A 1. facility 2. internal 3. sparkle
4. nightmare 5. explode 6. rescue

B 1. polish 2. cease 3. neglect
4. flame 5. approximately 6. drown

DAY 05-08

Review Test 02 pp. 42-45

A 1. durable 2. approach 3. bar
4. neighborhood 5. explode 6. faint

B 1. in depth 2. a maximum of 3. exceed
4. prohibited

C 1. opportunity 2. opt for 3. at random
4. a series of 5. burden 6. an excess of
7. stand out 8. penalty

D 1. benefits of 2. cheated on
3. protested against 4. efficient for
5. as soon as 6. as long as

E 1. b 2. c 3. a 4. c

F 1. a 2. c 3. a 4. b

G 1. a 2. b 3. a 4. b 5. c 6. a

H 1. violating 2. ceased 3. neglected
4. regulated

DAY 09

Check Up .... p. 48

A 1. suffer 2. struggle 3. symptoms
4. critical 5. relief 6. surgery / an operation

B 1. were paralyzed 2. critical 3. crucial
4. recovery 5. relieve

Build Up .... p. 49

A 1. stiff 2. paralyze 3. crucial
4. await 5. relieve 6. remarkable

B 1. symptom 2. therefore 3. nevertheless
4. rational 5. keep (something) in mind
6. patient

DAY 10

Check Up .... p. 52

A 1. vaccine 2. shot 3. bandage
4. addicted to 5. alternative
6. over-the-counter

B 1. has infected 2. were infected 3. sneeze
4. addicted 5. broke out

Build Up .... p. 53

A 1. virus 2. inject 3. nerve
4. therapy 5. marvel 6. heal

B 1. infect 2. tense 3. thumb
4. alternative 5. ultimate 6. snore

DAY 11

Check Up .... p. 56

A 1. companion 2. flexible 3. suspended
4. discipline 5. consult 6. give off

B 1. associate 2. existence 3. prejudice
4. spoiled 5. desperate

Build Up .... p. 57

A 1. resident 2. accompany 3. commute
4. destiny 5. spoil 6. divorce

B 1. companion 2. discipline 3. suspend
4. fate 5. despair 6. for good

DAY 12

Check Up .... p. 60

A 1. smash 2. seal 3. mild
4. generate 5. fuel 6. short of

B 1. Electric 2. blend with 3. refrigerator
4. function 5. preserve

Build Up .... p. 61

A 1. bunch 2. ingredient 3. blend
4. squeeze 5. smash 6. dairy

B 1. core 2. electric 3. utilize
4. preserve 5. generate 6. fuel

DAY 09-12

Review Test 03 pp. 62-65

A 1. patient 2. inject 3. shot
4. nerve 5. destiny 6. bunch

B 1. critical 2. has infected 3. give off
4. Electric

C 1. suffer 2. struggle 3. a sigh of relief
4. rational 5. alternative 6. over-the-counter
7. divorce 8. fuel

D 1. be patient 2. get a vaccine 3. addicted to
4. alternative to 5. suspended for
6. desperate to

E 1. c 2. a 3. c 4. b

F 1. c 2. b 3. c 4. a

G 1. c 2. b 3. c 4. a 5. c 6. a

H 1. paralyzed 2. underwent surgery
3. broke out 4. spoiled

DAY 13

Check Up .... p. 68

A 1. wealth 2. rent 3. deposit
4. temporary 5. frequent 6. input

B 1. in poverty 2. owes 3. inquire
4. disrupted 5. getting up

Build Up .... p. 69

A 1. wealth 2. poverty 3. temporary
4. permanent 5. spare 6. waterproof

B 1. rent 2. owe 3. frequent
4. disrupt 5. interfere 6. credit

DAY 14

Check Up .... p. 72

A 1. journal 2. submit 3. agent
4. forecast 5. predict 6. assemble

B 1. subscribe to 2. reform 3. restored
4. reproduce 5. threat

Build Up .... p. 73

A 1. subscribe 2. outcome 3. revive
4. assemble 5. reproduce 6. threat

B 1. institute 2. submit 3. acquire
4. forecast 5. take a risk 6. recruit

DAY 15

Check Up .... p. 76

A 1. up-to-date 2. converts 3. analyze
4. decline / decrease 5. fulfill
6. get rid of / dispose of

B 1. imports 2. distributed 3. transform
4. adjusted 5. postponed

Build Up .... p. 77

A 1. the latest 2. distribute 3. transform
4. modify 5. decline 6. dispose

B 1. contribute 2. convert 3. adjust
4. diminish 5. analysis 6. dismiss

DAY 16

Check Up .... p. 80

A 1. wage 2. prior 3. phase 4. conference
5. compromise 6. compensate for

B 1. prior 2. aspect 3. considerable
4. have collaborated 5. negotiating

Build Up .... p. 81

A 1. phase 2. conference 3. cooperate
4. negotiate 5. complement 6. neutral

B 1. finance 2. considerable 3. considerate
4. coordinate 5. to one's surprise 6. priority

DAY 13-16

Review Test 04 pp. 82-85

A 1. spare 2. waterproof 3. threat
4. up to date 5. dispose 6. conference

B 1. disrupted 2. forecast 3. reproduce
4. transform into

C 1. deposit 2. journal 3. predict
4. restore 5. the latest 6. analyze
7. wage 8. prior engagement

D 1. in poverty 2. owes 3. subscribe to
4. a risk of 5. adjusted to 6. compensate for

E 1. a 2. c 3. a 4. b

F 1. b 2. b 3. a 4. c

G 1. c 2. b 3. a 4. b 5. c 6. b

H 1. recruiting 2. analyzed 3. collaborated
4. negotiating

DAY 17

Check Up .... p. 88

A 1. historic 2. an era 3. a crown
4. royal 5. heritage 6. ruins of

B 1. Dynasty 2. loyal to 3. noble
4. has undergone 5. looked back

Build Up .... p. 89

A 1. ancient 2. contemporary 3. kingdom
4. tomb 5. remains 6. ruin

B 1. empire 2. crown 3. royal
4. undergo 5. date back to 6. knight

DAY 18

Check Up .... p. 92

A 1. victory 2. capture / occupy 3. declare
4. glory 5. withstand 6. surrounded

B 1. conquered 2. captured 3. vanished
4. moreover 5. descended

Build Up .... p. 93

A 1. invade 2. descend 3. glow
4. wander 5. vanish 6. fade

B 1. conquer 2. defense 3. capture
4. withstand 5. population 6. multiply

DAY 19

Check Up .... p. 96

A 1. immigration 2. migrating 3. origin
4. tribe 5. customs 6. involved in

B 1. immigrated 2. migrate 3. ethnic
4. distance 5. independent

Build Up .... p. 97

A 1. immigrate 2. migrate 3. obey
4. distant 5. dispute 6. independent

B 1. immigration 2. migration 3. custom
4. settle down 5. race 6. servant

DAY 20

Check Up .... p. 100

A 1. district 2. border 3. boundary
4. democracy 5. Embassy 6. welfare

B 1. suburb 2. counties 3. provinces
4. zone 5. known for

Build Up .... p. 101

A 1. urban 2. rural 3. county
4. border 5. govern 6. embassy

B 1. suburb 2. province 3. authority
4. republic 5. ambassador 6. diplomat

DAY 17-20

Review Test 05 pp. 102-105

A 1. crown 2. knight 3. remains
4. district 5. border 6. boundary

B 1. loyal to 2. ruined 3. surrounded
4. migration

C 1. historic 2. cultural heritage 3. ruins
4. declare 5. origin of 6. dispute
7. zone 8. ambassador to

D 1. in defense of 2. won a victory
3. wandered 4. descended from
5. immigrated to 6. in the distance

E 1. b 2. c 3. a 4. b

F 1. a 2. b 3. c 4. a

G 1. c 2. b 3. a 4. c 5. c 6. a

H 1. was conquered 2. were captured
3. multiplied 4. involved in

DAY 21

Check Up .... p. 108

A 1. religion 2. heaven 3. mercy
4. creation 5. sacrifice 6. temple

B 1. miracle 2. creatures 3. sacred
4. confessed to 5. silence

Build Up .... p. 109

A 1. worship 2. bless 3. creature
4. holy 5. silence 6. meditate

B 1. religious 2. miracle 3. sacred
4. heaven 5. hell 6. priest

DAY 22

Check Up .... p. 112

A 1. sculpture 2. crafts 3. abstract
4. contrast 5. artificial 6. pile

B 1. carved 2. sculpted 3. annual
4. attached 5. In contrast to

Build Up .... p. 113

A 1. sculpture 2. statue 3. antique
4. portrait 5. landscape 6. quarter

B 1. sculpt 2. contrast 3. contrary
4. artificial 5. in contrast to 6. craft

DAY 23

Check Up .... p. 116

A 1. string 2. ideal 3. conduct
4. compose 5. composers 6. the volume

B 1. classical 2. touched 3. ever
4. clip 5. composed of

Build Up .... p. 117

A 1. instrument 2. string 3. conductor
4. composer 5. clip 6. stream

B 1. classical 2. conduct 3. dynamic
4. touched 5. engage 6. be engaged in

DAY 24

Check Up .... p. 120

A 1. literature 2. theme 3. author / writer
4. science-fiction 5. philosophy
6. conscience

B 1. myth 2. summary 3. verbal
4. implied 5. did the trick

Build Up .... p. 121

A 1. novel 2. myth 3. paragraph
4. lyric 5. tragic 6. trick

B 1. fiction 2. philosophy 3. ethic
4. quote 5. take away 6. conscience

DAY 21-24

Review Test 06 pp. 122-125

A 1. temple 2. carve 3. craft
4. portrait 5. abstract 6. contrast

B 1. landscapes 2. Statue 3. composers
4. fiction

C 1. religion 2. silence 3. ice sculpture
4. contrary to 5. in contrast to 6. classical
7. author 8. conscience

D 1. creatures 2. sacrificed 3. confessed to
4. string instruments 5. streaming service
6. take away

E 1. a 2. b 3. c 4. a

F 1. c 2. a 3. a 4. b

G 1. c 2. a 3. b 4. c 5. a 6. c

H 1. are/were crafted 2. is composed
3. was engaged 4. is/was conducted

DAY 25

Check Up .... p. 128

A 1. Pole 2. horizontal 3. plant
4. yield 5. hybrid 6. versus / vs.

B 1. on the horizon 2. fertile 3. cultivate
4. soaked with 5. harvest

Build Up .... p. 129

A 1. grand 2. scenery 3. harsh
4. grain 5. absorb 6. soak

B 1. polar 2. horizon 3. crop
4. yield 5. on the horizon 6. give in (to)

DAY 26

Check Up .... p. 132

A 1. pave, with 2. founded / based
3. equipment 4. replace
5. substitute 6. located

B 1. established 2. founded 3. devices
4. equipped 5. substitute

Build Up .... p. 133

A 1. construct 2. fountain 3. metal
4. complex 5. device 6. split

B 1. architecture 2. establish 3. replace
4. envy 5. site 6. take over

DAY 27

Check Up .... p. 136

A 1. the environment 2. throughout 3. bury
4. pollution 5. avoid / prevent 6. a sudden

B 1. circumstance 2. conserve 3. sudden
4. prevented 5. in danger

Build Up .... p. 137

A 1. bloom 2. shade 3. mount
4. flood 5. lightning 6. secure

B 1. conserve 2. disaster 3. tide
4. put A in danger 5. bury 6. pollution

DAY 28

Check Up .... p. 140

A 1. summit 2. gap 3. earthquake
4. volcano 5. endangered 6. risk of

B 1. peak 2. in haste 3. species
4. prey 5. became extinct

Build Up .... p. 141

A 1. summit 2. steep 3. erupt
4. cell 5. prey 6. extinct

B 1. slope 2. earthquake 3. species
4. range 5. evolve 6. at risk of

DAY 25-28

Review Test 07 pp. 142-145

A 1. polar 2. bury 3. earthquake
4. volcano 5. food chain 6. evolve

B 1. fountain 2. devices 3. buried 4. peak

C 1. harvest 2. versus 3. equipment
4. replace, with 5. split 6. the environment
7. in any circumstance 8. endangered

D 1. fertile soil 2. soaked with
3. on the horizon 4. located on
5. in danger 6. rare species

E 1. a 2. a 3. b 4. c

F 1. a 2. c 3. c 4. b

G 1. a 2. c 3. c 4. a 5. b 6. c

H 1. was constructed 2. is paved with
3. was established 4. was taken over

DAY 29

Check Up .... p. 148

A 1. experiment 2. procedures 3. solid
4. magnet 5. innovation 6. Revolution

B 1. proceed 2. substance 3. mechanical
4. installed 5. chemistry

Build Up .... p. 149

A 1. laboratory 2. insert 3. solid
4. liquid 5. evaporate 6. upward

B 1. experiment 2. magnet 3. chemical
4. mechanical 5. logical 6. carry out

DAY 30

Check Up .... p. 152

A 1. satellite 2. parallel 3. object
4. the military 5. nuclear 6. horror

B 1. zero gravity 2. attracts 3. satellite
4. parallel 5. in terror

Build Up .... p. 153

A 1. attract 2. rotate 3. alien
4. weapon 5. vertical 6. parallel

B 1. gravity 2. satellite 3. encounter
4. military 5. nuclear 6. go around

DAY 31

Check Up .... p. 156

A 1. political 2. retire 3. Liberty
4. Party 5. legal 6. illegal

B 1. consists of 2. decay 3. resigned
4. justify 5. incident

Build Up .... p. 157

A 1. candidate 2. resign 3. party
4. folk 5. illegal 6. incident

B 1. corrupt 2. retire 3. civil
4. justify 5. coincide 6. consist of

DAY 32

Check Up .... p. 160

A 1. criminal 2. clue 3. witnesses
4. a trace 5. jail / prison 6. innocent

B 1. suspect 2. arrested 3. accused
4. guilty 5. in prison

Build Up .... p. 161

A 1. rob 2. witness 3. trace
4. pursue 5. arrest 6. prison

B 1. commit 2. murder 3. evidence
4. victim 5. guilty 6. not only A but also B

DAY 29-32

Review Test 08 — pp. 162-165

A 1. laboratory 2. evaporate 3. magnet
4. horror 5. candidate 6. witness

B 1. a solid 2. rotates 3. satellite 4. decay

C 1. experiment 2. chemicals 3. innovation
4. carry out 5. satellite 6. the military
7. weapon 8. victims

D 1. proceed with 2. good chemistry
3. zero gravity 4. flying object
5. consisted of 6. So far

E 1. a 2. b 3. c 4. c

F 1. c 2. a 3. c 4. b

G 1. a 2. b 3. c 4. b 5. a 6. c

H 1. installed 2. justified 3. pursued
4. was robbed

INDEX

D

E

A*List
VOCA

숙어·구문 표현 연습장

중학
고난도

DAY 01

1. 나는 **가상 현실**(VR)에 관심이 많다.

   I'm interested in ________ ________ (VR).

2. 그 이야기는 **상상의 세계에서** 일어난다.

   The story takes place ___in___ ________ ________ ________.

3. 정말 **기억에 남는[잊지 못할] 하루**였다.

   It was ___a___ truly ________ ________.

4. 나는 해변에서 **셀카를 찍었다**.

   I ________ ________ ________ at the beach.

5. 우리는 사진을 찍기 **위해 포즈를 취했다**.

   We ________ ________ photographs.

6. 그녀는 모델처럼 (멋지게) **포즈를 취했다**.

   She ___struck___ ________ ________ like a model.

7. 그것은 **즉각적인 효과가 있었다**.

   It ___had___ ________ ________ ________.

8. 신기술은 우리의 삶**에** 큰 **영향을 미친다**.

   New technology ___has___ ________ great ________ ________ our lives.

9. 나는 외모가 우리 엄마**를 닮았다**.

   I ________ ________ my mom in looks.

10. 그는 **혼자 힘으로** 그 프로젝트를 끝냈다.

    He finished the project ________ ________ ________.

1. virtual reality (VR) 가상 현실 2. in an imaginary world 상상의 세계에서
3. a memorable day 기억에 남는[잊지 못할] 하루 4. take a selfie 셀카를 찍다
5. pose for ~을 위해 포즈를 취하다 6. strike a pose (멋지게) 포즈를 취하다[잡다]
7. have an (immediate) effect (즉각적인) 효과가 있다 8. have an impact on ~에 영향을 미치다[주다]
9. take after (someone) ~을 닮다 10. on one's own 혼자서, 혼자 힘으로

DAY 02

1. 우리는 그 콘서트의 **생방송**을 시청했다.

   We watched ___a___ ______ ______ of the concert.

2. 그는 하룻밤 사이에 **유명인이 되었다**.

   He ___became___ ______ ______ overnight.

3. 그들은 그 팝스타**와 인터뷰를 했다**.

   They ___had___ ______ ______ ______ the pop star.

4. 그녀는 그것을 **본능적으로** 알았다.

   She knew it ______ ______.

5. 그녀는 그의 농담에 **불쾌감을 느꼈다[기분이 상했다]**.

   She ______ ______ by his joke.

6. 나는 그**에게 동정심을 느꼈다**[그**를 불쌍히 여겼다**/그**가 딱했다**].

   I ___felt___ ______ ______ him.

7. 나는 불우한 사람들**에게 연민을 느낀다**.

   I ___have___ ______ ______ the less fortunate.

8. 그 영화는 **극적인 반전**을 특징으로 한다.

   The movie features ___a___ ______ ______.

9. 그는 자신의 새 차를 **자랑하**기를 좋아한다.

   He likes to ______ ______ his new car.

10. 그 영화는 7월에 개봉될 **예정이다**.

    The movie ___is___ ______ ______ be released in July.

1. a live broadcast 생방송, 생중계 2. become a celebrity 유명인이 되다, 셀럽이 되다
3. have an interview with ~와 인터뷰를 하다 4. by instinct 본능적으로
5. feel offended 불쾌감을 느끼다, 기분이 상하다 6. feel pity for ~에게 동정심을 느끼다, ~을 불쌍히 여기다, ~가 딱하다
7. have sympathy for ~에게 연민을 느끼다[동정심을 갖다] 8. a dramatic twist 극적인 반전
9. show off (~을) 자랑하다, 으스대다, 과시하다 10. be scheduled to ~할 예정이다

DAY 03

1. 나는 어젯밤에 **기이한 꿈을 꾸었다**.

I ___had___ ________ ________ ________ last night.

2. 그녀는 그 원숭이들**에게 주문을 걸었다**.

She ________ ________ ________ ________ the monkeys.

3. 그 두 그룹은 서로 **완전히 다르다[뚜렷이 구별된다]**.

The two groups ___are___ completely ________ ________ each other.

4. 언어는 인간을 동물**과 구별 짓는다**.

Language ________ human beings ________ animals.

5. 그녀는 큰 결정을 내리는 **데 신중하다**.

She ___is___ ________ ________ making big decisions.

6. 그녀는 자신의 몸무게**에** 아주 **예민하다**.

She ___is___ very ________ ________ her weight.

7. 미리 예약하**는 것이 필수이다**.

___It's___ ________ ________ book in advance.

8. 그는 **일생을** 가난한 이들을 돕는 **데 바쳤다**.

He ________ ___his___ ___life___ ________ helping the poor.

9. 너 글린다**랑 화해했**니?

Did you ________ ________ ________ Glinda?

10. 그는 손실**을 메우**기 위해 열심히 일했다.

He worked hard to ________ ________ ________ the loss.

1. have a weird dream 기이한 꿈을 꾸다 2. cast a spell on ~에게 주문을 걸다
3. be distinct from ~와는 (완전히) 다르다[뚜렷이 구별된다] 4. distinguish A from B A와 B를 구별하다, A를 B와 구별 짓다
5. be cautious about ~에 대해 주의하다, ~에 신중하다 6. be sensitive about ~에 예민하다
7. it's essential to ~하는 것이 필수이다 8. dedicate one's life to (something) 일생을 ~에 바치다
9. make up with (someone) ~와 화해하다 10. make up for (손실 등을) 메우다, 보충하다, 만회하다

DAY 04

1. 그는 이 분야의 전문가**로 인정받고 있다.**

He ______is______ ____________ ____________ an expert in this field.

2. 그는 **가짜[위조] 신분증**을 소지하고 있었다.

He carried ______a______ ____________ ____________ ____________.

3. 나는 진실을 말할 **것을 맹세한다.**

I ____________ ____________ tell the truth.

4. 그는 그들**에게** 큰 소리로 **욕을 했다.**

He ____________ ____________ them loudly.

5. 너는 네 자신**을 부끄러워해**야 한다.

You should ____________ ____________ ____________ yourself.

6. 그는 공황[패닉] **상태에 있었다.**

He ______was______ ______in______ ____________ ____________ ____________ panic.

7. 그들은 마침내 그 계획(안)**에 동의했다**[계획**을 승낙했다**].

They finally ____________ ____________ the plan.

8. 그녀는 장학금**을 받을 자격이 있다**(요건에 부합한다).

She ____________ ____________ the scholarship.

9. 많은 사람들이 품질**을** 가격**과 동일시한다.**

Many people ____________ quality ____________ price.

10. 너는 그것이 진짜 다이아몬드인지 아닌지 **구별할 수 있니**?

____________ you ____________ if it's a genuine diamond or not?

1. be recognized as ~로 인정받다[인식되어 있다] 2. a fake ID card 가짜[위조] 신분증
3. swear to ~할 것을 맹세하다 4. swear at ~에게 욕을 하다
5. be ashamed of ~을 부끄러워하다 6. be in a state of ~한 상태에 있다
7. consent to ~에 동의하다, ~을 승낙하다 8. qualify for ~의 자격을 얻다, ~할 자격이 있다, ~에 부합하다
9. identify A with B A를 B와 동일시하다 10. can tell (~을) 구별하다, (~라는 것을) 알 수 있다

DAY 05

1. 당신의 재능을 보여 줄 이 **드문 기회**를 놓치지 마세요.

   Don't miss this ______________ ______________ to show your talents.

2. 우리는 그 문제에 대해 **설문 조사를 할** 예정이다.

   We're going to ___do___ ______________ ______________ about the issue.

3. 그 설문 조사는 500명의 **무작위 표본**을 사용했다.

   The survey used ______________ ______________ ______________ of 500 people.

4. 그의 집은 100만 달러**로 감정된다[평가된다]**.

   His house ___is___ ______________ ______________ one million dollars.

5. 나는 걷기와 같은 **적당한 운동**을 즐긴다.

   I enjoy ______________ ______________ like walking.

6. 그 책은 그녀**에게 깊은[심오한] 영향을 미쳤다**.

   The book ___had___ ______________ ______________ ______________ ___on___ her.

7. 우리는 **오래가는 건전지**가 필요하다.

   We need ___a___ ______________ ______________.

8. 우리는 그 주제에 대해 **깊이 있게** 논의했다.

   We discussed the topic ______________ ______________.

9. 참가자들은 **무작위로** 선정되었다.

   Participants were selected ______________ ______________.

10. 나는 더 이상 이 소음**을 참을** 수 없다.

    I can't ______________ ______________ ______________ this noise anymore.

1. a rare opportunity 드문 기회 2. do a survey 설문 조사를 하다
3. a random sample 무작위 표본[샘플] 4. be assessed at ~로 감정되다[평가되다]
5. moderate exercise 적당한 운동 6. have a profound impact on ~에게 깊은[심오한] 영향을 미치다
7. a durable battery 오래가는 건전지 8. in depth 깊이 있게
9. at random 무작위로, 임의로 10. put up with ~을 참다[참고 견디다]

DAY 06

1. 이 채널은 24시간 뉴스 및 **시사** 채널이다.

This channel is a 24-hour news and ________ ________ channel.

2. 그는 **무거운 짐을 지고** 있었다.

He was carrying ________ ________ ________.

3. 그는 시험**에서 부정행위를 했다**.

He ________ ________ the exam.

4. 그들은 그 정책**에 항의하여 시위를 했다**.

They ________ ________ the policy.

5. 많은 사람들이 그 시위**에 참가했다**.

Many people ________ ________ the protest.

6. 그녀는 **과도한 스트레스**를 겪고 있다.

She is suffering from an ________ ________ ________.

7. **제한 속도를 초과하지** 마세요.

Don't ________ ________ ________ limit.

8. 그 새 계획은 비용 절감**에 효율적이다**.

The new plan is ________ ________ reducing costs.

9. 거의 200팀이 그 경연**에 참가했다**.

Nearly 200 teams ________ ________ ________ the competition.

10. 그녀의 재능은 그 경연에서 정말 **돋보였다[두드러졌다]**.

Her talent really ________ ________ in the competition.

1. current affairs 시사 2. carry a heavy burden 무거운 짐을 지다
3. cheat on an exam[a test] 시험에서 부정행위를 하다 4. protest against ~에 항의하여[반대하는] 시위를 하다
5. participate in ~에 참가하다 6. an excess of stress 과도한 스트레스
7. exceed the speed limit 제한 속도를 초과하다 8. be efficient for ~에 효율적이다
9. take part in ~에 참가하다[참여하다] 10. stand out 눈에 띄다, 두드러지다, 돋보이다

DAY 07

1. 화재 발생 시 **비상 출구**를 사용하세요.

   Use the ______ ______ in case of fire.

2. 그 도둑은 **보안 카메라**에 찍혔다.

   The thief was caught on ___a___ ______ ______.

3. 그 문제**에 대해** 새로운 **접근 방식을 취하**자.

   Let's ___take___ ______ new ______ ______ the problem.

4. 그녀는 피아니스트**만큼** 피아노를 **잘** 친다.

   She plays the piano ______ ______ ______ a pianist.

5. 그는 초대 목록**에서 제외되었다**.

   He ___was___ ______ ______ the invitation list.

6. 그 클럽 출입은 회원들**로**만 **제한된다**.

   Access to the club ___is___ ______ ______ members only.

7. **교통 법규를 위반하지** 마세요.

   Don't ______ ______ ______.

8. 법규를 어기면 **벌금을 내**야 한다.

   If you violate the law, you should ______ ______ ______.

9. 폭우 **때문에** 우리는 나가지 **못했다**.

   The heavy rain ______ us ______ going out.

10. 도착하**는 대로** 네게 전화할게.

    I will call you ______ ______ ______ I arrive.

1. emergency exit 비상 출구 2. a security camera 보안 카메라
3. take a new approach to ~에 (대해) 새로운 접근 방식을 취하다 4. as well as ~와 마찬가지로 잘, ~만큼 잘
5. be excluded from ~에서 제외되다 6. be restricted to ~로 제한되다
7. violate traffic laws 교통 법규를 위반하다 8. pay a penalty 처벌을 받다, 벌금을 내다
9. keep[prevent] A from V-ing A가 ~하는 것을 막다[못하게 하다] 10. as soon as ~하자마자, ~하는 대로 곧

DAY 08

1. 우리 동네에는 좋은 **스포츠 시설**이 있다.

There is a good ______________ ______________ in my neighborhood.

2. 그 건물은 독특한 **내부 구조**를 가지고 있다.

The building has a unique ______________ ______________.

3. 그 스포츠 센터는 유지 보수를 위해 **운영을 중단했다**.

The sports center ___has___ ______________ ______________ for maintenance.

4. 그 건물은 수년간 **방치되었다**(방치되어 왔다).

The building ___has___ ______________ ______________ for years.

5. 그 건물은 **화염에 휩싸여 있었다**.

The building ___was___ ______________ ______________.

6. 그들은 **폭탄을 폭발시켰다[터뜨렸다]**.

They ______________ ______________ ______________.

7. 우리는 **버려진 애완동물들을 구조했다**.

We ______________ ___abandoned___ ______________.

8. 그녀는 아직도 그 사건에 대한 **악몽을 꾼다**.

She still ______________ ______________ about the accident.

9. **그때** 나는 9살이었다.

______________ ______________ ______________, I was 9 years old.

10. 네가 나를 필요로 하**는 한** 네 곁에 있을게.

I'll stay with you ______________ ______________ ______________ you need me.

1. sports facility 스포츠 시설 2. internal structure 내부 구조
3. cease operations 운영을[영업을] 중단하다 4. be neglected for years 수년간 방치되다
5. be in flames 화염에 휩싸이다, 불바다가 되다 6. explode a bomb 폭탄을 폭발시키다[터뜨리다]
7. rescue abandoned pets 버려진 애완동물들을 구조하다 8. have a nightmare 악몽을 꾸다
9. at the time 그때, 그 당시에 =at that time 10. as long as ~하기만 하면, ~하는 한

DAY 09

1. 그녀는 봄철에 알레르기**로 고생한다[고통받는다]**.

   She ________ ________ allergies in the spring.

2. 그들은 살아남**기 위해 발버둥쳤다[애썼다]**.

   They ________ ________ survive.

3. 그녀는 암**과 싸우고 있다**.

   She ___is___ ________ ________ cancer.

4. 뇌졸중**의 전형적인 증상들**은 무엇입니까?

   What are ___the___ ___typical___ ________ ________ a stroke?

5. 그는 **위독한 상태이다**.

   He ___is___ ________ ________ ________.

6. 비타민은 건강**을 위해 필수적이다**.

   Vitamins ___are___ ________ ________ good health.

7. 그는 수술**에서** 완전히 **회복되었다**.

   He ___made___ ________ full ________ ________ the surgery.

8. 그녀는 **안도의 한숨**을 내쉬었다.

   She breathed ___a___ ________ ________ ________.

9. 그는 폐암 **수술을 받았다**.

   He ________ ________ for lung cancer.

10. 정기 검진이 필요하다는 것을 **잊지 마세요[명심하세요]**.

    Please ________ ________ ________ that you need regular checkups.

1. suffer from ~로 고통받다[고생하다], ~에 시달리다 2. struggle to ~하기 위해 발버둥치다[애쓰다]
3. struggle against ~에 대항해 싸우다 4. the typical symptoms of ~의 전형적인[일반적인] 증상들
5. be in critical condition 위독한 상태에 있다 6. be crucial for ~에 필수적이다[결정적이다/아주 중요하다]
7. make a recovery from (수술·병 등)에서 회복되다 8. a sigh of relief 안도의 한숨
9. undergo surgery 수술을 받다 10. keep (something) in mind (~을) 명심하다, 잊지 않고 기억하다

DAY 10

1. 나는 독감 **예방 주사[백신]를 맞아**야 해.

I need to ______________ ______________ ______________ for the flu.

2. 수천 명의 사람들이 그 바이러스**에 감염되었다**.

Thousands of people ____were____ ______________ ______________ the virus.

3. 나는 지난주에 **독감 주사를 맞았다**.

I ____got____ ______________ ______________ ______________ last week.

4. 그녀는 **긴장을 풀기** 위해[**진정하**려고] 애썼다.

She tried to ______________ ____her____ ______________.

5. 그녀는 (베인) 상처에 **붕대를 감았다**.

She ____put____ ______________ ______________ on the cut.

6. 그는 온라인 게임**에 빠져[중독되어] 있다**.

He ____is____ ______________ ______________ online games.

7. 이 치료법은 수술**의 대안**이 될 수 있다.

This therapy can be ____an____ ______________ ______________ surgery.

8. 우리의 **궁극적인 목표**는 암을 극복하는 것이다.

Our ______________ ______________ is to overcome cancer.

9. 대부분의 비타민은 **처방전 없이 (약국에서)** 살 수 있다.

Most vitamins are available ______________ ______________ ______________.

10. 작년에 새로운 바이러스가 **발생했다**.

A new virus ______________ ______________ last year.

1. get a vaccine 백신을 접종받다, 예방 주사를 맞다 2. be infected with ~에 감염되다
3. get the flu shot 독감 주사를 맞다 4. calm one's nerves 신경을 안정시키다, 진정하다, 긴장을 풀다
5. put a bandage 붕대를 감다 6. be addicted to ~에 빠져[중독되어] 있다
7. an alternative to ~에 대한 대안 8. ultimate goal 궁극적인 목표
9. over the counter 의사의 처방전 없이 (약국에서) 살 수 있는 10. break out (전쟁·화재·전염병 등이) 발발하다, 발생하다

DAY 11

1. 고양이와 개는 흔한 **반려 동물**이다.

   Dogs and cats are common ________ ________.

2. 그런 사람들**과 어울리지** 마라.

   Don't ________ ________ those people.

3. 그는 직장**에서 정직을 당했다**.

   He ___was___ ________ ________ work.

4. 사람들은 뚱뚱한 사람들**에 대해 편견을 갖고 있다**.

   People ___have___ ________ ________ ________ fat people.

5. **변호사에게 상담하는** 게 어때요?

   Why don't you ________ ________ ________?

6. 그녀는 작년에 **이혼했다**.

   She ________ ________ ________ last year.

7. 그녀는 일자리를 얻**기 위해 필사적이었다**.

   She ___was___ ________ ________ get a job.

8. 그녀는 **절망하여** 울었다.

   She cried ________ ________.

9. 그들은 **영영** 헤어졌다.

   They broke up ________ ________.

10. 그 꽃들은 달콤한 향기**를 내뿜었다**.

    The flowers ________ ________ a sweet scent.

1. a companion animal 반려 동물 2. associate with ~와 어울리다
3. be suspended from ~로부터 정지[정직/정학/유예]당하다 4. have a prejudice against ~에 대해 편견을 갖다
5. consult a lawyer 변호사에게 상담하다 6. get a divorce 이혼하다
7. be desperate to ~하기 위해 필사적이다 8. in despair 절망하여, 절망에 빠져
9. for good 영영, 영원히 10. give off (냄새·열·빛 등을) 내뿜다, 발산하다

DAY 12

1. 나는 바나나 **한 다발**을 샀다.

   I bought _______ _______ _______ bananas.

2. 기름은 물**과 섞이지** 않는다.

   Oil does not _______ _______ water.

3. **전기 차**가 인기를 얻고 있다.

   _______ _______ are becoming popular.

4. 다음 주유소에서 **주유를 하는[연료를 채우는]** 것이 좋겠다.

   We'd better _______ _______ at the next gas station.

5. 남은 음식은 **냉장고에** 보관해야 한다.

   You should keep leftovers _______ _______ _______.

6. 버튼이 **제대로 작동하지[기능하지]** 않는다.

   The button does not _______ _______.

7. 치즈와 요구르트는 **유제품**이다.

   Cheese and yogurt are _______ _______.

8. 우리는 **환경을 보존해**야 한다.

   We should _______ _______ _______.

9. 여름에는 전력**이 부족할** 수 있다.

   We may ___be___ _______ _______ electricity during the summer.

10. 남은 음식**을** 점심으로 **활용할** 수 있다.

    You can _______ _______ _______ leftovers for lunch.

1. a bunch of ~ 한 다발[단/송이] 2. blend with ~와 섞이다
3. an electric car 전기 자동차 4. fuel up 주유를 하다, 연료를 채우다, 기름을 넣다
5. in the refrigerator 냉장고에 6. function properly 제대로 작동하다[기능하다]
7. dairy products 유제품 8. preserve the environment 환경을 보존하다
9. be short of ~이 부족하다[모자라다] 10. make use of ~을 활용하다[이용하다]

DAY 13

1. 많은 노인들이 **빈곤하게 산다**.

   Many elderly people ____live____ ________ ________.

2. 우리는 **차를 렌트하**기로 했다.

   We decided to ________ ________ ________.

3. 나의 성공은 당신 **덕분이다**.

   I ________ my success ________ you.

4. 그 일자리**에 대해 문의하**고 싶습니다.

   I would like to ________ ________ the job.

5. 그녀는 **임시직을 얻었다[구했다]**.

   She ____got____ ________ ________ ________.

6. 운 좋게도 그는 **정규직을 얻었다[정규직으로 취업했다]**.

   Luckily, he ________ ________ ________ ________.

7. 다른 사람의 일**에 간섭하지** 마세요.

   Don't ________ ________ other people's business.

8. **예비[여분의] 타이어**를 가지고 있나요?

   Do you have ________ ________ ________?

9. 그는 새 직장**에** 곧 **익숙해졌다**.

   He ________ ________ ________ his new job quickly.

10. 정기적으로 소프트웨어를 **꼭** 업데이트**하세요**.

    ____Make____ ________ ________ update your software regularly.

1. live in poverty 가난 속에 살다, 빈곤하게 살다 2. rent a car 차를 렌트하다[빌리다]
3. owe A to B A를 B에게 빚지다, A는 B 덕분이다 4. inquire about ~에 대해 문의하다
5. get a temporary job 임시직을 얻다[구하다] 6. get a permanent job 정규직을 얻다[구하다], 정규직으로 취업하다
*get a job 취직하다, 직장을 구하다 7. interfere in ~에 간섭하다[개입하다] 8. a spare tire 예비[여분의] 타이어
9. get used to N[V-ing] ~에 익숙해지다 10. make sure (to/that) 반드시 ~하도록 하다, 확실히 ~하다

DAY 14

1. 너는 **일기를 쓰**니?

   Do you ________ ________ ________?

2. 나는 넷플릭스**에 가입했다**[넷플릭스**를 구독하고 있다**].

   I ________ ________ Netflix.

3. 금요일까지 **(당신의) 신청서[지원서]를 제출해** 주세요.

   Please ________ your ________ by Friday.

4. 그는 예전에 **비밀 요원**이었다.

   He used to be ________ ________ ________.

5. **일기 예보**에 따르면 내일 눈이 올 것이다.

   According to the ________ ________, it will snow tomorrow.

6. **미래를 예측하**는 것은 쉽지 않다.

   It's not easy to ________ ________ ________.

7. 스포츠를 할 때는 부상**의 위험**이 있다.

   There is ________ ________ ________ injury when playing sports.

8. 그들은 그**를 협박했다**.

   They made ________ ________ ________ him.

9. 내가 너라면 **위험을 감수할** 것이다.

   If I were you, I would ________ ________ ________.

10. 야생 동물은 서식지 손실로 종종 **위협을 받는다[위험에 처한다]**.

    Wildlife is often ________ ________ due to habitat loss.

1. keep a journal 일기[일지]를 쓰다 *keep a diary 일기를 쓰다 2. subscribe to ~을 구독하다, ~에 가입하다
3. submit an application 신청서를 제출하다, 지원서를 내다 4. a secret agent 비밀 요원, 첩보원
5. a weather forecast 일기 예보 6. predict the future 미래를 예측하다
7. a risk of ~의 위험 8. make a threat against ~에게[를] 협박하다
9. take a risk[risks] 위험을 감수하다, 모험을 하다 10. be under threat 위협을 받고 있다, 위험에 처해 있다

1. 그 공장은 **수출용** 자동차를 생산한다.

   The factory produces cars ________ ________.

2. 너 **최근[최신] 뉴스** 들었니?

   Have you heard ________ ________ ________?

3. 이 기술은 매우 **최신식**이다.

   This technology is very ________ ________ ________.

4. 그 책들은 지역 학교**에 배포될** 것이다.

   The books will ____be____ ________ ________ local schools.

5. 그들은 그 오래된 공장을 미술관**으로 변모시켰다[탈바꿈시켰다]**.

   They ________ the old factory ________ an art gallery.

6. 그녀는 곧 새로운 환경**에 적응했다**.

   She soon ________ ________ the new environment.

7. 그 공장은 유독성 폐기물**을** 불법으로 **처리했다[버렸다]**.

   The factory ________ ________ toxic waste illegally.

8. 그는 마침내 자신의 어린 시절 **꿈을 이뤘다**.

   He finally ________ his childhood ________.

9. 그것은 **늦어도** 내일까지는 완료되어야 한다.

   It should be finished by tomorrow ________ ________ ________.

10. 재활용은 쓰레기**를 처리하**는[**없애**는] 가장 좋은 방법이다.

    Recycling is the best way to ________ ________ ________ waste.

1. for export 수출을 위한, 수출용의 2. the latest news 최근[최신] 뉴스
3. up to date 현대식의, 최신(식)의 4. be distributed to ~에 배포되다
5. transform A into B A를 B로 완전히 바꾸다[탈바꿈시키다/변신시키다] 6. adjust to ~에 적응하다
7. dispose of ~을 버리다[없애다/처리하다] 8. fulfill one's dream 꿈을 이루다[달성하다]
9. at the latest (아무리) 늦어도 10. get rid of ~을 제거하다[없애다], ~을 처리하다

DAY 16

1. 그는 **주당** 900달러**의 임금**을 받는다.

   He earns ______a______ ____________ ____________ ____________ $900.

2. 나는 **선약**이 있다.

   I have ____________ ____________ ____________.

3. 건강이 돈**보다 우선이다**.

   Health ______is______ ____________ ____________ money.

4. 그녀는 **연례 회의[대회]**에 참석했다.

   She attended ____________ ____________ ____________.

5. 그들은 서로 **협력하**기로 합의했다.

   They agreed to ____________ ____________ each other.

6. 그 밴드는 다양한 아티스트**와 협업(콜라보)을 했다**.

   The band ____________ ____________ various artists.

7. 직원들은 여전히 회사**와 협상 중**이다.

   The employees are still ____________ ____________ the company.

8. 그들은 손실**을 보상하**기로 결정했다.

   They decided to ____________ ____________ the loss.

9. 회의**에 앞서** 그는 보고서를 검토했다.

   ____________ ____________ the meeting, he reviewed the report.

10. **놀랍게도** 그들은 타협에 이르렀다.

    ____________ ______my______ ____________, they reached a compromise.

1. a weekly wage of ($900) 주급 (900달러), 주당 (900달러)의 임금 2. a prior engagement 선약(먼저 한 약속)
3. A is prior to B A가 B보다 먼저[우선]이다 4. an annual convention 연례 회의[대회]
5. cooperate with ~와 협력하다 6. collaborate with ~와 협업(콜라보)을 하다
7. negotiate with ~와 협상하다 8. compensate for ~을 보상하다
9. prior to ~에 앞서, ~ 전에 10. to one's surprise 놀랍게도, 뜻밖에

DAY 17

1. 그것은 세상을 바꾼 **역사적인 순간**이었다.

   That was ______ ______ ______ that changed the world.

2. 나는 **현대 미술**을 좋아한다.

   I like ______ ______.

3. **대영 제국**은 한때 세계를 지배했다.

   ___The___ ______ ______ ruled the world once.

4. 그는 **왕관을 쓰**기를 거부했다.

   He refused to ______ ___the___ ______.

5. 그들은 조국**에 충성했다**.

   They ___were___ ______ ______ their country.

6. 피라미드는 **파라오들의 무덤들**이었다.

   Pyramids were ______ ______ ______ ___the___ ___pharaohs___.

7. 그들은 고대 사원**의 잔해**를 발견했다.

   They discovered ______ ______ ______ an ancient temple.

8. 그 도시는 많은 **변화를 겪어 왔다**.

   The city ___has___ ______ many ______.

9. 이 유적들은 로마 시대**까지 거슬러 올라간다**.

   These ruins ______ ______ ___to___ the Roman era.

10. 그는 자신의 어린 시절**을 되돌아봤다**.

   He ______ ______ ___on___ his childhood.

1. a historic moment 역사적인 순간 2. contemporary art 현대 미술
3. the British Empire 대영 제국 4. wear a crown 왕관을 쓰다, 왕위에 오르다
5. be loyal to ~에 충성하다[의리를 지키다] 6. the tombs of the pharaohs 파라오들의 무덤들
7. the remains of ~의 잔해 8. undergo (many) changes (많은) 변화를 겪다
9. date back to ~까지 거슬러 올라가다 10. look back on ~을 되돌아보다[회상하다]

DAY 18

1. 페루는 1532년에 스페인**에 의해 정복되었다**.

   Peru ___was___ ________ ________ the Spanish in 1532.

2. 그들은 조국**을 지키기 위해** 싸웠다.

   They fought ________ ________ ________ their country.

3. 그들은 그 전투에서 **승리를 거두었다**.

   They ________ ________ ________ at the battle.

4. 많은 병사들이 적**에게** (포로로) **잡혔다**.

   Many soldiers ___were___ ________ ________ the enemy.

5. 정부는 **비상 사태를 선포했다**.

   The government ________ ________ ________ ________ ___emergency___.

6. 그것은 그에게 **최고의 영광의 순간**이었다.

   That was ___the___ ___best___ ________ ________ ________ for him.

7. 태양이 떠오르면서 별들은 **서서히 사라진다**.

   Stars ________ ________ as the sun rises.

8. 그들은 **혹독한 날씨를 견뎌 냈다**.

   They ________ ___harsh___ ________.

9. 그 성은 높은 돌담**으로 둘러싸여 있다**.

   The castle ___is___ ________ ________ a high stone wall.

10. 그들은 바이킹**의 후손[후예]이다**.

    They ___are___ ________ ________ the Vikings.

1. be conquered by ~에 의해 정복되다 2. in defense of ~을 지키기 위해
3. win a victory 승리를 거두다, 승리하다 4. be captured by ~에게 붙잡히다, ~에 사로잡히다
5. declare a state of emergency 비상 사태를 선포하다 6. the best moment of glory 최고의 영광의 순간
7. fade out 서서히 사라지다 8. withstand harsh weather 혹독한 날씨를 견뎌 내다
9. be surrounded by ~에 둘러싸이다[포위되다] 10. be descended from ~의 후손[후예]이다

DAY 19

1. 그의 조부모님은 미국**으로 이민을 왔다**.

His grandparents ______ ______ America.

2. 그들은 **출입국 관리소[입국 심사]를 통과했다**.

They __went__ ______ ______.

3. 많은 새들이 겨울을 나기 위해 **남쪽으로 이동한다**.

Many birds ______ ______ for the winter.

4. **핼러윈의 기원**은 무엇일까요?

What's ______ ______ ______ __Halloween__?

5. 미국에는 500개 이상의 **아메리카 원주민 부족들**이 있다.

There are over 500 ______ ______ ______ in the United States.

6. 우리는 그것에 대한 **추가 정보**가 필요하다.

We need ______ ______ about it.

7. 그들은 작은 마을**에 정착했다**.

They ______ ______ a small town.

8. 인도는 1947년에 **독립했다**.

India ______ ______ in 1947.

9. 그는 이웃과의 분쟁**에 휘말렸다**.

He ______ ______ ______ a dispute with his neighbor.

10. 나는 언젠가 **정착하**여 가족을 갖고 싶다.

I want to ______ ______ and have a family someday.

1. immigrate to ~로 이민을 오다 2. go through immigration 출입국 관리소[입국 심사]를 통과하다
3. migrate south 남쪽으로 이동하다 4. the origin of Halloween 핼러윈의 기원
5. Native American tribes 아메리카 원주민 부족들 6. further information 추가 정보, 자세한 정보
7. settle in ~에 정착하다 8. become independent 독립하다, 자립하다
9. be involved in ~에 연루되다[관련되다] 10. settle down (한곳에 자리 잡고) 정착하다

DAY 20

1. 그녀는 **시골 지역에서** 자랐다.

   She grew up ___in___ ______ ______ ______.

2. 그는 뉴욕의 **금융 지구**에서 일한다.

   He works in New York's ______ ______.

3. 그 도시는 **지진 지대에** 위치해 있다.

   The city is located ___in___ ______ ______ ______.

4. 그들은 내일 캐나다로 **국경을 넘을** 계획이다.

   They plan to ______ ______ ______ into Canada tomorrow.

5. 사실**과** 의견**의 경계**가 명확하지 않다.

   The ______ ______ fact ___and___ opinion is not clear.

6. **대한민국**은 민주주의 국가이다.

   ___The___ ______ ______ ______ is a democratic country.

7. 그녀는 **주일 미국 대사**가 되었다.

   She became ___the___ ___U.S.___ ______ ______ ___Japan___.

8. 서울 주재 **영국 대사관**은 어디에 있나요?

   Where is ______ ______ ______ in Seoul?

9. 그 나라는 좋은 복지 시스템**으로 잘 알려져 있다.**

   The country ___is___ ______ ______ its good welfare system.

10. 그 작가는 한국 독자들**에게** 잘 **알려져 있다.**

    The author ______ well ______ ______ Korean readers.

1. in a rural area 시골 지역에서 2. financial district 금융 지구
3. in an earthquake zone 지진 지대에 4. cross the border 국경을 넘다
5. boundary between A and B A와 B 사이의 경계 6. the Republic of Korea 대한민국
7. the U.S. ambassador to Japan 주일 미국 대사 8. the British Embassy 영국 대사관
9. be (well) known for ~로 (잘) 알려져 있다, ~로 유명하다 10. be (well) known to ~에 (잘) 알려져 있다

DAY 21

1. 모든 사람은 **종교의 자유**가 있다.

Everyone has the ________ ________ ________.

2. 그 섬은 **지상 낙원**(지상 위의 천국)과 같은 곳이다.

The island is like ___a___ ________ ________ ________.

3. 사람들은 **신에게 예배를 드리**기 위해 교회에 간다.

People go to church to ________ ________.

4. 그는 **자비를 구했다[간청했다]**.

He ___begged___ ________ ________.

5. 그 사고에서 아무도 죽지 않은 것**은 기적이다**.

___It's___ ________ ________ (that) nobody was killed in the crash.

6. 소는 힌두교도들**에게 신성시된다**.

Cows ___are___ ________ ________ Hindus.

7. 그녀는 자녀**를 위해** 모든 것을 **희생했다**.

She ________ everything ________ her children.

8. 그는 절도**를 자백했다**.

He ________ ________ the theft.

9. 우리는 사원에서 **말 없이[조용히]** 앉아 있었다.

We sat ________ ________ in the temple.

10. 그녀는 가끔 **혼잣말을 했다**.

She sometimes ________ ________ ________.

1. freedom of religion 종교의 자유 2. a heaven on earth 지상 위의 천국, 지상 낙원
3. worship God 신을 숭배하다, 신에게 예배를 드리다 4. beg for mercy 자비를 구하다[간청하다]
5. It's a miracle (that) ~인 것은 기적이다 6. be sacred to ~에게 신성시되다
7. sacrifice A for B B를 위해서 A를 희생하다 8. confess to ~을 자백하다[시인하다]
9. in silence 조용히, 말 없이 10. talk to oneself 혼잣말을 하다

DAY 22

1. 그들은 돌**에** 별 모양을 **새겼다**.

They ______________ a star ______________ the stone.

2. 그는 대리석**으로** 아름다운 여성을 **조각했다**.

He ______________ a beautiful woman ______________ ______________ marble.

3. **자유의 여신상**은 유명한 랜드마크이다.

___The___ ______________ ______________ ______________ is a famous landmark.

4. 그는 자신의 **초상화를 그렸다**.

He ___painted___ ______________ ______________ of himself.

5. 일반적인 믿음**과는 반대로** 많은 고양이들은 우유를 싫어한다.

______________ ______________ popular belief, many cats dislike milk.

6. 그 **연례 전시회**는 8월에 열린다.

The ______________ ______________ is held in August.

7. 그들은 케이크를 **4등분으로 잘랐다**.

They ___cut___ the cake ______________ ______________.

8. 이 제품은 **인공 색소**가 들어 있지 않다.

This product contains no ______________ ______________.

9. 작년**에 비해** 올해는 매우 춥다.

______________ ______________ ______________ last year, it's very cold this year.

10. 그 책은 재미있지만, **반면에** 깊이가 부족하다.

The book is entertaining, but ______________ ______________ ______________ ______________, it lacks depth.

1. carve A into B B에 A를 새겨 넣다 2. sculpt A out of B B로 A를 조각하다
3. the Statue of Liberty 자유의 여신상 4. paint a portrait 초상화를 그리다
5. contrary to ~와는 달리, ~에 반하여 6. annual exhibition 연례 전시회
7. cut A into quarters A를 4등분으로 자르다 8. artificial colors 인공 색소
9. in contrast to ~와는 대조적으로, ~에 비해 10. on the other hand 한편, 반면에

DAY 23

1. **끈으로** 소포를 묶어라.

   Tie up the package ___with___ ________ ________.

2. 그녀는 **클래식 음악** 듣는 것을 즐긴다.

   She enjoys listening to ________ ________.

3. 이 프로그램은 초보자**에게 이상적이다.**

   This program ___is___ ________ ________ beginners.

4. 그는 음향을 확인하기 위해 **테스트를 (실시)할** 것이다.

   He will ________ ________ ________ to check the sound.

5. 그 오케스트라는 존 윌리엄스**가 지휘한다.**

   The orchestra ___is___ ________ ________ John Williams.

6. 나는 그의 친절한 말**에** 깊이 **감동했다.**

   I ________ deeply ________ ________ his kind words.

7. 너는 발레를 (한 번이라도) 본 **적이 있니**?

   ________ ________ ________ seen a ballet?

8. 나는 **스트리밍 서비스**를 구독 중이다.

   I subscribe to ___a___ ________ ________.

9. 오케스트라는 많은 악기**로 구성되어 있다.**

   An orchestra ________ ________ ________ many instruments.

10. 그는 당시 그 프로젝트**에 관여하고 있었다.**

    He ________ ________ ________ the project at that time.

1. with a string 끈으로 2. classical music 클래식[고전] 음악
3. be ideal for ~에(게) 이상적이다 4. conduct a test 테스트를 하다[실시하다]
5. be conducted by ~에 의해 지휘되다, ~가 지휘하다 6. be touched by ~에 의해 감동받다, ~에 감동하다
7. Have you ever + 과거분사? 너는 (한 번이라도) ~해 본 적 있니? 8. a streaming service 스트리밍 서비스 (하나)
9. be composed of ~으로 이루어지다[구성되다] 10. be engaged in ~에 관여하다[참여하다]

DAY 24

1. 그녀는 대학에서 **영문학**을 공부했다.

   She studied __________ __________ in college.

2. 그 책의 **주요 주제[테마]**는 무엇입니까?

   What is ____the____ __________ __________ of the book?

3. 그 영화는 **소설을 바탕으로 하고 있다**.

   The movie ____is____ ____based____ __________ __________ __________.

4. 나는 **공상 과학 영화** 보는 것을 즐긴다.

   I enjoy watching __________ ____films____.

5. **고대 그리스 신화**를 읽어 본 적이 있나요?

   Have you ever read ____ancient____ __________ __________?

6. 그 소설**의 첫[시작] 단락**은 독특했다.

   ____The____ __________ __________ ____of____ the novel was unique.

7. **요약하자면[요컨대]**, 그것은 읽을 가치가 있었다.

   __________ __________, it was worth reading.

8. 그는 내**게 장난을 쳤다**.

   He ____played____ __________ __________ __________ me.

9. 소금을 조금 추가해 봐. 그러면 **될** 거야.

   Add a bit of salt. That'll __________ __________ __________.

10. 내 장난감을 **빼앗지** 마세요.

   Don't __________ __________ my toys.

1. English literature 영문학 2. the main theme 주요 주제[테마]
3. be based on a novel 소설을 기반으로[바탕으로] 하다 4. science-fiction films 공상 과학 영화들
5. ancient Greek myths 고대 그리스 신화 6. the opening paragraph of ~의 첫[시작] 단락
7. in summary 요약하자면, 요컨대 8. play a trick on ~에게 장난을 치다
9. do the trick 문제를 해결하다, 효과가 있다 10. take away ~을 가져가다[데려가다], ~을 없애다, ~을 빼앗다

DAY 25

1. 우리는 **경치를 즐기**기 위해 멈췄다.

   We stopped to ___enjoy___ ________ ________.

2. **북극곰**은 북극에 산다.

   ________ ________ live in the Arctic.

3. 태양이 **수평선[지평선] 위로 떠오르고** 있다.

   The sun is ___rising___ ________ ________ ________.

4. 이 지역의 **비옥한 토양**은 농사에 좋다.

   The ________ ________ in this region is good for farming.

5. 봄에 농부들은 **땅을 경작한다**.

   In spring, farmers ________ ________ ________.

6. 식물의 뿌리는 **물을 흡수한다**.

   Plant roots ________ ________.

7. 그의 셔츠는 땀**으로 흠뻑 젖었다**.

   His shirt ___was___ ________ ________ sweat.

8. **수확철**이다.

   It's ________ ________.

9. 더 많은 폭풍이 **다가오고** 있다.

   More storms are ________ ________ ________.

10. 그들은 결코 **굴복하지** 않고 계속 싸웠다.

    They never ________ ________ but kept fighting.

1. enjoy the scenery 경치를 즐기다 2. polar bears 북극곰들
3. rise on the horizon 수평선[지평선] 위로 떠오르다 4. fertile soil 비옥한 토양
5. cultivate the land 땅을 경작하다 6. absorb water 물을 흡수하다
7. be soaked with ~에[로] 흠뻑 젖다 8. harvest season 수확철
9. on the horizon (어떤 일이) 곧 일어날 듯한 10. give in (to) (~에) 굴복하다, 항복하다

DAY 26

1. 그 도로는 아스팔트**로 포장되어 있다**.

   The road ___is___ ______ ______ asphalt.

2. 그 학교는 1912**년에 설립되었다**.

   The school ______ ______ ______ 1912.

3. 그 문은 **금속으로 만들어져 있다**.

   The gate ___is___ ______ ______ ______.

4. 모든 **전자 기기**를 꺼 주세요.

   Please turn off all ______ ______.

5. 그 체육관에는 다양한 운동 기구**가 갖추어져[구비되어] 있다**.

   The gym ___is___ ______ ______ a variety of exercise equipment.

6. 탄산음료를 물**로 바꿔**도[**대체해**도] 된다.

   You can ______ soda ___with___ water.

7. 버터 **대신** 마가린을 **사용해**도 된다.

   You can ______ margarine ___for___ butter.

8. **(계산서를) 나눠서 내**자. / **각자 계산하**자.

   Let's ______ ______ ______.

9. 그 건설 현장은 맨해튼**에 위치해 있다**.

   The building site ______ ______ ______ Manhattan.

10. 새 매니저가 그 프로젝트**를 넘겨받았다**.

    The new manager ______ ______ the project.

1. be paved with ~로 포장되다 2. be established[founded] in ~년에 설립되다
3. be made of metal 금속으로 만들어지다 4. electronic devices 전자 기기들
5. be equipped with ~가 갖추어져[구비되어] 있다 6. replace A with B A를 B로 바꾸다[대체하다]
7. substitute A for B B 대신 A를 사용하다 8. split the bill (계산서를) 나눠서 내다, 각자 계산하다
9. be located in[on] ~에 위치해 있다 10. take over ~을 인계받다, ~을 인수하다

DAY 27

1. 우리는 **환경을 보호해**야 한다.

   We must ___protect___ ______ ______.

2. **어떤 상황에서든** 최선을 다하세요.

   Do your best ______ ______ ______.

3. 벚꽃이 **공원 곳곳에** 피었다.

   Cherry blossoms bloomed ______ ______ ______.

4. 잔디는 꽃에 **묻혀**(꽃으로 뒤덮여) **있었다**.

   The grass ______ ______ under the blossoms.

5. **대기[공기] 오염**이 점점 더 심해지고 있다.

   ___The___ ______ ______ is getting worse.

6. **자연재해**가 증가하고 있다.

   ______ ______ are increasing.

7. 태풍은 종종 **홍수를 일으킨다**.

   Typhoons often ___cause___ ______.

8. 그 나무는 **벼락을 맞았다**.

   The tree ___was___ ___struck___ ______ ______.

9. 플라스틱 쓰레기는 바다 생물을 **위험에 빠뜨릴** 수 있다.

   Plastic waste can ___put___ sea creatures ______ ______.

10. **갑자기** 불이 나갔다(정전이 되었다).

    ______ ______ ______ ______, the lights went out.

1. protect the environment 환경을 보호하다 2. in any circumstance 어떤 상황에서든
3. throughout the park 공원 곳곳에 4. be buried (파)묻히다, 뒤덮이다
5. air pollution 대기[공기] 오염 6. natural disasters 자연재해, 천재지변
7. cause floods 홍수를 일으키다[야기하다] 8. be struck by lightning 벼락을 맞다
9. put A in danger A를 위험에 빠뜨리다 10. all of a sudden 갑자기

DAY 28

1. 그들은 에베레스트 산 **정상**에 도달했다.

   They reached ____the____ ________ ________ Mount Everest.

2. 교통량은 오전 8시에 **최고조에 달한다**.

   Traffic ____reaches____ ________ ________ at 8:00 AM.

3. **활화산**은 매우 위험하다.

   ____An____ ________ ________ is very dangerous.

4. 그들은 **서둘러** 마을을 떠났다.

   They left the village ________ ________.

5. 열대우림은 많은 **희귀종**의 서식지이다.

   Rainforests are home to many ________ ________.

6. 모든 생물은 **먹이 사슬**의 일부이다.

   All living things are part of ____a____ ________ ________.

7. 인간은 침팬지**에서 진화했**나요?

   Did humans ________ ________ chimpanzees?

8. 바다거북은 현재 **멸종 위기에 처해 있다**.

   The sea turtle ____is____ now ________.

9. 많은 종들이 멸종 **위험에 처해** 있다.

   Many species are ________ ________ ________ extinction.

10. **내가 아는 한**, 거의 100만 종이 멸종 위험에 처해 있다.

   ________ ________ ________ ____I____ ____know____, nearly 1 million species are at risk of extinction.

1. the summit[peak] of ~의 정상[꼭대기] 2. reach one's peak 절정에 이르다, 최고조에 달하다
3. an active volcano 활화산 4. in haste 서둘러
5. a rare species 희귀종 6. a food chain 먹이 사슬
7. evolve from ~에서 진화하다 8. be endangered 멸종 위기에 처하다
9. at risk of ~할 위험에 처한[위험이 있는] 10. as far as (거리·범위·정도가) ~까지, ~하는 한

DAY 29

1. 그들은 **실험실에서** 실험을 진행하고 있다.

   They are conducting experiments ______ ______ ______.

2. 항상 **안전 절차를 따르세요**.

   Always ___follow___ ______ ______ ______.

3. 그들은 프로젝트**를 계속 진행하**기로 결정했다.

   They decided to ______ ______ the project.

4. 얼음이 녹으면 **고체에서 액체로** 변한다.

   When ice melts, it changes ___from___ ______ ______ ___to___ ______ ______.

5. 플라스틱을 태우면 **독성 화학 물질**이 생성될 수 있다.

   Burning plastic can produce ______ ______.

6. 그 항공편은 **기계적 결함**으로 인해 취소되었다.

   The flight was canceled due to ______ ______.

7. 그는 현금 자동 인출기(ATM)**에** 카드를 **넣었다**.

   He ______ his card ______ the ATM.

8. AI 분야의 **기술 혁신**은 놀랍다.

   ___Technological___ ______ in AI is amazing.

9. 우리는 그 문제에 대해 설문 조사**를 실시할** 것이다.

   We will ______ ______ a survey about the matter.

10. 나는 내 동료들**과 잘 맞는다[케미가 좋다]**.

    I ___have___ ______ ______ ______ my colleagues.

1. in the laboratory 실험실에서 2. follow the safety procedures 안전 절차를 따르다
3. proceed with ~을 (계속) 진행하다 4. (change) from a solid to a liquid 고체에서 액체로 (변하다)
5. toxic chemicals 독성 화학 물질 6. mechanical problems 기계적 결함
7. insert A into B A를 B에 넣다[삽입하다] 8. technological innovation 기술 혁신
9. carry out ~을 수행하다, ~을 이행하다 10. have good chemistry with ~와 잘 통하다, ~와 케미가 좋다

DAY 30

1. **무중력 상태에서** 물체는 떨어지지 않고 떠다닌다.

In ______ ______, objects float instead of falling.

2. 달은 **지구의 위성**이다.

The moon is a ______ ______ Earth.

3. UFO는 '**미확인(정체불명의) 비행 물체**'를 나타낸다.

UFO stands for unidentified ______ ______.

4. 그 두 선은 서로 **평행하다**.

The two lines are ______ ______ each other.

5. 그는 2년간 **군 복무를 했다**.

He served ______ ______ ______ for two years.

6. **원자력[핵에너지]**은 전기를 생성하는 데 사용된다.

______ ______ is used to generate electricity.

7. 그는 **총을 소지하고** 있었다.

He was carrying ______ ______.

8. 정부는 **테러와의 전쟁을 선포했다**.

The government declared the war ______ ______.

9. 그는 종종 맨발로 **돌아다닌다**.

He often ______ ______ barefoot.

10. 오늘 내가 누구**와 마주쳤**는지 알아맞혀 봐!

Guess who I ______ ______ today!

1. in zero gravity 무중력 상태에서 2. a satellite of Earth 지구의 (하나의) 위성
3. unidentified flying object 미확인(정체불명의) 비행 물체 4. be parallel to ~와 평행하다
5. serve in the military 군에서 복무하다, 군 복무를 하다 6. nuclear energy 원자력, 핵에너지
7. carry a gun 총을 소지하다 8. declare the war on terror 테러와의 전쟁을 선포하다
9. go around ~ 주위를 돌다, (여기저기) 돌아다니다, (병·소문 등이) 돌다 10. run into ~와 우연히 마주치다, ~와 충돌하다[부딪치다]

DAY 31

1. 우리나라에는 두 **주요 정당**이 있다.

Our country has two ____main____ ________ ________.

2. 그는 강력한 **대통령 후보**이다.

He is a strong ________ ________.

3. 관료들[공무원들]은 탐욕**으로 인해 부패했다.**

Officials ____were____ ________ ________ greed.

4. 그는 그 스캔들 이후 (그의 직**에서**) **사임했다.**

He ________ ________ his post after the scandal.

5. 그녀는 2년 전에 교직**에서 은퇴했다.**

She ________ ________ teaching two years ago.

6. 우리는 우리의 **시민권**을 보호해야 한다.

We should protect our ________ ________.

7. **불법 주차 구역**에 주차해서는 안 된다.

You should not park in ________ ________ ________.

8. 어젯밤에 **총격 사건**이 있었다.

There was ____a____ ________ ________ last night.

9. 축구 팀은 11명의 선수**로 이루어져 있다.**

A soccer team ________ ________ eleven players.

10. 그는 의장직에서 **물러났다.**

He ____has____ ________ ________ as chairperson.

1. main political parties 주요 정당들 2. presidential candidate 대통령 후보(자)
3. be corrupted by ~로 부패하다 4. resign from ~에서 사임하다[물러나다]
5. retire from ~에서 은퇴하다[퇴직하다] 6. civil rights 시민권
7. illegal parking areas 불법 주차 구역 8. a shooting incident 총격 사건
9. consist of ~로 이루어지다, ~로 구성되다 10. step down (from) (요직 등에서) 물러나다, 사임하다

DAY 32

1. 그는 심각한 **범죄를 저질렀다.**

He ______________ a serious ______________.

2. 그들은 시내의 **한 은행을 털었다.**

They ______________ ______________ ______________ downtown.

3. 경찰은 그 총격 사건**의 목격자를 찾고** 있다.

Police are ___looking___ ___for___ ______________ ______________ the shooting.

4. 경찰은 그를 살인 **혐의로 의심하고 있다.**

The police ______________ him ______________ murder.

5. 용의자는 **흔적도 없이 사라졌다.**

The suspect ___vanished___ ______________ ______________ ______________.

6. 그는 강도 **혐의로 체포되었다.**

He ___was___ ______________ ______________ robbery.

7. 그녀는 거짓말한 것에 대해 **죄책감을 느꼈다.**

She ______________ ______________ about lying.

8. 그 강도는 **교도소로 보내졌다**(교도소에 수감되었다).

The robber ___was___ ______________ ______________ ______________.

9. **지금까지** 모든 것이 계획대로 잘 진행되고 있다.

______________ ______________, everything is going well as planned.

10. 그는 절도**뿐만 아니라** 강도 혐의**로도** 기소되었다.

He was accused of ______________ ______________ theft ______________ ______________ robbery.

1. commit a crime 범죄를 저지르다 2. rob a bank 은행을 털다, 은행 강도질을 하다
3. look for witnesses to ~의 목격자를 찾다[수소문하다] 4. suspect A of B A를 B 혐의로 의심하다
5. vanish without a trace 흔적도 없이 사라지다 6. be arrested for ~ 혐의로 체포되다
7. feel guilty 죄책감을 느끼다 8. be sent to prison 교도소로 보내지다, 교도소에 수감되다
9. so far 지금까지, 이 시점까지 10. not only A but also B A뿐만 아니라 B도 역시

MEMO

MEMO

MEMO